The American Revolution
and the French Alliance

The American Revolution
and the French Alliance

WILLIAM C. STINCHCOMBE

SYRACUSE UNIVERSITY PRESS

For J. L. S.

Preface

The purpose of this book is to examine the implementation of the French alliance in the United States and the ways in which American leaders considered and coped with the alliance in formulating foreign and military policy. More specifically, I consider the extent to which the French alliance affected the politics of the American Revolution. For instance, when did foreign policy issues become matters of internal conflict in the United States and why? How did American leaders in Congress, the clergy, the press, and the military respond to and maintain the alliance? This study discusses the different views of foreign policy and national objectives that became evident in the course of the alliance. Particular attention is given to alignments in the Continental Congress over peace ultimata, increasing French influence on American policy, military aid and cooperation, and French propaganda in the United States.

Of all the people who have aided me in this project my greatest debt is to Bradford Perkins, who originally suggested the topic as a possible dissertation subject. His scholarship, patience, and continuing interest, combined with a belief in intellectual freedom for the student, made him an ideal advisor. Others who gave me many helpful suggestions and who read the entire manuscript at various times include Howard H. Peckham, John Bowditch, and Shaw Livermore, Jr. My colleague, J. Roger Sharp, read several chapters and gave me needed advice. The Gilbert Chinard Prize Committee and John J. Meng, in particular, indicated a number of weaknesses and clarified my thinking on various points. My thanks to all of them.

Anyone working in this period of American history owes a great deal to the directors and staffs of the many historical societies and libraries; I thank them for unfailingly making my visits enjoyable as well as profitable. Particular thanks must go to William Ewing, curator of manuscripts at the William L. Clements Library, whose advice and assistance on many matters went beyond his duties at Clements. I would also like to thank John F. Kilfoil for his assistance in enabling me to use the Samuel Cooper Papers in the Huntington Library.

The American Philosophical Society and the International Relations

Program at Syracuse University generously provided me with funds to examine the Luzerne Papers in Paris.

To my wife, Jean Stinchcombe, I am greatly indebted for her help throughout the study.

W. C. S.

Syracuse, New York
Fall, 1968

Contents

Abbreviations Used in Footnotes

APS   American Philosophical Society
AAE   Archives du Ministère des Affaires Étrangères
AN   Archives Nationales
BPL   Boston Public Library
CU   Columbia University
CHS   Connecticut Historical Society
DC   Dartmouth College
DU   Duke University
GHS   Georgia Historical Society
HL   Huntington Library
HSP   Historical Society of Pennsylvania
HU   Harvard University
LC   Library of Congress
LMCC   Edmund C. Burnett, editor, *Letters of Members of Continental Congress* (Washington, 1921–1936)
MHS   Massachusetts Historical Society
NA   National Archives
N-YHS   New-York Historical Society
NYPL   New York Public Library
NCSA   North Carolina State Archives
PU   Princeton University
SCHS   South Carolina Historical Society
SHC   Southern Historical Collection, University of North Carolina
UP   University of Pennsylvania
UV   University of Virginia
WCL   William L. Clements Library

I. The Advent of the French Alliance

"The roar of the British Lion will no more be heard," a disgruntled American Loyalist wrote after hearing of the French-American alliance of 1778, "the French cock may now crow and strut undisturbed." A total revolution had occurred in American diplomacy, and the United States had, he contended, foolishly "allied itself to her natural, professed, and most dangerous enemy." [1] The Loyalists continued to regard the American Revolution as a civil war, but the Patriots had abandoned this view eighteen months before with the Declaration of Independence and eagerly sought formal entrance into the family of nations. An alliance with the foremost enemy of Great Britain became natural and in the best interest of the United States.

The American Revolution attempted to achieve goals which required the United States to become an active participant in international politics; independence itself ultimately depended on the shifting balance of power among European nations. Before the alliance was signed, the precarious balance of power made Great Britain reluctant to commit its full resources in the Western Hemisphere to defeat the rebellious colonies. France and Spain, allied by the Bourbon pact, had mutual interests in undermining British hegemony in both Europe and the Americas, and awaited only the right opportunity to seek revenge on their common adversary.

The growing American nationalism, fanned by revolution and its ideology, was affected by the new country's connections with France and Spain as well as its independence from Great Britain. Yet few Americans considered the significance of their struggle against Great Britain within the context of the European balance of power. Rather, they viewed their conflict with the mother country as a strictly bilateral war with but one purpose: to achieve independence. Other nations were welcome to join the struggle against British tyranny, but they could expect thanks only to the degree that they speeded the independence of the United States. The alliance was a temporary means to a noble end, rather than a long-term commitment to France or European politics.

Paradoxically, the very concepts for which Americans fought were

[1] Curwen to Smith, Feb. 25, 1778, *Journal and Letters of Samuel Curwen* (4th ed.; Boston, 1864), p. 192.

antithetical to fundamental features of French society. In government, the centralized powers of the French monarchy and the privileges of the aristocracy stood in stark contrast to the limited power of American representative assemblies. In religion, the contrast was even greater. John Winthrop's "city upon a hill" was assumed to mean that the United States was to be a Protestant preserve unsoiled by the worldly church of Rome. Freedom of religion for all denominations was much more widespread in the United States than in France. The American press, too, had acquired freedom from the governmental control imposed on French papers.

Americans, however, had little knowledge of their new ally. Instead, they relied on stereotypes nurtured during the repeated imperial wars in which Great Britain and France struggled for dominance on the North American continent. The Seven Years' War had exacerbated American hostility toward Frenchmen, often depicted as driven by an unscrupulous Catholic monarch with insatiable ambition. In addition, individual Frenchmen, particularly diplomats and priests, were characterized as cunning, devious, and above all, subtle. The widely held American stereotype of Frenchmen, at least before 1775, suggested an incarnation of the Devil, who sought in many ways to seduce Americans into abandoning the path of righteousness they had followed since colonization.[2]

Americans, deceived by their own stereotypes, failed to see the wide support their struggle aroused in France. The American Revolution received eager encouragement from Voltaire, Condorcet, Turgot, and other thinkers of the Age of Enlightenment. Many French intellectuals saw in the American Revolution the beginnings of a new era soon to open in Europe, that would eliminate injustice and arbitrary rule. The enthusiasm extended to international relations, where some thinkers foretold the end of the old alliance system and the decline of imperial rivalries. However mistaken the "philosophes'" view of America as a wilderness utopia, their advocacy of the Revolution immensely aided American diplomacy in Europe.[3]

Although dissimilar in politics, religion, and social structure, and little understood to each other, France and the United States were drawn together by a temporary bond of mutual interest that enabled both to pursue their respective objectives by signing an alliance. The value of the alliance for both countries depended on their interest in diminishing

[2] Samuel Woodward, *A Sermon Preached October 9, 1760* (Boston, 1760), pp. 11–16.

[3] Durand Echeverria, *Mirage in the West* (Princeton, 1957), pp. 17, 42, 71; Robert R. Palmer, *The Age of the Democratic Revolution* (Princeton, 1959), vol. I, pp. 239–82; Felix Gilbert, *The Beginnings of American Foreign Policy: To the Farewell Address* (rev. ed.; New York, 1965), pp. 54–66.

the power of Great Britain. The bond of interest which proved so important during the war had not been self-evident before 1776, nor would it be durable after 1783. The brief, yet timely, opportunity for a French-American alliance resulted from changes in the Thirteen Colonies during the fifteen years preceding the Revolution.

The peace settlement of the Seven Years' War quite inadvertently allowed the opportunity for an alliance to develop. By the Treaty of Paris in 1763, France abandoned all territorial claims in North America except for certain fishing islands near Newfoundland, and Spain ceded East and West Florida, leaving Great Britain in control of most of the settled portion of North America except for Mexico. Great Britain, by gaining control of strategic and profitable islands, emerged as the most powerful nation in the Caribbean. Although dominant, Great Britain was not invulnerable, however, since France and Spain had divided Santo Domingo and Spain still held Cuba and Puerto Rico. With the exception of the Floridas, Spain also continued to hold the entire coastline of the Caribbean, and the Dutch, relegated to the role of a second-rate power, nevertheless held St. Eustatius. Spain, moreover, controlled the mouth of the Mississippi, the key to future development in the upper Mississippi and Ohio valleys.

After 1763 the American colonies seemed to be Great Britain's safest possession, and the colonists rejoiced in the victory the mother country had achieved over France. The results of the war were clear to Americans. One minister proclaimed, "She [Great Britain] now, better than ever, understands the Worth and Importance of her Colonies, and, instead of requiring any *Check* upon their Growth, knows that her own Wealth and Glory greatly depend upon their Increase, Extent, and Numbers." Now the last major obstacle for the Colonies had been removed, Mellen continued. "*Canada,* in the Hands of *France,* has always stinted the Growth of our Colonies. But with *Canada* in our Possession, our People in America will increase amazingly." [4]

The West appeared to hold unlimited possibilities. Benjamin Franklin, typical of many Americans, seemed mesmerized by the prospects of expansion.[5] Expansion in any form, be it increased population, territory, or commerce, was fast becoming a cardinal tenet of American belief. Many American leaders had acquired vast holdings in the western territory, and others also looked westward as they contemplated the rapid growth of the Thirteen Colonies. With a tenfold increase in the co-

4 John Mellen, *A Sermon Preached at the West Parish in Lancaster, October 9, 1760* (Boston, 1760), p. 36, italics in original.

5 Gerald Stourzh, *Benjamin Franklin and American Foreign Policy* (Chicago, 1954), pp. 54–65.

lonial population since the turn of the century, and a marked expansion of commerce, there seemed to be no barrier to developing the vast western area except that of restrictions imposed by the mother country.

Yet the growth of the Colonies produced many unsolved problems. While they were small commercial enclaves along the coast, the need for sophisticated governmental machinery was minimal. Colonial assemblies, no matter what the provisions of their charters, at first had little to do. As the Colonies grew, however, the assemblies determined the confines of boundaries, instituted judicial systems, and established machinery to allow commerce to operate efficiently. At various times, different Colonies also handled Indian problems on the frontiers, printed money, and selected their own judiciary.[6]

The increased responsibilities of the assemblies gave colonial leaders an opportunity to gain experience in handling the problems of government. When controversy with the mother country erupted, largely over western lands and Indian problems, the Colonies had developed the institutions and leadership which would greatly facilitate their early resistance to Great Britain. This resistance culminated in 1774 when the state legislatures called the first Continental Congress, the organization that started the critical debate on foreign affairs and independence.

During the years of controversy prior to the Revolution, the colonists did little creative thinking about the international implications of their dispute with Great Britain. Not until independence became an issue did the international situation seem relevant. In the quarrels concerning the Stamp Act, the Townshend Duties, the Wilkes Affair, the Boston Tea Party, the Quebec Act, and finally the Boston Port Bill, the colonists, even those in the Continental Congress, justified their resistance by asserting their legal rights as Englishmen. Until the colonists decided that they were Americans and not Englishmen, they did not attempt to exploit their position in international politics.[7] Once they started to regard themselves as Americans their attitudes toward Great Britain changed, and they came to view her as one of four competing powers in the Western Hemisphere. A potential enemy of Great Britain became a possible ally of the colonists. France and Spain were no longer natural enemies, but countries whose interests coincided with those of the thirteen newly independent colonies.

An apparent obstacle to an alliance with either France or Spain was

---

[6] Jack Greene, *Quest for Power* (Chapel Hill, 1963), pp. 109, 219, 360.

[7] Max Savelle, "The Appearance of an American Attitude toward External Affairs," *American Historical Review* (hereafter *AHR*), Vol. LII (1946), pp. 655–66; Wonyung Hyun Oh, "American Opinion Relative to International Affairs," (unpublished dissertation, University of Washington, 1963), pp. 93, 118, 177.

their Catholicism. On the other hand, Great Britain and the United States were both Protestant countries, although most Americans had long since renounced any affinity to Anglicanism. The colonists, in their struggle with the mother country, resurrected the Puritans' rallying cry of religious freedom. During the controversy over political issues, a festering battle over the establishment of Anglican bishops in New England aligned the clergy with the Patriots in resisting any fundamental change sought by partisans of the mother country. In New England, the clergy overwhelmingly supported the Revolution.[8]

Even in the South, where the Anglican Church had been established, it reflected the republican nature of America rather than the class structure of Great Britain. In Virginia, as many as a third of the Anglican ministers joined the rebels, and the remainder fled before 1776. One minister who remained later lost his parish in a church subscribers' election to an opponent who campaigned "under the denomination of the poor man's parson." [9]

Nevertheless, it was difficult to see how a conflict between Protestants could aid a reconciliation with Protestantism's most powerful foe. But because the religious controversy was so closely intertwined with the political struggle against Great Britain, the American clergy adapted to the new circumstances; political liberties and religious freedom in America were seen as interdependent. Clearly the clergy and their parishioners were virulently anti-Catholic, but they were not prepared to participate in a religious crusade against Catholicism when other issues seemed more important.

Even earlier, during the Seven Years' War, when anti-Catholic invective was at its height, some Americans "had grown indifferent to and weary with the archaic battle line of the Reformation. The notion of an Armageddon between Protestants and Papists was one of the dogmas of a stormy past that proved inadequate to a stormier present." [10] In victory sermons at the time of the conquest of Canada, clergymen lambasted Catholicism as an evil, but recognized that the primary cause of the war was not religion but imperial rivalry for the American continent. Victory, to be sure, was due to Protestant purity, but the future seemed bright because the main cause of the war had been removed.[11]

---

8 Carl Bridenbaugh, *Mitre & Sceptre* (New York, 1962), p. 172.

9 *Ibid.*, p. 323; Wallace Brown, *The King's Friends* (Providence, 1965), p. 188. Quote from Pendleton to Woolford, July 26, 1779, Edmund Pendleton Papers, SHC.

10 Alan Heimert, *Religion and the American Mind: From the Great Awakening to the Revolution* (Cambridge, 1966), p. 85.

11 Woodward, *A Sermon*, pp. 11–14; Mellen, *A Sermon*, pp. 34–35; Eli Forbes, *A Sermon Preached October 9, 1760* (Boston, 1761), pp. 12–13.

By the late eighteenth century, references to the Pope carried such universal unpopularity, yet so little content, that Americans accused King George III of assuming a "popish title" during the Seven Years' War, and hung the Pope in effigy at rallies which accorded the like honor to Lord North and George III immediately before the Revolution.[12] "The Pope" became synonymous with "the enemy." In a transformation characteristic of revolution, the Catholicism of the Bourbon powers was not feared as much as the "popery" of the King of Great Britain.

As the colonists increasingly committed themselves to an all-out assault on the mother country's position, they inevitably had to reconsider the source of Great Britain's vast power. William Livingston, a leader in the separation movement and later Governor of New Jersey, declared that the American Colonies were the real makeweight in the international balance of power. Great Britain's power in Europe, he reasoned, depended on the Colonies which made her stronger than any one rival in Europe.[13]

Livingston's dubious assertion of this critical position was not an uncommon interpretation of the source of national wealth and power in the second half of the eighteenth century. Englishmen who opposed Great Britain's deep involvement in Europe, particularly through the Hanoverian connection, advocated a foreign policy giving priority to the Colonies. These critics, generally anti-Administration Whigs, charged that the King of England, who was also the King of Hanover, subordinated the true interests of Great Britain to defend his other possessions. William Pitt, when a young man, expressed the feelings of many Englishmen when he stated in Parliament, "This great, this powerful, this formidable kingdom, is considered only as a province to a despicable electorate." [14]

Long before they thought of independence, the colonists supported any foreign policy which gave them primary consideration. Pitt was acclaimed when he changed Great Britain's traditional foreign policy during the Seven Years' War by emphasizing colonial possessions and commerce. The pacifist Whigs, who decried the balance of power and advocated non-entanglement with Europe, also received American support. The arguments of pacifist Whigs who hoped to replace the old alliance system with purely commercial ties between nations were widely read

---

[12] Heimert, *Religion and the American Mind,* p. 85; Arthur M. Schlesinger, *Prelude to Independence: The Newspaper War on Britain* (2d ed.; New York, 1965), p. 26.

[13] Savelle, "Appearance of an American Attitude toward External Affairs," p. 658.

[14] Quoted in Gilbert, *The Beginnings,* p. 25 and ch. II.

and accepted in the Colonies. Early American hopes for political isolation and commercial ties found their best expression in January, 1776, with the publication of Thomas Paine's *Common Sense,* written not long after the author himself emigrated from Great Britain.[15]

In its first two sessions, Congress hoped to achieve its objectives without taking the final step in the break with Great Britain. It deliberately stifled any moves toward independence, and only after independence could foreign alliances be considered. Until 1776 the conflict remained a domestic quarrel, and Congress, true to the pacifist Whig legacy, believed that trade was its strongest weapon.[16] It had declared all ports closed in 1775, thus depriving itself of needed war supplies. A Philadelphia paper expressed the prevailing Congressional opinion that trade controls would resolve political conflicts, "Every nation which enjoyed a share of our trade would be a guarantee for the peaceable behavior and good conduct of its neighbours." [17] The self-imposed trade embargo failed to force Great Britain to compromise, and George III, declaring the American Colonies to be in a state of rebellion, forbade any nation to trade with them.[18]

In the meantime, Congress refused to lift the embargo, because opening the ports would represent a critical step for action as an independent power. Early in 1776 Congress was still unwilling to admit that independence was its only recourse besides capitulation.[19] But in April, after receiving news that the King had declared the Colonies to be in a state of rebellion, Congress, out of necessity, ordered all American ports opened for commerce with any nation except Great Britain.[20] It postponed formal action on independence and with it a possible alliance, however. Richard Henry Lee broke the impasse on June 7, 1776, when he proposed a declaration of independence, because "it is expedient forthwith to make the most effectual measures for forming Alliances." Thus independence was not intended primarily as a break from Europe, but as a means to expand connections with the Continent.[21]

After declaring independence, Congress worked throughout the summer of 1776 drafting a model treaty to prepare for the legal entrance of the United States into the family of nations. By September,

[15] *Ibid.,* pp. 33–34.

[16] *Ibid.,* p. 44.

[17] Quoted in Arthur M. Schlesinger, *The Colonial Merchants and the American Revolution* (2d ed.; New York, 1957), pp. 598–99.

[18] Samuel F. Bemis, *The Diplomacy of the American Revolution* (rev. ed.; Bloomington, 1961), pp. 29–30.

[19] *Ibid.,* p. 30; Oh, "American Attitudes," p. 154.

[20] Gilbert, *The Beginnings,* p. 45.

[21] *Ibid.,* pp. 44, 45, 48; Gilbert Chinard, ed., *The Treaties of 1778* (Baltimore, 1928), pp. 3–18.

Congress had passed instructions for a model treaty, drafted largely by John Adams. The instructions to the newly appointed commissioners to France—Benjamin Franklin, Arthur Lee, and Silas Deane—stipulated that the United States desired only commercial relations with France and no political ties.[22]

Adams and his colleagues were not so naive as to believe that commerce provided a panacea for political problems. Rather, they saw a commercial treaty with France as a way for the United States to open alternatives in its struggle against Great Britain. A commercial agreement with France would accomplish a number of political objectives unrelated to commerce. Trade itself was not as important as recognition at this time. If France recognized the United States and other European powers followed its lead, then Great Britain would have to choose between war with a European power to enforce her trade regulations or tacit recognition of the United States as a belligerent by allowing neutral trade.

A commercial treaty with France would postpone the delicate question of a political alliance until the commissioners reported the French reaction to the proposals. Congressmen had not reached agreement on a political alliance, because they assumed that France would demand territorial compensation in North America—probably Canada or her former possessions in the Ohio Valley. Either request would conflict with New England desires to acquire Canada or the Middle States' hopes for the Ohio Valley. Besides, American leaders realized that a commercial treaty with France would assuredly bring her into war with Great Britain, and this was the first goal of United States foreign policy.[23] American leaders who wanted a political alliance and those who sincerely desired only commercial connections, probably a minority, united on the necessity of commercial relations with Europe. But the model treaty as drafted by John Adams was intended to strengthen independence, with trade relations being of secondary importance.

Some Americans criticized reliance on commercial incentives to bring France into the war, since the United States already allowed French ships to enter her ports duty-free. Such a situation would never encourage France to enter the war according to a Philadelphia merchant, who commented, "I never thought that France would commence a War with Great Britain, while she could enjoy the benefits of the American Trade at a less Expence." [24] Furthermore, negotiation, alli-

[22] Gilbert, *The Beginnings,* pp. 51–54.

[23] Although Gilbert stresses the commercial motive in the origins of American foreign policy, he admits that the purpose of an agreement with France at this time was to bring her into the war against Great Britain, *ibid.,* pp. 52–53.

[24] Shippen to Yeates, Jan. 27, 1778, Balch Papers, HSP, Vol. II.

ances, and the balance of power were regarded in France as more reliable considerations in diplomacy than trade relations. Benjamin Franklin, while Minister to France, warned Congress that France would not respond to American requests on the basis of commercial interest, "Trade is not the admiration of their noblesse, who always govern here. Telling them their *commerce* will be advantaged by our success, and that it is their *interest* to help us, seems as much to say, help us, and we shall not be obliged to you." [25]

The model treaty included provisions typical of old-fashioned territorial agreements. Article 11 of the treaty allowed France the right of conquest in British West Indian possessions, while Article 9 asked France to refrain from conquest on the North American continent. Throughout the war Congress appealed to France's other ally, Spain, primarily on the basis of projected conquest, not future trade agreements. In 1776 Congress offered Spain West Florida and a declaration of war against Portugal, if Spain would recognize and aid the United States.[26]

Meanwhile, France and, to a lesser extent, Spain began clandestine aid shipments to the United States. Caron de Beaumarchais, playwright and high-level courier for the French Foreign Minister, Count de Vergennes, made contact with Arthur Lee in London in 1775. Beaumarchais recommended that immediate aid be given to the Americans, and shortly thereafter the French Cabinet approved Beaumarchais' plan to have Hortalez and Company channel military supplies, many of them rendered obsolete by the French Army reforms of 1770, to the Americans. Vergennes was willing to go much farther and was prepared to recognize the United States in the summer of 1776, but the fall of New York City to the British strengthened the position of the anti-war party within the French Cabinet. Vergennes retreated, carefully preparing to take advantage of any new circumstances to recognize the United States while allowing increased shipments of secret goods. The aid shipped to the United States through French sources in 1776 and 1777 was critical to the continuing war effort; the American Army at Saratoga received 90 per cent of its arms and ammunition from French merchants.[27]

It became obvious in late 1776 and 1777 that the model treaty with its commercial incentives would not be enough to lure France into

[25] Franklin to Livingston, March 24, 1782, Francis Wharton, ed., *Revolutionary Diplomatic Correspondence of the United States* (Washington, 1889), Vol. V, p. 215, italics in original.

[26] Chinard, ed., *Treaties of 1778*, pp. 5–6; Franklin to D'Amanda, April 7, 1777, Wharton, ed., *Diplomatic Correspondence*, Vol. II, p. 304.

[27] Claude Van Tyne, "French Aid Before the Alliance of 1778," *AHR*, Vol. XXXI (1925), pp. 37–40.

recognizing the United States. Yet the eighteen months between the Declaration of Independence and the signing of the alliance proved fortunate for developing American self-confidence in eventual victory. Benjamin Rush, who viewed the Revolution as the advance of republicanism, argued that the delay by France was beneficial because "we were in a great danger of being ruined by a too speedy rupture between France and England." Rush believed it would require one or two independent campaigns "to purge away the monarchical impurity we contracted by laying so long upon the lap of Great Britain." [28]

The growing identification of republicanism as the dominant ideology of the Revolution stimulated Americans to consider their effort as separate and distinct from European politics. At the time when a majority of Americans made their choice between Great Britain and the United States, the issues of freedom of religion and republicanism seemed clear. With no international complications to consider, the overwhelming majority of Americans in all sections supported the United States, or at least did not go over to the British. By the time the alliance had been signed, the American commitment to the Revolution, and with it independence and republicanism, was irrevocable. Consequently, the tie to the old enemy, France, caused no appreciable defections to the British.[29]

Nevertheless, Americans had been impatient with France's refusal to recognize the United States. The mutual interest of both countries coincided, and Americans could not understand French hesitation. Samuel Cooper, pastor of the Brattle Street Church in Boston and long a Patriot leader in Massachusetts, wondered how long France would take to see her own interests clearly:

> Will France let such an opportunity for her own advantage slip out of her hands? Can Britain give her an equivalent for the independence of these states? Will the House of Bourbon not exert itself to prevent any more foreign troops from coming to America? Can we have no men-of-war to open our ports and trade, and secure our most necessary supplies? Will not France employ its influence in Canada and on the foreigners that are here? [30]

28 Rush to John Adams, Aug. 8, 1777, Lyman H. Butterfield, ed., *The Letters of Benjamin Rush* (Princeton, 1951), Vol. I, p. 152.

29 William H. Nelson, *The American Tory* (New York, 1961), p. 92. Nelson states that only in New York is it reasonably certain that Loyalists may have constituted half of the population. Paul H. Smith, "The American Loyalists: Notes on Their Organization and Numerical Strength," *William & Mary Quarterly,* third series, Vol. XXV (1968), pp. 269–70, estimates that the Loyalists comprised no more than 16 per cent of the total population and about 19.8 per cent of the white population.

30 Cooper to Franklin, Feb. 27, 1777, Edward Hale and Edward Hale, Jr., *Franklin in France* (Boston, 1887), Vol. I, p. 105.

William Carmichael, serving in Paris, commented, "We are now acting a play which pleases all the spectators, but none seem inclined to pay the performers. All that we seem likely to obtain from this is applause." Although Carmichael did not seek political isolation from Europe, he continued realistically, "The want of resolution in the House of Bourbon to assist us in the hour of distress will be an argument with our people, if successful, to form no binding connections with them." [31] Despite their impatience with France, Americans could do little but await a propitious event which would strengthen the hand of the war party in France and lead to recognition.

The capitulation of Burgoyne at Saratoga in 1777 gave the American cause the necessary boost. Vergennes opened negotiations for an alliance after receiving the news of Saratoga. Conrad Alexandre Gérard— Vergennes' first secretary and later the first French Minister to the United States—and the American commissioners conducted the negotiations. Two treaties, a commercial treaty following the model treaty and a defensive treaty in case of the expected war with Great Britain, were signed on February 6, 1778. Without consultation with Congress, the American commissioners, Silas Deane, Benjamin Franklin, and Arthur Lee, agreed to a binding political alliance which provided that neither power would sign a separate peace treaty without the prior consent of the other country; the alliance would continue at least until Great Britain officially acknowledged United States independence.[32]

Americans at home, not learning of the new alliance for almost three months, had confidence in their own ability to survive without formal recognition by France. After Saratoga recognition would, in their view, follow demonstrated proof that the United States could defend itself. Americans now believed that they did not need to make supplications for aid. Instead, they expected to enter an alliance on a basis of equality. Americans attributed their changed circumstances not to the appeal of the model treaty or the justice of the Declaration of Independence, but to the proven military prowess of the United States. This would surely bring recognition where all else had failed.

Americans believed the tables were now turned and France would have to react quickly. One of Franklin's correspondents observed, "Fortunate would it be for Brittian [sic] if she could secure the alliance of America before *your* Negotiations with Foreigners effectually reduces her to a State of being a Province of France. She has been warned of her Danger." [33] John Carroll, a Catholic priest who accompanied Franklin

[31] Carmichael to Dumas, April 28, 1777, Wharton, ed., *Diplomatic Correspondence*, Vol. II, pp. 308–309.

[32] Bemis, *Diplomacy of the American Revolution*, pp. 58–59.

[33] Wendell to Franklin, Oct. 30, 1777, Franklin Papers, APS, Vol. VII, italics in original.

on his ill-fated trip to Canada in 1775, expressed the feelings of American leaders after Saratoga, "To tell the truth, we begin to be a little out of humour at the delay of the Bourbon Princes in taking some decisive measures." [34]

Henry Laurens, his anti-French suspicions fanned by fellow South Carolinian Ralph Izard in Paris, fumed at what he considered the degrading treatment accorded the American commissioners. Laurens, however, and most others who shared his views, could separate their anti-French sentiments and their belief in the desirability of an alliance.

> Will sober men rely upon the faith or the benevolence of Kings: Has France done one act of kindness towards us, but what has been plumply for the promotion of her own interest? Has she not played off our commissioners—ambassadors like puppets? She has bountifully offered us the loan of money, provided we should furnish her with the means of raising. . . . [However] It is not necessary that we should break off with France. We might make use of her.[35]

William Livingston, Laurens' correspondent, considered an alliance necessary, but he was too much of a republican in politics to think the King of France would openly aid a revolution which would read "a pernicious lesson to his own subjects." [36] Livingston was one of a decided minority which believed that ideology would deter France from recognizing the United States after Saratoga. Mutual interest was the only attraction the United States could offer, and most Americans believed that it would eventually be compelling. Washington, dismayed by French delays, still believed that France would aid the United States, because it "cannot be fairly supposed, that she will hesitate a moment to declare War, if she is given to understand, in a proper manner, that a reunion of the two Countries may be the consequence of procrastination." [37] Other Americans also believed that a threat of reconciliation, if nothing else, would bring France into the war. Congressman James Lovell wrote, "I suspect that England will more easily draw France into open War by talking about Reconciliation than by boasting of subduing us by force. Louis thinks the latter impossible: his only fears are about the former." [38]

---

[34] Carroll to Franklin, Jan. 18, 1778, *ibid.,* Vol. VIII.

[35] Laurens to Livingston, Jan. 27, 1778, Theodore Sedgwick, Jr., *A Memoir of William Livingston* (New York, 1833), pp. 253–58.

[36] Livingston to Laurens, Feb. 5, 1778, Livingston Papers, MHS, box I.

[37] Washington to Banister, April 21, 1778, John C. Fitzpatrick, ed., *The Writings of George Washington* (Washington, 1931–1944), Vol. XI, p. 288.

[38] Lovell to Samuel Adams, Feb. 19, 1778, Adams Papers, NYPL.

Americans did not know what to expect in the early months of 1778. Every arriving ship produced a spate of wild rumors about the prospects of an alliance, but no one had any clear idea what France might ask in return. In late March a Providence paper reported,

> It is asserted here [Bordeaux] as a Fact, that Dr. Franklin hath been presented to the King of France, and acknowledged by the latter to be Ambassador from the Thirteen United States of America: That Dr. Franklin engaged that the Americans would deliver Canada into the hands of France: That 20,000 French Troops are to embark for Canada: and that France, Spain, Portugal have entered into an alliance with the Americans.[39]

A Philadelphia druggist recorded the same rumor in his diary.[40]

To the dismay of the Patriots, news of the North reconciliation proposals reached New York and Philadelphia in mid-April before word arrived from the commissioners in France. Colonel John Laurens, an aide to Washington and Henry Laurens' son, wrote to his father after learning of the North proposals, "If France has not declared war, she does not merit our alliance." [41] Whether France merited the alliance or not became meaningless, because on April 19 Simeon Deane, Silas' brother, arrived in Boston with official news of the treaties signed between France and the United States.

[39] *Providence Gazette,* March 28, 1778.
[40] Christopher Marshall Diary and Letterbook, HSP, diary entry March 29, 1778.
[41] Laurens to Laurens, April 20, 1778, William G. Simms, *Memoir and Correspondence of Col. Laurens in the Years 1777–78* (New York, 1867), p. 161.

II. Initial American Reaction

On April 19, 1778, the anniversary of the Battle of Lexington, the Reverend Samuel Cooper was preparing to enter his pulpit when Simeon Deane, who had just arrived from Paris, presented him with a letter from Benjamin Franklin. Breaking the seal, Cooper had just time to read the first paragraph announcing the conclusion of the alliance. "I gave public Thanks & implor'd the Blessings of Heaven, on the King of France & his Dominions," Cooper reported to Franklin. "It was such a new Thing in more senses than one, and struck the whole Congregation with agreeable Surprise, who most cordially joy'nd in that act of Devotion." [1]

Simeon Deane was no silent diplomatic courier. In each city or army camp between Boston and York he gave a general account of the treaties. Frederick MacKenzie, a British officer stationed at Newport, heard of Deane's arrival, but at first refused to believe the rumors of the alliance. MacKenzie quickly changed his mind, and on May 4 he recorded in his diary, "Great rejoicings have been made of late all over the Country, on account of their Alliance with France, which they say is now certain." [2]

Citizens from Providence fired a thirteen-gun salute at sunrise and sunset to celebrate the news.[3] After leaving Providence, Deane made his way through New York State, stopping at Fishkill, where Governor George Clinton first heard the news. Another New Yorker, Phillip Schuyler, learned of the alliance by letter and immediately sent messengers to inform various Indian tribes convened at Onondaga. The *New York Journal,* displaying greater restraint than the New England papers, decided not to print the news of the alliance until it had received permission from Congress.[4]

Simeon Deane delivered the dispatches to Congress at York on April

[1] Cooper to Franklin, May 13, 1778, Franklin Papers, UP, Vol. II.
[2] *Diary of Frederick MacKenzie* (Cambridge, 1930), Vol. I, pp. 271, 275–76, diary entries April 25, 1778, May 4, 1778.
[3] *Providence Gazette,* April 25, 1778.
[4] Clinton to Conway, April 29, 1778, Hugh Hastings, ed., *Public Papers of George Clinton* (Albany, 1899–1914), Vol. III, p. 231; Schuyler to Washington, May 22, 1778, Washington Papers, LC, Vol. LXXIV; *New York Journal,* May 16, 1778, quoted in Frank Moore, ed., *Diary of the Revolution* (Hartford, 1876), p. 565.

30. Congressmen welcomed the news, and after a weekend adjournment, they voted unanimously on May 4 to ratify the treaties.[5] In the spring of 1778, despite the Saratoga victory, the British still had two armies intact, a sea monopoly, and control of New York and Philadelphia, while the American Army had been greatly depleted by the devastating winter at Valley Forge. Under these circumstances, Congress did not carefully weigh the possible disadvantages, but swiftly embarked on a policy which tied United States independence to French policy in Europe. Members of Congress took time only to note that France stipulated that it retain all of its West Indian possessions at the end of the war and that neither party could agree to a separate peace with Great Britain. No Congressman protested that the American commissioners had violated their instructions. In fact, the commercial pact provided for in the instructions was overshadowed by the defensive treaty, which, it was observed, granted France no territorial compensation in North America. Congress, by its quick acceptance of the alliance, changed the entire political and military course of the war.

The public reception of the news of the alliance justified Congress' hasty and unanimous move. The alliance caused no appreciable defections to the British, and no anti-Catholic or anti-French articles appeared in the press. The lack of dissent resulted from events of the previous two years rather than from a deliberate consideration of the alliance. Americans siding with the British had already moved within British lines, and those remaining within American lines welcomed news of the alliance. "America is at last saved," Henry Livingston wrote, "by almost a Miracle." [6]

The initial reaction to the alliance stressed the magnanimity and generosity of the French and their king—almost a complete reversal of previous American stereotypes.

> The Treaty between the United States of America & the *Most Christian* king proves that his Majesty of France is not only so, but also the most wise, most just, & magnanimous Prince not only in the World at present but to be found in history. The treaty was unanimously approved of by Congress, and the King of France has the signal honor of the thanks of Congress.[7]

[5] Edmund Burnett, *The Continental Congress* (New York, 1941), pp. 331–32. Burnett's book is still the best account of the Continental Congress, although he tends to slight its role in foreign affairs as well as the relation of congressional controversy to French policy.

[6] Livingston to Walter Livingston, May 11, 1778, Livingston Papers, N-YHS, box IV.

[7] McKean to Sally McKean, May 11, 1778, McKean Papers, HSP, Vol. VI, italics in original.

Citizens in the South responded to news of the treaty as enthusiastically as had their compatriots in the North. Mann Page wrote that Virginians appeared "to be much pleased with the Intelligence." In New Bern, North Carolina, a celebration was held and according to the local newspaper, "Universal joy appeared in every countenance; great plenty of liquor was given to the populace, and the evening was concluded with great good humour and social mirth." [8]

Henry Laurens wrote John Gervais, his business partner in Charleston, that he would not say "The Treaty, specious & engaging as it appears, is altogether unexceptionable—but all circumstances considered I re[cord] 'tis very well." Gervais, showing less restraint, stated that the news of the alliance "gave great Satisfaction to all except Tories," and added, "The Court of France I [do] not think have acted with a Conduct which I should have expected in her however they have taken the best way." Another Charleston merchant viewed the alliance "as a special act of a kind providence in our favour." [9]

The liberal terms of the alliance excited particular admiration in the press throughout the nation.

> The part he [King of France] acted upon this occasion, was truly noble and magnanimous. No monopoly of our trade was desired; it is left open to all we chuse to trade with. This is wise as it is generous; it being undoubtly the interest of France that this treaty should be durable, which would not have been so likely had hard terms been exacted of us.[10]

Loyalists greeted the news at first with skepticism and later with disgust. The rumors of an alliance were intended for "the credulous Multitude, [which] tho' so often deceived, still grasp at the Delusion." [11] Another Loyalist charged that the alliance, the last effort of desperate men, represented the "keystone of the arch that supports that system of lies with which the good people of America have been gull'd and deceived: but the foundation is rotten, and the whole fabric must soon fall to the ground." Claiming that the alliance would be of little benefit to the states even in the event of war between France and England, he con-

[8] Mann Page, Jr. to Richard Henry Lee, May 28, 1778, Lee Family Papers, UV, R. 4; *North Carolina Gazette* (New Bern), May 29, 1778.
[9] Laurens to Gervais, May 4, 1778, Henry Laurens Papers, SCHS, R. 7; Gervais to Laurens, June 19, 1778, *ibid.,* R. 19; Smith to Zubly, July 13, 1778, Josiah Smith Papers, SHC.
[10] *Independent Chronicle* (Boston), April 23, 1778.
[11] *Newport Gazette,* May 21, 1778.

cluded, "The truth is, the leaders of rebellion are alarmed for their own safety; they see peace and happiness held out to the people in the clearest and most unreserved terms [North proposals], but for themselves, there is no retreat, only what must ultimately end in infamy and disgrace." [12]

James Allen, who remained neutral during the war but held definite Loyalist sympathies, was dismayed on May 11. "The face of politics is much alter'd for the worse, as war with France being inevitable, as she has recognized the Independence of America & entered into a Commercial treaty with the United States." The sun rose again for the former chief justice of Pennsylvania; on June 8 he wrote confidently, "Things now wear a different face. War with France, is not declared, not likely to take place, troops are coming over here & if Congress will not treat, as there is reason to expect, this will be an active campaign." [13] But Henry Laurens noted that Loyalist efforts to discount or criticize the alliance often backfired, "The French Court are illiberally charged with insidious practices—this gives much offense." [14]

Initially the news of the alliance had minimal effect on the loosely organized moderate and radical blocs in Congress, an alignment that had its origins in the conflicts of 1775 and 1776 over the timing of independence. The radicals, who had advocated an early and complete break with Great Britain, urged immediate independence; they further argued that, once independence was declared, self-interest would compel France to recognize and aid the United States. The moderate bloc included those who opposed independence and those who feared that a premature declaration would foreclose possibilities of reconciliation with Great Britain. The argument was substantive and its effects long lasting in foreign policy, because the radicals believed the moderates' contention would discourage any foreign aid and destroy the opportunity for independence. Moreover, the radicals never ceased to believe that the moderates opposed a final break, and therefore were more likely to accept an end to the conflict with less than complete independence from Great Britain.

The radical bloc, under the leadership of the Massachusetts delegates, received consistent support from New Englanders such as Roger Sherman, William Ellery, Oliver Wolcott, William Whipple, and Josiah Bartlett. Outside of New England the radicals were numerically weak,

[12] *Royal Gazette* (New York), May 20, 1778.
[13] "Diary of James Allen, Esq. of Philadelphia, Counsellor-at-Law, 1770–1778," *Pennsylvania Magazine of History and Biography* (hereafter *PMHB*), Vol. IX (1885), pp. 435, 438, May 11, 1778, June 8, 1778.
[14] Laurens to Gates, June 17, 1778, Gates Papers, N-YHS, box IX.

their ranks including only Thomas McKean from the Middle States and the Lee brothers and Henry Laurens in the South. Until 1779, Thomas Burke of North Carolina and John Witherspoon of New Jersey generally supported the radicals in foreign policy.

The moderates, led by John Jay, Robert Morris, George Clymer, John Dickinson, and Meriwether Smith, were not as well organized as the radicals and did not achieve dominance in Congress until the end of 1779. By 1778, however, the moderates were as firm as the radicals in their demand for total independence from Great Britain. They were less imbued with republican ideals than radicals such as Samuel Adams and William Whipple, however, and they failed to accept the radicals' conviction that American objectives could not be secured without unceasing vigilance against the intentions of even friendly nations. Nor did they share the radicals' belief that particular territorial demands were essential to safeguard independence and the republic's security. "The fishing Banks are at least as important as Tobacco yards, or Rice Swamps, or the flourishing Wheat Fields of Pennsylvania," Samuel Adams preached in an argument that few moderates could accept. "The Name only of Independence is not worth the Blood of a single Citizen. We have not been so long contending for Trifles. A *Navy* must support our Independence; and Britain will tell you, that the *Fishery* is a grand Nursery of Seamen." [15]

Radicals viewed the alliance as a confirmation of their belief that self-interest would lead France to the aid of the United States. Washington succinctly stated the prevailing view of this group, "France appears to have acted with politic generosity towards us, and to have timed her declaration in our favor most admirably for her own interest and abasing her ancient rival." [16] Nevertheless, the lack of demands by France surprised the radicals and Oliver Wolcott was puzzled that nothing in the treaty "indicates any Design of obtaining any advantage over us, But seems adapted to secure a lasting Friendship which it is certainly in the highest Interest of France to cultivate." William Ellery agreed with Wolcott, "I have only time to say that these Treaties are magnanimous and founded in our Independency, equality, and reciprocity." [17]

Although the radicals had long considered self-interest the mainspring of foreign relations, they were surprised at the benefits it brought in practice. France, in following its own immediate self-interest, had

[15] S. Adams to McKean, Aug. 29, 1781, McKean Papers, Vol. I, italics in original.

[16] Washington to MacDougall, May 1, 1778, Fitzpatrick, ed., *Washington,* Vol. XI, p. 325.

[17] Wolcott to Mrs. Wolcott, May 9, 1778, Wolcott Papers, CHS, Vol. II; Ellery to Vernon, May 6, 1778, *LMCC,* Vol. III, p. 222.

greatly enhanced the cause of the United States. Elbridge Gerry, ecstatic at the turn of events, wrote in virtual disbelief:

> I congratulate you on the late events in Europe. What a miraculous change in the political world! The ministry of England advocates for despotism, and endeavouring to enslave those who might have remained loyal subjects of the King. The government of France an advocate of liberty, expousing [sic] the cause of protestants and risking a war to secure their independence. The king of England considered by every whig in the nation a tyrant, and the king of France applauded by every whig in America as the protector of the rights of man! The king of Great Britain aiding the advancement of popery, and the king of France endeavouring to free his people from ecclesiastical power! Britain at war with America! France in Alliance with her! These, my friend, are astonishing changes. Perhaps one principle, self interest, may account for all.[18]

The moderates welcomed the alliance, being confident that it would bring independence and a quick end to the war. Perhaps because they desired less and foresaw an early conclusion to the war, they were less distrustful of French motives and objectives than were the radicals. Gouverneur Morris, for example, was convinced the United States would be in possession of her independence within three months if France and Great Britain had representatives in the United States. Samuel Chase of Maryland believed the alliance would enable the United States to gain independence. "America," he wrote, "has now taken her rank among the nations and has it in her power to secure her Liberty and Independence." [19]

The moderates included a number of men who feared that a protracted war might upset or fundamentally alter the pre-revolutionary social order. Robert R Livingston, for one, dreaded the consequences of any change in the social order. "I sincerely rejoice with you in our flattering prospect of a happy termination of this war, our allies have stepped in in very good time," he wrote, "we began to need their assistance and I do not doubt John Bulls hatred of his old enemy will induce him to close with us on our own terms in order to go to loggerheads with Lewis." The patrician Livingston continued, "They love the sport, let them go at it, & God send us a good deliverance for I do not

[18] Gerry to ———, May 26, 1778, James T. Austin, *Life of Elbridge Gerry* (Boston, 1828), Vol. I, p. 276.

[19] Morris to Jay, April 28, 1778, Henry Johnson, ed., *Correspondence and Public Papers of John Jay* (New York, 1891), Vol. I, pp. 178–79; Chase to Johnston, May 3, 1778, *LMCC*, Vol. III, p. 218.

find that this war has produced the effect I expected from it upon the manners of the people, or rendered them [more?] worthy or making them more virtuous of the blessing of a free government." [20]

Many moderates accepted the break with Great Britain without protest, but they had mixed feelings about an alliance with France. The ties of religion and language could not be eradicated overnight. John Jay, a Huguenot, stated that Great Britain must grant independence, but if she did this he would rather have an alliance with Great Britain than with any other power on earth. He admitted to Gouverneur Morris, "The destruction of Old England would hurt me; I wish it well; it afforded my ancestors an asylum from persecution." [21]

James Iredell, a judge in North Carolina, had feelings similar to Jay's. Upon hearing of the alliance, Iredell resigned his post in order to devote more time to his law practice, convinced that United States independence was now assured. In 1778 Iredell described the reception of the news of the alliance in New Bern to his wife, "There was also an affecting prospect to a man who still feels for the condition of his native country, and laments the miserable but necessary disunion from her. The British flag reversed, and the French and American meeting, and laid by the side of each other." Iredell, like most moderates, did not oppose the alliance, but regretted the sad turn of events. "The advantage of the connection, upon its present honorable principles, is undoubtedly great; but old attachments, and the possibility there once existed with prudent management of happier circumstances, will sometimes unavoidably be uppermost." [22]

The moderates and radicals still agreed on the fundamental point of independence, and both groups believed the alliance would hasten the time when Great Britain would recognize the United States. Americans were sincerely grateful to France, for no longer did they have to appeal to the temperance of Great Britain. Instead, the United States could now look forward confidently to defeating Great Britain militarily with the aid of France. Both moderate and radical leaders became slightly overconfident, seeing the United States in a strong bargaining position to achieve beneficial terms by exploiting the ancient rivalry of France and Great Britain.

Robert Treat Paine, a signer of the Declaration of Independence from Massachusetts, best summarized the exaggerated view of American power in a letter explaining the advantages of the alliance. The alliance,

[20] Livingston to Morris, June 13, 1778, Livingston Papers, N-YHS, box IV.

[21] Jay to Morris, April 29, 1778, John Jay Papers, CU.

[22] For his resignation, see Iredell to Arthur Iredell, June 30, 1783, Charles E. Johnson Papers, NCSA, Vol. 67.3; quote is from Iredell to Mrs. Iredell, May 23, 1778, *ibid.,* Vol. 67.1.

he wrote, was "made upon equal terms & the most liberal principles . . . [and] not all of [the] Sagacity and trustful invention of the most fanciful tory can [state] one objection."

> As to that Treaty of Alliance or defense, which in ye most explicit terms makes our independence its Object, both in matters of Gov-[ernment] & Commerce. The first article is so well framed, that if we should make peace with G[reat] B[ritain] preserving our independence & the next moment a war should take place between G[reat] B[ritain] & France, we should be under no obligation to join in either of their quarrels farther than would be our interest. . . .
>
> The 4th Article takes [care] of all difficulties which may have been conceived about Canada or Nova Scotia, or any part of North America, being a perpetual [renunciation] thereof [by France]. . . . In these matters France is no doubt governed by her own interest; that moment America cant defend herself alone, she conversely obtain[s] the aid of Britain, upon the terms she has offered us (if nothing else) of being her humble slaves.[23]

The terms of accommodation to which Paine referred are the North proposals for reconciliation. Lord North had reacted to the news of the expected French alliance by making the first serious effort to compromise British differences with the United States. With Parliament's approval, he appointed a commission, headed by Lord Carlisle, to negotiate with Congress. The Carlisle Commission had limited powers but was prepared to offer amnesty, repeal of internal taxation, and recognition of the rights of colonial assemblies in exchange for Congressional recognition of the supremacy of Parliament. Because the Commission could not even negotiate on the cardinal point of the war, independence, Congress never seriously considered the North proposals. A Loyalist paper sensed the impending failure of the proposals when Patriots in New Jersey received the terms, "some [are] looking upon them to be quite satisfactory, and others say, nothing less than Independency will suffice." [24] The proposals, perhaps acceptable in 1775, now seemed only a ruse. George Washington commented, "I shall candidly declare to you, that they appear to me to be a compound of Fear, art, villainy, and these ingredients so equally mixed, that I scarcely know which predominates." [25]

[23] Paine to George Phillips, draft, no date [early May, 1778?], Robert Treat Paine Papers, MHS.

[24] *New York Gazette,* April 27, 1778.

[25] Washington to John Washington, June 10, 1778, Fitzpatrick, ed., *Washington,* Vol. XII, p. 43.

News of the Carlisle Commission reached the United States ten days before that of the alliance, although the members of the commission did not arrive until June. Congress rejected the North reconciliation proposals before officially hearing of the alliance. The quick rejection was a political move to demonstrate unanimity against peace without independence, or as Henry Laurens expressed it, "what answer can be given but that which was returned to the foolish virgins—'the Door is Shut.' " [26] Many leaders, including John Jay, Thomas Burke, and William Livingston, believed erroneously that the Carlisle Commission did have the power to offer independence, and therefore the United States would ultimately have to negotiate with it, even though Congress had officially rejected its offer; much public and private discussion of this point ensued.

"Camillus," probably a pseudonym for William Livingston, strongly attacked the reconciliation proposals, "Yes, My Lord, the graduation in shame was too great, or you would have done it last year; but it is now too late. We are united (we believe) to your powerful rival the French and we glory in the connection." There was no fear, "Camillus" asserted, of an intimate union with France, and "with such an ally as France in Europe, What power will dare to molest us?" [27] In spite of the bravado of "Camillus," the news of the reconciliation proposals before official confirmation of the alliance alarmed many officials.

Henry Laurens, the president of the Continental Congress, wrote Washington and William Livingston, stressing the approaching political crisis for the United States. Laurens feared that the United States would have to negotiate with the Carlisle Commission, since an offer of independence would be irresistible.[28] Livingston agreed with Laurens, but believed that the United States could bargain with both powers. "France and Great Britain seem to be like two great merchants recurring to America for a market and I hope we shall not be such block-heads as to sell our commodities too cheap." [29]

The news of the alliance delayed any final decision on what to do about the Carlisle Commission. Americans, with the assurance of French support, became more strident in their communications. James Thaxter wrote that the reconciliation proposals were "founded on his

[26] Laurens to Gates, June 17, 1778, Gates Papers, Box 19D.
[27] *New Jersey Gazette* (Trenton), April 29, 1778.
[28] Laurens to Washington, April 27, 1778, *LMCC*, Vol. III, pp. 191–92; Laurens to Livingston, April 29, 1778, Laurens Papers, R. 7. Thomas McKean agreed with Laurens' assessment. McKean to Caesar Rodney, April 28, 1778, George H. Ryden, ed., *Letters to and from Caesar Rodney* (Philadelphia, 1933), pp. 264–65.
[29] Livingston to Laurens, May 7, 1778, Laurens Papers, R. 9.

[Lord North's] fears. He will tremble more yet."[30] General John Sullivan returned the copies of the North proposals sent to him by Robert Pigot, the commander of the British troops at Newport.

> Had proposals of This kind been properly & Sincerely made by the Court of Britain to the Supreme Authority of America, before the wanton Cruelty which has marked the progress of the British Arms in this Country had taken place, or prior to our Declaring ourselves Independent, & Entering into an Alliance with Foreign Powers; They would have been accepted with Sentiments of Gratitude. But at this time all proposals Except for peace upon Honourable & Equal terms must be ineffectual.[31]

After it gradually became obvious that the Carlisle Commission would not offer independence, the chance of negotiating with Great Britain was eliminated until the completion of the campaign of 1778. The alliance with France became the foundation of United States policy when Americans discovered that there were still no grounds for negotiation with Great Britain. The pact explicitly stated that neither party could conduct separate peace talks, but Americans would have broken the alliance in its first months if they could have ended the war with recognition of United States independence. Fortunately for the future of the alliance, the French Minister did not arrive until the United States had determined that the Carlisle Commission could not offer independence. A correspondent of Horatio Gates ably summed up the influence of British failures, rather than French successes, in the United States commitment to the alliance.

> Our Treaty with France, has, I think been wisely concerted on our part; and exhibits a degree of Generosity and disinterestedness on the part of France which was hardly expected from a Court grown old in Intrigues, and remarkably sedulous in securing advantages by negotiation. I wait with Impatience to hear further about the Expected arrival of Commissioners from the Court of London. Their Errand, if founded on the two Bills we have seen, will doubtless be unsuccessful. Amer [?] *Novumus Taxare* [,] a Repeal of certain detestable Acts, and a tender of pardon,

[30] Thaxter to Abigail Adams, April 30 and May 3, 1778 (one letter), Adams Family Papers, MHS, R. 349. Quotations from the Adams Papers are from the microfilm edition, by permission of the Massachusetts Historical Society.

[31] Sullivan to Pigot, April 27, 1778, Otis G. Hammond, ed., *Letters and Papers of Major-General John Sullivan of the Continental Army* (*Collections of the New Hampshire Historical Society*, Vols. XIII–XIV; Concord, 1930–1939), Vol. II, p. 40.

the acceptance of which would necessarily imply a guilt, must be very unsavory to the American Taste expecially after an acknowledgment of our Independence by one of the first powers in Europe.[32]

After the failure of the Carlisle Commission, Americans turned their attention to the new possibilities created by the alliance. Two issues came to the forefront, the territorial aspirations of the United States and its obligations to France. The territorial issue had remained dormant while independence held priority, but once independence was assumed, Americans began to debate the possibility of gaining increased territory through the alliance. The alignment on this question saw the radicals generally demanding more territory, while the moderates were content to settle for the territory within the Thirteen Original Colonies.

The New England delegates had an especially large appetite for additional territory, particularly Canada, Nova Scotia, and Newfoundland. The acquisition of these areas required large land armies and naval support which could be gained only by convincing France to back New England demands. Although France had renounced her claims to territory in North America, it would not support American demands for northern territory unless the United States held possession when peace talks commenced. The New Englanders remained convinced that the alliance offered an opportunity to gain the territory they considered essential for economic and security reasons. William Ellery described the expanded vision of the United States which came to his mind after the alliance:

> I should with you, perhaps, have been willing that France should have continued in her usual way to have supported us, [supplies, loans] had I not in contemplation the divesting of Britain of every foot of land upon this Continent. I think it absolutely necessary to a future lasting peace that we should be possessed of Canada, Nova Scotia and the Floridas, which we cannot effect without the open assistance of France.[33]

Samuel Adams agreed with Ellery, "I hope we shall secure to the United States, Canada, Nova Scotia, and *the Fishery* by our Arms or by Treaty. Florida too is a tempting object at the South." William Whipple, the recipient of Ellery's letter, agreed with his New England colleagues about the desirability of acquiring Canada and Nova Scotia, and, if pos-

---

[32] [M]orin[fie]ld to Gates, May 16, 1778, Gates Papers, box IX.
[33] Ellery to Whipple, May 31, 1778, *LMCC*, Vol. III, p. 269.

sible, dividing Florida with Spain.[34] John Adams proclaimed to Ralph Izard that the primary interest of Massachusetts was agriculture, but in a letter to Congress Adams was also adamant about additional territory.

> The few men of the nation [Great Britain] who think seriously see clearly, in the long train of consequences of American independence, the loss of their West India islands, Nova Scotia, the Floridas, all the American fisheries, a dimunition of their naval power, as well as national bankruptcy and a revolution in their government in favor of arbitrary power.[35]

John Adams and most radicals had an exaggerated view of French generosity, hoping to reap large benefits from the alliance with limited obligations in return. Samuel Adams, for example, agreed with his cousin on the desirability of annexing all British possessions in North America while avoiding United States involvement in French or European affairs. After talking to the French Minister, Gérard, Samuel Adams believed that the United States could accomplish its goals but remain clear of France's European policy.

> Under an Apprehension that our connection with France might lead us to partake in her wars, which be grounded on Views of Ambition and Conquest, I took occasion to hint to him that the sole object of America was independence. He frankly said that whenever Great Britain should acknowledge our Independence, there would be an End of Dispute between her and us, and it would not be the Inclination as it was not the Interest of France to continue the War.[36]

To Adams' way of thinking, France fought wars of conquest, but American territorial ambitions came under the principle of independence.

Richard Henry Lee attempted to elicit Washington's views on territorial demands, but Washington remained noncommittal. This was not enough for Lee. "Should G.B. be engaged in war with the Bourbon family it furnishes us an opportunity of pushing the former quite off this Northern continent," Lee instructed Washington, "which will secure us peace for a Century, instead of War in 7 years, which the British posses-

[34] Adams to Warren, Nov. 2 or 3, 1778, *ibid.*, p. 476; Whipple to Bartlett, Feb. 7, 1779, Josiah Bartlett Papers, DC, Vol. II. Italics in original in Adams' letter.
[35] Adams to Izard, Sept. 25, 1778; Adams to Congress, Dec. 8, 1778, Wharton, ed., *Diplomatic Correspondence,* Vol. II, pp. 743, 857. Adams' views about the consequences of the Revolution were almost identical to those of George III. See Piers Mackesy, *The War for America, 1775–1783* (Cambridge, 1964), p. 461.
[36] Adams to Thacher, Aug. 11, 1778, *LMCC,* Vol. III, p. 368.

sion of Canada, N. Sco. & the Floridas, will inevitably produce." [37] Lee's views were exceptional among southern delegates, although Jefferson agreed with him that the United States should have the fisheries.[38]

The leaders in the Middle States took the moderate position on additional territory. Representatives of New Jersey, Maryland, New York, and Delaware generally opposed demanding Canada or the Floridas. They sought only to end the war as quickly as possible on terms of independence.

Southern delegates harbored greater ambitions, aspiring to the Mississippi territory as well as Florida. Governor Patrick Henry sent an expedition under George Rogers Clark into the Illinois country to claim that territory for Virginia; Georgia and South Carolina organized and sent expeditions against the Indians in the British-occupied territory along their borders; but after 1779 delegates from the Southern States relaxed their demands for Florida and the West due to a desire to end the war honorably without further loss of territory. The French successfully exploited southern fears of military reverses and territorial losses to assert Spanish claims in Florida and the Mississippi territory. The decline of southern territorial aspirations also doomed New England's ambitions.

The French took an ambivalent and somewhat devious position on United States territorial goals. In the Mississippi area, Gérard believed that the United States should compromise and allow Spain to gain most of the territory in order to induce her to assist France and the United States. Gérard did not have any firm instructions on the question of navigation or territory along the Mississippi. In the winter of 1779, however, he discouraged an expedition against Florida by the Southern States, and the French policy became one of preventing the United States from conquering any territory in the lower Mississippi Valley and Florida.[39]

Vergennes had a firm policy on Canada. France had ceded its claims to the United States, but was not averse to British possession of Canada.

[37] Washington to Lee, May 25, 1778, Fitzpatrick, ed., *Washington*, Vol. XI, pp. 450–51; Lee to Washington, June 24, 1778, James C. Ballagh, ed., *The Letters of Richard Henry Lee* (New York, 1911), Vol. I, pp. 419–20.

[38] Jefferson to Lee, Aug. 30, 1778; Lee to Jefferson, Oct. 5, 1778, Julian Boyd, ed., *The Papers of Thomas Jefferson* (Princeton, 1950–   ), Vol. II, pp. 210, 214.

[39] For Gérard's refusal to aid the United States, see Laurens to the President of South Carolina, Jan. 29, 1779, *LMCC*, Vol. IV, p. 48; for the entire problem of western lands, see Thomas P. Abernethy, *Western Lands and the American Revolution* (2d ed.; New York, 1959), pp. 237, 284; Philip C. Phillips, *The West in the Diplomacy of the American Revolution* (Urbana, 1913), pp. 59, 107; Edward S. Corwin, *French Policy and the American Alliance of 1778* (Princeton, 1916), p. 240; see also for the Spanish side, John W. Caughey, *Bernardo De Galvez in Louisiana* (Berkeley, 1934), pp. 92, 246.

Vergennes explained the French position to Gérard before the latter left France for the United States.

> The Congressional Deputies [American commissioners] have suggested to the King that he promise to favor the conquest of Canada, Nova Scotia, and the Floridas which the Americans would undertake; and there is reason to believe that this undertaking is of the utmost importance to Congress. But the King feels that the possession of these three countries, or at least that of Canada by England, would be a serviceable principle for keeping the Americans uneasy (*d'inquiétude*) and cautious; that it will make them feel to an even greater extent the need which they have for friendship and alliance with the King; and that it is not in his [Majesty's] interest to destroy this principle. Accordingly His Majesty thinks that he must make no promises relative to the proposed conquest.[40]

Vergennes warned Gérard not to refuse to cooperate if French good intentions were questioned, but to insist that none of the three territories became an ultimatum in American peace instructions. Vergennes did not deviate from this position during the war, although he did say that if France had to make a choice, Gérard should support United States acquisition of Nova Scotia rather than Canada.[41]

Americans constantly urged a Canadian expedition, but Gérard was equally consistent in refusing to support one. Lafayette, however, favored a Canadian expedition in the winter of 1778–1779, if he were named to lead it. Gérard opposed Lafayette's plans on the basis of his instructions, which he never explicitly revealed to Congress, and Washington himself had strong objections to the proposed invasion. In a private letter to Henry Laurens, Washington wrote that a Canadian expedition led by a Frenchman alarmed "all my feelings for the true and permanent interests of my country." French occupation of Canada, particularly Quebec, which was "attached to them by all the ties of blood, habits, manners, religion, and former connexion of government" would, he feared, "be too great a temptation to be resisted by any power ac-

---

[40] Vergennes to Gérard, March 29, 1778, John J. Meng, ed., *Despatches and Instructions of Conrad Alexandre Gérard* (Baltimore, 1939), p. 129. Meng reprints all of the correspondence between Gérard and Vergennes concerning the United States, and I have used this text for the dispatches. We differ, however, on Gérard's success as a diplomat. See Meng's excellent introduction on Gérard in the United States in *ibid.*, pp. 91–122.

[41] Vergennes to Gérard, March 29, 1778; Oct. 26, 1778; Nov. 18, 1778; Jan. 28, 1779, *ibid.*, pp. 129, 359, 373, 494.

tuated by the common maxims of national policy." Washington continued by stating the position he would take toward France for the remainder of the war:

> Men are very apt to run into extremes; hatred to England may
> carry some into an excess of Confidence in France; especially
> when motives of gratitude are thrown into the scale. Men of this
> description would be unwilling to suppose France capable of act-
> ing so ungenerous a part. I am heartily disposed to entertain the
> most favourable sentiments of our new ally and to cherish them as
> others to a reasonable degree; but it is a maxim founded on the
> universal experience of mankind, that no nation can be trusted
> farther than it is bound by its interests; and no prudent statesman
> or politician will venture to depart from it.[42]

By the fall of 1778 the basic outlines of the final territorial settlement had taken shape, although neither side realized this at the time.
Each year the radicals pressed for an invasion of Canada and insisted
that the fisheries be included in the peace ultimata, with the latter demand becoming the most persistent source of tension between the allies
for the remainder of the war. It slowly became evident that desires for
territorial acquisition could be fulfilled only by negotiation and diplomacy, not by military conquest. Each country protected what it conceived to be its own interest, thus guaranteeing that no large-scale expedition would be launched against the Floridas or Canada as a result of
the alliance. The high hopes of Americans who at first regarded it as the
key to territorial expansion faded under the methodical reasoning of
men like Washington and Vergennes, who recognized the limits of mutual interest.

The debate over territorial ambitions involved the complicated question of the extent to which the United States was, and should be obligated to France. Few Americans doubted French power or denied that
the alliance would bring substantial benefits. But a Philadelphia merchant wondered, as did Samuel Adams, whether the alliance would "en-
tangle us in European Connections, which may engage us in ruinous
Wars, in which we shall have no interest." [43] Many Americans either
ignored this apprehension, or contended that conflicts over France's European commitments need not occur if the United States adhered to the
letter and spirit of the alliance. The alliance, it was explained, was for
independence only.

[42] Washington to Laurens, Nov. 18, 1778, Fitzpatrick, ed., *Washington,* Vol.
XIII, pp. 254–57.
[43] Ingersoll to Reed, June 17, 1778, Reed Papers, N-YHS, Vol V.

After the rejection of the Carlisle Commission, Americans supported close but cautious cooperation with France. Moderate leaders believed that the United States should pursue a policy which would quickly achieve independence, and they were convinced that restricted territorial ambitions and the French alliance would serve this purpose. The radical leaders who had first urged the alliance also considered it essential to securing American independence. Although fearful of long-range commitments to a foreign nation, they chose a policy of cooperation with France while still advocating territorial expansion. The need for the alliance received virtually universal recognition. "Surely," Patrick Henry wrote, "Congress will never recede from our French friends. Salvation to America depends on our holding fast to our attachment to them." John Adams agreed. "The longer I live in Europe and the more I consider our affairs, the more important our Alliance appears to me. It is a rock upon which we may safely build." [44]

Although they well understood the importance of French assistance, Americans, especially the radicals, were wary of their new ally. A realization of what France could do for the United States, rather than friendship or gratitude, determined the American reaction to the alliance. Samuel Adams commented that if war should break out between Great Britain and France, "I should think France must be our Pole Star, while it continues, and our Connections must be formed with hers." Nevertheless, there continued to be apprehension about the new direction of American policy. The radical group sought to assure itself that the connection with France and the defensive alliance were only temporary. William Ellery feared that British policy would "destroy every spark of affection which may still remain in the breasts of Americans, and force us and our commerce irrecoverably into the arms of France, which have been and still are extended to receive both." [45]

Americans, by late summer of 1778, believed they could honorably fulfill their obligations to France if she acted on the supposition that United States independence in itself was a sufficient reward for her assistance. France did not need to engage in a war of conquest, Horatio Gates lectured French naval commander Count D'Estaing, in a letter outlining the American position. Gates explained that Great Britain had armed herself with a balance of power and maintained it with such art that it had been difficult to see any defects. But the alliance now offered

---

[44] Henry to Richard Henry Lee, June 18, 1778, Lee Family Papers, R. 4; Adams to Warren, Aug. 4, 1778, Wharton, ed., *Diplomatic Correspondence*, Vol. II, p. 676.

[45] Adams to John Adams, Oct. 25, 1778, *LMCC*, Vol. III, p. 462; Henrietta C. Ellery, ed., "Journal of Route and Occurrences in a Journey to Philadelphia from Dighton, begun October 24, 1778," *PMHB*, Vol. XII (1888), p. 198.

France a chance to demonstrate the cruelty and oppression of Great Britain to all Europe.

> He [the King of France] fights their Battles against England, by whom they have all been insulted. He enables them all to partake with him of the Addition of relative power, which our Independence gives him. He checks a Set of Tyrants, who fancied themselves strong enough not to dissemble their Design to oppress all the States of the Earth.[46]

Gates added that he was sure that the King of France would seek no territory for the sake of ambition, and that early victory "must be the Reward of his Moderation and it is natural to believe that the use he will make of his Success will silence Envy." [47] Realizing the precarious position of the United States, Gates could only hope that France would fulfill her commitments under the alliance. If she did not, there would be little that the United States could do except make a humiliating peace with Great Britain.

There seemed to be little justification for fearing the alliance with France. The Americans had achieved most of their desires in the commercial treaty, and the defensive treaty was moderate and generous by the standards of statecraft of that day. France had not raised any questions about religion or required the United States to divide territory with her as the price for an alliance. Instead, France provided an initial subsidy without political strings and sent a fleet to America to aid the war effort against Great Britain. It would have been surprising if Americans had not been pleased with the alliance. Its enthusiastic reception truly indicated public feeling, but did not imply a blind trust in France or a sacrifice of American self-interest.

The first moves of the United States in foreign relations seemed to be successful. The reasons for success included the European balance of power, the tenacity of Americans in fighting alone for three years, and British blunders. Whatever the explanation of the alliance, the Continental Congress received credit for directing a foreign policy which seemed to insure independence beyond a doubt without sacrificing essential interests. What future steps needed to be taken were still unknown and more often ignored. Spain remained a mystery, and Great Britain would certainly change her policy after the failure of the Carlisle Commission. Nor were there answers on what France would do in the future to assist independence.

These serious questions, which received scant attention in the initial

[46] Gates to D'Estaing, Dec. 30, 1778, Gates Papers, box 19C.
[47] *Ibid.*

American reaction to the alliance, lay dormant while Americans celebrated their diplomatic success. Even the puritanical William Livingston could be frivolous about the prospects.

> His Christian Majesty is certainly a very clever fellow, and I drink to his health whenever I can get wine to do it in (and without any scruple about the difference between the French King and the King of France), thinking it an abomination, and highly derogatory to the dignity of Le Grand Monarch, to toast him in a toddy. I hope his Catholic Majesty will soon give us an opportunity to express our affection for him in the like sociable manner; and if there be any foundation for the treaty which English newswriters have fabricated for us in the Mediterranean, depend upon it, I shall not forget the Emperor of Morocco, as great a Mahometan as he is.[48]

[48] Livingston to Laurens, June 18, 1778, Laurens Papers, R. 9.

III. Conrad Alexandre Gérard

On July 11, 1778, the French frigate *La Chimère* docked at Chester, just below Philadelphia, after completing a ninety-one day trip with a French fleet commanded by Vice Admiral Count D'Estaing. On board *La Chimère* was the first French Minister to the United States, Conrad Alexandre Gérard. The next day a Congressional reception committee headed by John Hancock officially greeted Gérard, who made a triumphal entry into Philadelphia.[1] A Rhode Island delegate described the auspicious event, "I had the Honor last Sabbath of welcoming in Person the Plenipotentiary of France to these United States. Grand and important is the year of 1778. We behold with wonder and Astonishment a Leap of at least a Century." [2]

Gérard, an experienced diplomat, was surprised at the warmth of his reception. "Nothing, My Lord, equals the zeal which almost all members of Congress and the other major figures displayed in coming to see me and in expressing to me their feelings on the alliance and on the courtesies of the King," he reported in his first dispatch. "I would fear to be exaggerating, were I to reproduce the wording which the calmest people used and still use every day in their conversations with me." [3]

Although the term "French diplomat" was virtually synonymous with deceit to many Americans, Gérard's conduct impressed even the suspicious radical members of Congress, causing Josiah Bartlett to observe, "The behavior of Mons. Gerard seems to indicate a greater degree of sincerity in that nation than my prejudices formerly allowed them." The skeptical Henry Laurens noted, "very seldom, Sir, do I suffer myself to pronounce an opinion of any Man upon so short and slight an acquaintance; even the present Case although I have seen many works which induce me to [be impressed?] with this Gentleman's candor and integrity." [4]

Gérard represented a type of Frenchman quite unlike the merchants, soldiers of fortune, and glory-seekers who had preceded him in the United States. The son of an upper middle-class Alsatian family, he en-

[1] *Pennsylvania Packet* (Philadelphia, hereafter *Packet*), July 14, 1778.
[2] Marchant to Carter, July 14, 1778, *LMCC*, Vol. IV, p. 330.
[3] Gérard to Vergennes, July 15, 1778, Meng, ed., *Gérard*, p. 148.
[4] Bartlett to Whipple, July 20, 1778, Whipple Papers, LC; Laurens to Lowndes, July 15, 1778, Laurens Papers, R. 7.

tered the foreign service in 1749 after receiving a law degree from the University of Strasbourg. Gérard had a successful, but unspectacular, career, advancing to *premier commis* (first secretary) under the Duc de Choiseul in 1766. When Vergennes was appointed minister of foreign affairs in 1774, he retained Gérard as first secretary and in 1776 assigned him additional responsibilities as Commissioner of Boundaries.[5] Gérard had also negotiated the treaties with the United States before his appointment as minister.

Gérard was thus one of the most informed and experienced diplomats in the French government. Intimately acquainted with French policy toward Great Britain and the United States, he was more qualified for American service than any other French diplomat. Vergennes was confident that Gérard could present French policy accurately in Philadelphia.

Vergennes directed Gérard to assure American ratification and adherence to the alliance, while seeing that the United States did not enter into separate negotiations with Great Britain or sign a separate peace. In addition, Gérard would have to make certain that the United States did not take any action which might permanently alienate Spain. Vergennes did not have a rigid policy in other areas. He made it clear that France would not prolong the war to insure United States inclusion in the fisheries, and, significantly, he failed to mention the conflict between Spain and the United States over the navigation of the Mississippi river. Gérard had wide latitude in the actions he could take to execute the basic outlines of French policy.[6]

In spite of his experience, Gérard arrived in the United States with several attitudes which were to cause tension. He assumed that Americans recognized the great power that France was bringing to the aid of an insignificant country. The alliance, in Gérard's opinion, represented a meritorious act by the powerful in aid of the weak. Americans, if they understood the situation, could be expected to follow French suggestions. Given Gérard's assumptions, the possibility of American opposition did not seem consistent with loyalty to the alliance.

Americans, like Gérard, supported the alliance, but they viewed it with different assumptions. Remembering the eighteen months that France had waited after independence, they did not regard the alliance as a favor. The alliance, as Americans understood it, was a partnership resulting from the demonstrated ability of the United States to be an independent country. Americans felt gratitude, but not subservience, in

[5] All of the information on Gérard's background is from Meng's introduction, Meng, ed., *Gérard*, pp. 35–42.
[6] Vergennes to Gérard, March 29, 1778, *ibid.*, pp. 126–30.

1778. A newspaper account of Gérard's formal recognition by Congress reflected the new American self-confidence in their position as an independent nation.

> Thus has a new and noble sight been exhibited in this new world—the Representatives of the United States of America, solemnly giving public audience to a Minister Plenipotentiary from the most powerful Prince in Europe. Four years ago, such an event, at so near a day, was not in the view even of imagination; But it is the Almighty who raiseth up: he hath stationed America among the powers of the earth and cloathed her in robes of Sovereignty.[7]

Gérard's attitude of superiority was of little import in his efforts to secure congressional adherence to the alliance and rejection of the Carlisle Commission offers. Even before Gérard arrived, Congress had decisively refused to enter into negotiations with any person connected with the Carlisle Commission. Gérard quickly concluded that Congress was sincere in not seeking to explore separate peace talks.[8]

After the Carlisle Commissioners announced their intention to return to Great Britain, John Berkenhout and John Temple, acting under orders from Lord George Germain, sought to open peace talks with certain members of Congress.[9] John Temple had important connections in the United States. A former resident of Boston and the son-in-law of a leading Boston politician, James Bowdoin, he arrived in Philadelphia after interrogation by the State Council of Massachusetts, which expressed "entire satisfaction at his return" from England. Temple carried letters of introduction to Samuel Adams from John Winthrop and Samuel Cooper.[10] Berkenhout, traveling on his own, made his way from New York through New Jersey, but his mission was terminated when he was jailed by order of Congress. Temple met with more success, dining with the Massachusetts delegation in the first week of December.[11] A Philadelphia paper soon published a letter signed "Centinel," scolding Samuel Adams for entertaining Temple.[12]

Gérard could not understand how Adams had allowed such a stupid

---

[7] *Connecticut Courant* (Hartford), Aug. 25, 1778.

[8] Gérard to Vergennes, July 25, 1778; Aug. 12, 1778, Meng, ed., *Gérard*, pp. 178–79, 213.

[9] Gérard to Vergennes, Sept. 1–3, 1778, *ibid.*, p. 251; for Berkenhout's account of his experience, see Howard Peckham, ed., "Dr. Berkenhout's Journal, 1778," *PMHB*, Vol. LXV (1941), pp. 69–82.

[10] *Continental Journal* (Boston), Oct. 1, 1778; Winthrop to Adams, Nov. 9, 1778; Cooper to Adams, Nov. 7, 1778, NYPL.

[11] Samuel Holten Diary, Dec. 2, 1778, *LMCC*, Vol. III, p. 516.

[12] *Packet*, Dec. 8, 1778.

political mistake to occur. He informed Adams that, despite Temple's credentials, such conviviality would create a bad impression in France. Adams, seeking to cooperate, immediately agreed not to see Temple again. After his meeting with Gérard, Adams ruefully wrote his wife, "It may reasonably be supposed that he is determined to merit the Character of his own Court of a vigilant and faithful Minister." [13]

Gérard impressed Congress with the necessity of insuring that it did not appear to be holding conversations with Temple or Berkenhout. Unnoticed and disgraced, Temple finally left Philadephia to return to Great Britain via Holland, and Berkenhout was released from jail to return to New York.[14] Gérard reached agreement with Congress on Temple and Berkenhout, because the delegates realized how dangerous such actions might appear in France. Furthermore, Congress was determined not to negotiate without assurances of independence. Gérard's success was due to understanding on both sides of the need for a common line of action.

Spain presented a more difficult problem for Gérard. Vergennes had instructed him to protect Spanish interests, but never to speak officially for Spain. Without mentioning the Mississippi River, Vergennes asked Gérard to limit United States ambitions for East and West Florida so that they might serve as an inducement for Spain to enter the war. At a minimum, Vergennes declared, Spain should have West Florida, including the territory around Pensacola.[15]

Vergennes viewed Spanish policy toward the American Revolution with disdain, failing to consider that Spain had her own interests in the Americas. Floridablanca, the Spanish Foreign Minister, believed that his country had more to lose than to win by aiding the rebels and entering the war against Great Britain. A tenuous, but operative, division of territory existed in North America between Great Britain and Spain. Floridablanca, being reasonably satisfied with this division, believed that Spanish policy should be directed toward re-acquiring Minorca and Gibraltar.[16]

Moreover, Floridablanca had additional reservations about aiding the United States. He objected to supporting rebels in any colony, especially one in the Western Hemisphere. In addition, he thought that a

---

[13] Adams to Mrs. Adams, Dec. 13, 1778, Harry A. Cushing, ed., *The Writings of Samuel Adams* (New York, 1908), Vol. IV, pp. 96–97.

[14] After Berkenhout returned to England he wrote that Congress had "predetermined to listen to no terms of accommodation with Britain." He added, "No terms which Britain can offer to America will ever persuade the republican faction, by whose arts the southern colonies were stimulated to revolt, to relinquish the independent system of religion and government." John Berkenhout, *Lucubration on Ways and Means* (London, 1780), p. 18.

[15] Vergennes to Gérard, March 29, 1778, Meng, ed., *Gérard*, p. 128.

[16] Richard Morris, *The Peacemakers* (New York, 1965), pp. 14–17.

newly united nation would pose a greater threat to Spanish possessions in the Mississippi Valley than had British policy. Also, if Great Britain retained the Colonies, Floridablanca was sure that Spain could exert more pressure on her by threatening British interests in Europe and Africa.[17]

Don Juan de Miralles served as Spain's unofficial observer in Philadelphia. Gérard worked with Miralles, but disputed his view that the United States presented a threat to Spanish interests. Miralles declared that the United States was inimical to Spanish interests, insisting that Spain have exclusive navigation of the Mississippi and possession of the Floridas.[18]

Control of the Western territory fast became a pressing issue for Gérard, because George Rogers Clark had already been sent into the Illinois country to secure the area for Virginia. Gérard, forced to walk a tightrope between American and Spanish interests, sought a prior agreement with the United States on the division of British territory. By requesting Congress to limit its goals in the West, he attempted to forestall actions which could produce an irreconcilable difference between Spain and the United States.[19]

Miralles, too, put Gérard, in a difficult position by demanding that he support Spanish territorial demands. Gérard persuaded the United States to sacrifice some of its territorial aspirations for possible Spanish adherence to the alliance. He proposed a joint expedition to capture the Floridas, with the United States taking East Florida and Spain West Florida.[20] Beyond this, Gérard could only cajole and persuade in seeking to lessen the mutual distrust between the United States and Spain.

Gérard appeared to balance the two forces while actually favoring Spanish claims. Although he could not resolve all the problems, he did persuade the United States to limit its objectives. Congress offered to compromise on the navigation of the Mississippi if Spain would allow United States trade to pass through New Orleans. Gérard believed that he had worked out an equitable compromise, but he made it clear that he could make no commitments for Spain.[21] In later instructions Vergennes asked Gérard to keep the United States position on the Mississippi flexible, a task he had already accomplished.[22]

---

[17] *Ibid.*

[18] Gérard to Vergennes, July 25, 1778, Meng, ed., *Gérard,* pp. 186–87.

[19] Gérard to Vergennes, Sept. 1, 1778; Oct. 21–22, 1778, *ibid.,* pp. 242, 344–45.

[20] Gérard to Vergennes, Dec. 19–22, 1778, *ibid.,* pp. 434–35; Laurens to Lowndes, Jan. 31, 1779, *LMCC,* Vol. IV, p. 50; Whipple to Bartlett, Feb. 7, 1779, Bartlett Papers, Vol. II.

[21] Gérard to Vergennes, Feb. 18, 1779, Meng., ed., *Gérard,* p. 532.

[22] Vergennes to Gérard, Feb. 19, 1779, *ibid.,* p. 537.

Sweet persuasion was not the only tool Gérard used to convince Congress that it should follow his recommendations. He informed several delegates in a private conference that if the United States forced France to choose between Spain and the United States over territorial issues, Spain would receive priority. Toward the end of his tenure in the United States, Gérard wrote that he had accomplished a major goal of his instructions by convincing the United States not to ask France for anything without considering Spanish demands.[23]

Occasionally Gérard intervened in domestic problems having only a peripheral relation to diplomacy, thus causing unnecessary tension in the alliance. In the spring of 1779 Gérard assigned John Holker, a merchant and French consul general, responsibility for collecting flour for Count D'Estaing's fleet, which was expected to arrive in the fall. Consequently, the price of flour skyrocketed in the Middle States, and a committee was formed in Philadelphia to enforce price controls on foodstuffs. Agents of the committee, without regard for Holker's official position, seized flour in Philadelphia and Baltimore.

Gérard, protesting the seizure, assured Congress and Pennsylvania that Holker was acting as an agent of the French government. The flour was released, and Congress expressed its approval of Holker's purchases.[24] Although the committee had acted unwisely, its very existence suggested a sinister conspiracy to Gérard. He saw the committees as a revolt of the farmers against the merchants, an interpretation which is scarcely credible since the farmers benefited the most from large French purchases with solid currency.[25] The Philadelphia committee, in fact, included many small merchants reacting to the price control resulting from large purchases by Holker and his partner, Robert Morris.

Meriwether Smith, a strong supporter of Gérard, observed how distorted the French Minister's analysis had become.

> I will take the liberty of adding, that I have it expressly from the Mouth of Mr. Gerard, that he believes from Circumstances the most convincing to him, that they [the committees] are instruments in the Hands of designing Men, who are not friends of the Alliance, and wish to throw all Government into the Hands of the

23 Gérard to Vergennes, July 14–17, 1779; Sept. 10–17, 1779, *ibid.*, pp. 781, 886.

24 *Packet*, July 27, 1779; *ibid.*, Aug. 14, 1779; for a discussion of this episode, see Kathryn Sullivan, *Maryland and France, 1774–1789* (Philadelphia, 1935), ch. III.

25 "Minutes of the French Legation in the United States," July 20, 1779, LC, Vol. I; also enclosures in Gérard to Vergennes, July 6, 1779, Meng, ed., *Gérard*, pp. 753–61.

People by those Means, the better to enable them to attain their favorite purpose.[26]

Gérard had a deep distrust of democracy in any form; he assumed that merchants formed the strength of the revolutionary movement in the United States. Gérard's intervention to help Holker and Morris identified him with the group which gave the strongest support to Silas Deane, who was to be the source of Gérard's greatest difficulties. Proponents of the Philadelphia price control committee were politically allied with the New England faction, which was openly anti-merchant and anti-Deane.

Within a year of his arrival, Gérard labeled any opposition to what he construed as the French interest as being anti-French and hostile to the alliance. At first Gérard had noted members of an opposition without casting aspersions on their support for the alliance. Gradually he started to categorize any opposition, referring to it first as the "faction of the East" or the "party of the East." He admitted, however, that he could not yet ferret out its intentions.

Daniel Jenifer willingly supplied Gérard with the information that the goal of the opposition "was to form a coalition with England while breaking directly or indirectly with France." [27] Jenifer, one of the strongest French supporters in Congress, frequently conveyed such nonsense to Gérard, and later to Luzerne. Although Gérard at first discounted most of Jenifer's allegations, within a month he accepted the major contention and began calling the opposition "the English faction." Any person in the English faction was also an enemy to peace.[28]

Vergennes did not accept Gérard's interpretation of the opposition without modification. He believed that the ambitions of the Eastern States were too large for them to reach an accommodation with Great Britain. After receiving Vergennes' interpretation, Gérard changed the terms but not his suspicions of the opposition. He called members of the opposition "anti-Gallicans" until his departure for France in early October, 1779.[29]

Gérard's attitude toward the opposition became evident in the persistent controversy caused by the Silas Deane affair. Ultimately Gérard's involvement on the side of Deane caused sustained personal hostility to him by the entire radical bloc in Congress. The controversy antedated

---

[26] Smith to Jefferson, July 30, 1779, *LMCC*, Vol. IV, p. 348.

[27] Gérard to Vergennes, Feb. 18, 1779; March 3, 1779; March 4–6, 1779, Meng, ed., *Gérard*, pp. 532, 549, 556–60; for Jenifer's comments, see Gérard to Vergennes, March 13, 1779, *ibid.*, p. 584.

[28] Gérard to Vergennes, April 20, 1779; May 29, 1779, *ibid.*, pp. 605, 687.

[29] Vergennes to Gérard, Feb. 19, 1779; Gérard to Vergennes, July 14, 1779, *ibid.*, pp. 540, 777.

the alliance, having started in 1776 when Silas Deane was sent to France as one of three commissioners. Deane worked with Beaumarchais to channel goods to the United States before Franklin and Arthur Lee arrived as the other commissioners. Later, Franklin gladly left commercial matters to Deane, who was a merchant before the war. Both agreed not to tell Arthur Lee the full facts, because the French court let it be known that Lee did not have its confidence. A violent conflict broke out when Lee accused Deane of speculating with public funds.

While serving as a commissioner, Deane continued to act as a private merchant; his connections in the United States included his brothers, Barnabas and Simeon, Benjamin Harrison, Jr., of Virginia, and Robert Morris in Philadelphia. Deane mixed his public and private roles to his own pecuniary advantage, thereby losing the respect of those who expected self-denial from their public officials, a strong tenet in the radicals' conception of public office. He also lost the confidence of Congress by flagrantly violating his instructions. Instead of enlisting four or five engineers from the French Army, as directed, Deane enlisted over two hundred Frenchmen, apparently considering it politically useful to enlist as many as possible. This unauthorized action, in addition to Arthur Lee's letters to fellow radicals, served to enrage many members of Congress, which in November, 1777, recalled Deane and sent John Adams to replace him.[30]

Deane returned to the United States with Gérard and was frequently seen in his company thereafter. Congress, meanwhile, established a committee to investigate Deane's activities as commissioner. The opponents of Deane, led by his fellow New Englanders, prolonged the hearing through the summer and fall of 1778. Deane returned without vouchers or personal papers, so the Congressional committee could not come to a definite conclusion.

The Congressional controversy revolving around Silas Deane became the most prolonged and divisive conflict in American politics during the alliance. Actually Deane's commercial activities had limited support in Congress; the conflict centered on the future role of Arthur Lee, formerly commissioner to France and now United States commissioner to Spain. Well before his exposure of Deane's misdeeds, Lee had aroused the distrust of the French government, and at Gérard's urging an effort was initiated to recall him as commissioner to Spain. Radical members of Congress viewed the recall effort as an attempt by moderates, supported by the French, to punish a radical who dared to expose the wrongdoing of a fellow American. It was the combination of these

[30] Wharton, ed., *Diplomatic Correspondence,* Vol. II, from Continental Congress record, Nov. 21, 1777, p. 424; *ibid.,* Nov. 28, 1777, p. 431.

two separate controversies, and Gérard's involvement in both, which prolonged the conflict and shattered the fragile unity within Congress.

Vergennes had warned Gérard before his departure not to become involved in the domestic quarrels which would inevitably ensue when Deane returned to the United States. Vergennes hoped that Deane would be elected to Congress again, because he considered him one of the staunchest supporters of the alliance.[31] During his first few months in the United States Gérard was confident that Deane would receive a fair hearing before Congress, and he did not foresee damaging controversy. Deane, however, decided to return to France instead of seeking re-election to Congress, contrary to Gérard's wishes. By August Gérard was growing uneasy as he noted that members of Congress opposed to Deane were becoming more obstinate about giving him a fair hearing.[32]

Deane waited patiently, but after months of delay finally decided that Congress intended to deny him a fair hearing. Believing that the committee would never come to any conclusion, Deane broke the impasse by writing "To the Free and Virtuous Citizens of America," a defense which was published in December, 1778.[33] Deane justified his actions while commissioner as being innocent in thought and deed. Nor did he stop with this. He accused his opponents of being motivated by a desire for reconciliation with Great Britain and of seeking a separate peace in violation of the treaty with France. Deane also alleged that the British emissaries then in Philadelphia, John Temple and John Berkenhout, were in secret consort with the Lee family, particularly Arthur Lee, and radical members of Congress from New England.

Gérard had asked Deane to show him a copy of the essay before publication, sensing that he would have to persuade the author to modify certain passages, but Deane ignored the request.[34] Although Gérard objected to many statements in Deane's apologia, he failed to inform members of Congress of the points with which he agreed or disagreed. Gérard made his worst mistake as Minister at this point; he should have insisted that his opinions on Temple and Berkenhout were separate and distinct from his support of Deane. Gérard's refusal to make his position clear allowed many misconceptions to arise about his role. He appeared to support a statement charging a sizable number of Congressional delegates with wanting to disrupt the alliance and negotiate separately with Great Britain.

The controversy widened when Thomas Paine appointed himself the

[31] Vergennes to Gérard, April 22, 1778, Meng, ed., *Gérard*, pp. 136–37.
[32] Gérard to Vergennes, July 16, 1778; Aug. 16, 1778, *ibid.*, pp. 169, 227.
[33] *Packet*, Dec. 5, 1778.
[34] Gérard to Vergennes, Dec. 6, 1778, Meng, ed., *Gérard*, p. 406.

executioner of the public reputation of Silas Deane. In a series of articles during the winter of 1778–1779, Paine replied to Deane's accusations by proclaiming the innocence of New England delegates. He then attacked Deane's commercial activities, arguing that Deane had little or nothing to do with the original French decision to aid the United States. Paine further noted that aid came to the United States from France before the alliance was signed.[35]

Gérard was furious at Paine's disclosures. He could not allow an American official to declare that France had aided the United States before formal recognition of independence, and Paine's intemperate remarks eventually cost him his job as secretary to the Committee of Foreign Affairs. Congress, led by Gouverneur Morris, disavowed Paine's published charges against France.[36]

Gérard could not believe that Paine had acted alone. "Everyone assures me," he wrote Vergennes, "that Messieurs [Richard Henry] Lee and Samuel Adams have prevented M. Payne [sic] from giving me the satisfaction I have asked." [37] Just after his arrival in Philadelphia, Gérard had inaccurately reported that Samuel Adams and John Witherspoon belonged to a party whose hopes of reaching an accommodation with Great Britain were frustrated by the alliance.[38] Gérard also noted that Samuel Adams opposed Deane, but gave no special attention to this until Adams dined with John Temple. Then he began to conjure up visions of a conspiracy headed by Samuel Adams and Richard Henry Lee; Deane's critics were cast in the role of subverting the alliance. As Gérard's distrust of the opposition increased, the Deane controversy, which had only limited international overtones at its inception, blossomed into a direct threat to the future of the alliance.

The Deane controversy extended into other issues of the time. The Spanish mediation proposals of 1779 provided an opportunity for the pro-Deane forces and Gérard to cooperate in ridding themselves of Deane's most rabid enemy, Arthur Lee. Gérard had private reasons for suspecting Arthur Lee long before the Deane controversy, since both he and Vergennes mistakenly believed that Lee had leaked news of the alliance to Lord Shelburne in Great Britain.

Late in December, as the Deane controversy raged in the American press, Samuel Adams and Richard Henry Lee inquired how the French government viewed Arthur Lee. Gérard was evasive, but stated that he believed Lee to be an honest and upright man. He added, however, that

[35] *Packet,* Dec. 30, 1778.
[36] Congress denied that the United States received any aid before the alliance was signed and printed its repudiation of Paine in the *Packet,* Jan. 16, 1779.
[37] Gérard to Vergennes, Jan. 10, 1779, Meng, ed., *Gérard,* p. 468.
[38] Gérard to Vergennes, July 25, 1778, *ibid.,* pp. 179–80.

Lee had friends who were not respected by his court, and he refused to say that Lee had the confidence of either the Spanish or French courts.[39]

Gérard violated political wisdom rather than diplomatic custom in revealing his court's opinion of Arthur Lee, since Lee supporters were generally anti-Deane. He wished to have Lee replaced as commissioner to Spain by John Jay in April, 1779, in order to have a more trustworthy man in Madrid, the site of the proposed Spanish mediation.[40] Yet by his response to the Deane affair and his revelation of the court's opinion of Arthur Lee, Gérard merged, to the disadvantage of French policy, what might have been two separate issues. The Deane controversy and the recall of Arthur Lee became inextricably mixed, both to Gérard and to the radicals. When the recall motion failed on May 3, it prolonged Congressional discussion of the mediation and the Deane controversy.

Gérard compounded his initial mistake of fully supporting Deane by openly advocating the recall of Lee. He twice revealed his sympathies. Instead of using conciliation and discretion to accomplish French objectives, Gérard overtly aligned himself with one group in what became a divisive public issue. As a result, Gérard and the opposition could not reach amicable agreements during the remainder of his tenure as Minister to the United States. By his inept handling of the entire affair, Gérard had confirmed the suspicions that some radicals felt toward France and helped create a permanent bloc in Congress which was antagonistic to French suggestions.

Gérard returned to France in the wake of controversy in October, 1779. He left the United States due to illness, perhaps malaria, rather than Vergennes' disapproval of his work as Minister. Gérard was in poor health most of the time he spent in Philadelphia, and within four months of his arrival he had requested that a replacement be sent at the first opportunity. His appeals to Vergennes became increasingly urgent as time passed. He reported that he had been sick five of his first seven months in the United States, and often could not read or write. "I venture to beg you to believe that I would sacrifice my life rather than leave Philadelphia at the wrong moment," Gérard wrote in late February, adding, "I intend to leave as soon as the opportunity presents itself." [41]

The brevity and acrimony of Gérard's tenure caused Americans to speculate about his motives for leaving. Jefferson heard "that he [Gé-

[39] Richard Henry Lee, Statement, April 21, 1779; Henry Laurens, Statement, April 21, 1779; Thomas Burke, Statement, April 21, 1779, *LMCC*, Vol. IV, pp. 166–71; Gérard to Vergennes, April 20, 1779, Meng, ed., *Gérard*, p. 605.

[40] Gérard to Vergennes, Feb. 25, 1779, *ibid.*, p. 542.

[41] Gérard to Vergennes, Oct. 25, 1778; Feb. 5, 1779; Feb. 24, 1779, *ibid.*, pp. 354, 531, 541.

rard] thinks of return to his country, ostensibly for better health, but in truth through disgust. Such an event would be deplored here as the most dreadful calamity." Jefferson's correspondent assured him that the rumor was erroneous.[42] Washington also expressed concern about the effects of Gérard's departure on public opinion.

> The rumor of the camp is that Monsieur Gérard is about to return to France. Some Speak confidently of its taking place. If this be a fact, the motives doubtless are powerful, as it will open a wide field for speculation, and give our enemies, whether with or without real cause, a handle for misrepresentation and triumph.[43]

Gérard officially informed Congress that he was leaving the United States because of illness. The public learned of his departure by a short announcement in a Philadelphia paper, "The Minister Plenipotentiary of France is intending shortly to set out for France, all those who have any demands upon him are desired to send in their bills to the Housekeeper in the course of the next week that they may be immediately paid off." Later in the same week the paper announced that Gérard's successor, Luzerne, had arrived in Boston.[44]

Gérard received memorials from Pennsylvania and a group of merchants thanking him for his service to the United States and the alliance. He answered both with stiff and polite thanks.[45] To complete his duties in the United States, Gérard made a final visit to Washington to make a personal appraisal of the strengths and weaknesses of the American army.[46]

Gérard's supporters, generally merchants and the moderates of 1776, lamented his departure. Although John Holker complained that Gérard did not fully understand business transactions, Robert Morris believed that Gérard had served both countries superbly. "I hope he [Luzerne] may compensate for the loss of Mr. Gérard who carried with him the Perfect Esteem of all men not biassed by selfish party Views," Morris wrote. Another Philadelphia merchant stated that Gérard "has given all the satisfaction possible in his public and private character." [47]

Unfortunately for the alliance, men's opinions did reflect party

[42] Jefferson to Fleming, June 8, 1779, Boyd, ed., *Jefferson*, Vol. II, p. 288; Fleming to Jefferson, June 22, 1779, *ibid.*, Vol. III, p. 10.
[43] Washington to Jay, April 23, 1779, Fitzpatrick, ed., *Washington*, Vol. XIV, p. 436.
[44] *Packet*, Aug. 28, 1779; *ibid.*, Aug. 31, 1779.
[45] *Ibid.*, Sept. 23, 1779; *ibid.*, Sept. 30, 1779.
[46] *New Jersey Gazette*, Oct. 6, 1779.
[47] Holker to Morris, Nov. 19, 1778, Holker Papers, LC, Vol. I; Morris to Franklin, Sept. 18, 1779, Franklin Papers, APS, Vol. XV; Griffin to Franklin, Sept., 1779, *ibid.*, Vol. XV.

views. Gérard did not leave without some scathing observations by his opposition. Surprisingly, however, the radical members of Congress who had most strenuously opposed him were not too vehement in their criticism. James Lovell, the most persistent critic of France in Congress and strongly anti-Deane, believed that Vergennes had not wanted Gérard to become involved in the controversy between Arthur Lee and Silas Deane. Lovell could make a balanced judgment about Gérard's difficulties, "He [Luzerne] will judge for himself and will expecially take care not to ally himself with dirty Schemes of money making which others [Gérard] have been entrapped [or] at least appear to patronize." [48] Lovell separated Gérard's denigration of Arthur Lee from the Silas Deane controversy, maintaining a greater sense of proportion than either Gérard or the Lees.

Richard Henry Lee, who had retired to Chantilly due to ill health, wished that France had originally sent Luzerne instead of Gérard. "She brings a new Minister from France, Le Chevalier de la Luzerne, who is a gentleman, of much too high and honorable extraction and sentiment to enter into the dregs of party, thereby injuring the Alliance and disgracing his Master." [49] Lee, whose adherence to the alliance was indisputable, had a legitimate grievance against Gérard. While held in suspicion by Gérard, he had admonished the anti-French Charles Lee, "The true policy of the U.S. I apprehend to be universal peace and friendship with the whole world. Whatever excess may be shewn of friendship for any it should be for France." [50]

Lee strongly supported the alliance, but the course of the Deane controversy had caused him to focus his hostility on Gérard. He informed his brother Arthur that Gérard was more his enemy than Silas Deane, adding that Gérard, by misunderstanding the nature of political alignments in the United States, made his closest associations with men who had originally opposed independence and the alliance. Although partisan and written from personal pique, Lee made a sound assessment of Gérard's fundamental mistake as minister:

> It is very remarkable that those men who from the beginnings of the contest have been the most decided friends to the Liberties of America and the firmest opposers of British Tyranny, and who in the hour of Trial will be found most true to the Alliance, are the men whom Gerard has shewn the least desire to deal with. Another sort of Men have shared his friendship and familiarity.[51]

[48] Lovell to Adams, Sept. 21, 1779; Lovell to Gates, Sept. 16, 1779, *LMCC*, Vol. IV, pp. 426–27, 421.

[49] Lee to Laurens, Aug. 13, 1779, Ballagh, ed., *Lee*, Vol. II, p. 119.

[50] Richard Henry Lee to Charles Lee, Aug. 31, 1779, *ibid.*, Vol. II, pp. 142–43.

[51] Richard Henry Lee to Arthur Lee, May 23, 1779, *LMCC*, Vol. IV, pp. 227–28.

Gérard had failed to maintain friendly relations with the radical bloc. Radicals resented his identification with moderate leaders, including men such as John Jay, John Dickinson, Robert Morris, and Robert R Livingston. This latter group had opposed the timing of independence, and only after it was a fact did they advocate an alliance. The radical Adams-Lee bloc, by contrast, advocated independence in order to achieve an alliance; independence, they saw, depended on an alliance, while the reverse was equally true. Radicals were more confident than their opponents about American ability to resist Great Britain, and, although anxious to make the alliance function harmoniously, they were tenacious in their defense of national honor. Gérard preferred to work with opponents of the Adams-Lee bloc, because they did not subject French policies to unremitting scrutiny or defend inconvenient notions of national honor. Like Gérard, they feared any type of democracy and resisted potential changes in the social order.

Nevertheless, Arthur Lee, not Gérard, planted the first seeds of distrust between Gérard and the radicals. Lee, having observed prolonged French inaction before the alliance, thought that French intentions toward the United States required continued examination. In a letter to Samuel Adams, delivered by Gérard on his arrival in Philadelphia, Lee wrote that France's greatest fear was that the United States would make a separate peace treaty. This, he suggested, was why France had sent a fleet under D'Estaing, and Gérard as Minister to the United States. Invoking the familiar pre-war stereotype of French duplicity, Lee also warned that Gérard "was not wanting in political finesse and therefore not to be listend [sic] to, too implicitly." [52]

Samuel Adams accepted Lee's warning without giving Gérard the benefit of the doubt. Using wording identical to Lee's, Adams advised a political colleague, "The French Minister is a sensible prudent man, not wanting in political Finesse, and therefore not to be listend [sic] to, too implicitly." [53] These remarks spread through New England, where they were accepted by many. If he was to succeed, Gérard had to overcome an initial distrust by radicals and allay fears of personal insincerity. Unfortunately for France and the United States, Gérard had neither the personality nor the finesse in congressional politics to accomplish this.

Gérard's departure signified a change in the personalities connected with the politics of the French alliance. Luzerne, in contrast to Gérard, sought and won the trust of all groups in Congress. Gérard returned to France weakened and irritable; he acted only in an infrequent advisory role for the remainder of the war. [54] Many of the men who were deeply

[52] Lee to Adams, April 1, 1778, Adams Papers, NYPL.
[53] Adams to Warren, July 20, 1778, *LMCC*, Vol. III, p. 339.
[54] See Gérard's memorandum advising Rochambeau on his American expedition in the Rochambeau Papers, LC, Vol. II, p. 84, dated March, 1780.

involved in the Silas Deane controversy never regained their former positions of influence. Samuel Adams served only part of one year in Congress after 1779. Richard Henry Lee, sullen and ill, did not return to Congress. The diplomatic careers of Silas Deane and Arthur Lee were ruined. John Jay and John Adams, who steered a middle course in the controversies of 1779, were awarded foreign posts and served in Europe until the end of the war.

Gérard's service in the United States was not an outright failure, but it must be classified as a disappointment.[55] When he arrived, he received the acclaim of Congress and the American public, but when he departed, it was amidst divisive controversy in which he had been deeply involved. Gérard's health contributed to his inability to work successfully with all groups, because he had to depend on meetings with Congressmen invited to his residence; and after the outbreak of the Deane-Lee controversy in January, 1779, members of the radical opposition were rarely included in these invitations. Gérard's shortcomings stemmed, in large part, from his failure to recognize that many groups supported the Revolution, not just merchants and the moderates of 1776.[56] Because he understood neither the Revolution nor American politics, Gérard could not acknowledge the loyalty of Americans who disagreed with him on policy.

Although Vergennes did not express disapproval of Gérard's work, there are a number of strong indications that he was disappointed. Foremost among these is Gérard's failure to receive another diplomatic appointment. Although in ill health, Gérard did live for ten more years, receiving only the post of *prêteur royal* instead of an honorary diplomatic position. Luzerne, his successor, became Ambassador to Great Britain after completing his mission to the United States.

Another indication that Vergennes was not satisfied with Gérard can be seen in his instructions to Luzerne. Vergennes restated the French

[55] John J. Meng, "French Diplomacy in Philadelphia: 1778–1779," *Catholic Historical Review,* Vol. XXIV (1938), presents a different view. Meng argues that Gérard had two major accomplishments as Minister, protecting French interests in the fishery and securing the binding nature of the alliance, p. 57. The United States, however, did not seek to curtail French fishery rights, but sought access rights to the British fishery. The binding nature of the alliance, however interpreted, was never seriously questioned by Congress after it ratified the treaties even before Gérard's arrival.

[56] See Edmund S. Morgan, "The Puritan Ethic and the American Revolution," *William and Mary Quarterly,* third series, Vol. XXIV (1967), pp. 25–33, for a discussion of the merchant-Puritan antagonism involved in the Silas Deane controversy. However, the importance of the Deane-Lee dispute was that it evolved into an open conflict between Gérard and the supporters of Arthur Lee; Silas Deane's commercial activities were of secondary importance after the discussion of the peace ultimata began in February, 1779.

position on the fisheries and the navigation of the Mississippi, and he continued to accuse the opposition of being enemies of peace and of attempting to prolong the war by making exorbitant demands for the fishery. He then provided explicit directions on the way to handle any opposition in the United States, a subject he had never mentioned to Gérard. Despite a diplomatic opening, Vergennes clearly did not want Luzerne to repeat the mistakes of Gérard.

> In this case, the best that we can hope for is that you follow in the direction set by your predecessor, that is to say that without linking yourself openly to the patriotic party, and without declaring yourself to be against the ones said to be anti-French, you try to support with discretion the courage of the one group and bring the others back to the proper course by showing them the dangerous situation into which the Republic will be led by their principles and present conduct. It is all the more important, Monsieur, that these steps be kept measured and wise, [since] by placing yourself at the head of one party you would lose once and for all the trust of the other, and you would combat it in such a way as to counteract all of your advances. This would produce a scission and a spirit of opposition which it would not be possible to uproot and which would present a most annoying perspective both for the present and for the future.[57]

This served as Gérard's epitaph as a French diplomat.

[57] Vergennes to Luzerne, Sept. 25, 1779, Archives du Ministère des Affaires Étrangères, correspondance politique, (États-Unis), [hereafter AAE-cp-(EU)], LC, Vol. X.

IV. Newport: First Attempt at Allied Cooperation

In the spring of 1778 the military situation in the United States remained uncertain. Sir Henry Clinton, new commander of the British forces, ordered the evacuation of Philadelphia and scurried back to New York, pausing only long enough for a sharp but indecisive battle at Monmouth on June 28. Clinton reached New York and prepared for the expected assault, optimistic that the Carlisle Commission would be able to open negotiations with Congress. The American Army had left Valley Forge with misplaced confidence in its ability to deliver a mortal blow to the British in New Jersey. As both sides maneuvered there, the Americans received word that France had sent a fleet under Count D'Estaing to cooperate with the American forces. The unexpected military assistance was welcomed by most Americans, whose final verdict on the value of the alliance still depended on the amount of tangible military cooperation received from France. As soon as D'Estaing arrived off the Delaware Capes on July 7, 1778, he made contact with American liaison officers to determine the most suitable target for a joint assault.

Due to the delay in crossing the Atlantic, D'Estaing arrived in the middle of the campaign, and plans had to be quickly devised on an *ad hoc* basis. The most obvious target was Philadelphia, but the British, ordered to evacuate because of the possible arrival of a French Fleet, had left the city by land in the last week of June. D'Estaing therefore sailed for New York Harbor for a proposed combined assault. Plans for the siege of New York required that the French enter the harbor and blockade the city against the expected naval relief from Great Britain, but the deep draft of French vessels prevented the fleet from entering over Sandy Hook. This was probably fortunate, since the American Army was still ill-supplied and undermanned from the previous winter and probably could not have supported a long siege against a numerically superior and well-fortified British force.[1]

[1] For the military situation in the summer of 1778, see Douglas S. Freeman, *George Washington,* Vol. V (New York, 1952), pp. 44–54, 60–76; George Sheer and Hugh Rankin, *Rebels and Redcoats* (Cleveland, 1957), pp. 324–44; for the

Newport, where the British had an estimated four to six thousand men, was the only remaining target vulnerable to a land-sea siege. Although Newport was of trivial military significance in comparison with New York, its capture would serve as a symbol of French-American cooperation which would strengthen the ties of the alliance. Americans viewed the proposed assault on Newport as a test of what France would do militarily to aid independence. An American staff officer wrote, "Mr. M[athews] hopes Miss [Susan] L[ivingston] no longer continues an unbeliever respecting the good intentions of our Ally. If she does he is ready to take her down to Newport where she may have ocular proof of it." [2]

The Americans, however, lacked the quickness and strength necessary to mount an assault force superior to the British. The main army under Washington remained in the highlands of New York, while General Heath's forces were located near Boston. General John Sullivan, an early patriot and ambitious military leader, was appointed commander of the United States forces for the Allied attack on Newport. He had few Regular Army units under his command and relied heavily on a call-up of militia from New England. Nathanael Greene and Lafayette were assigned to aid Sullivan; John Laurens, who was educated in Geneva and spoke fluent French, served as liaison to Washington and to D'Estaing.

The siege of Newport commenced in late July after D'Estaing arrived. A local paper expressed the confidence that most Americans felt about the joint assault:

> Wednesday last to the great Joy of every good Subject, the Fleet of his most Christian Majesty, the great and wise Ally of these States, commanded by Admiral Count de Estaing, arrived off Point Judith, where a Number of Pilots belonging to this town went immediately on board, and brought them safe to anchor off the Harbour of Newport, whereby our savage Enemies are in their Turn completely blockaded. . . . The Britons with their Friends the Tories, are in great Consternation: and a few Days will probably produce Events of the utmost Importance.[3]

The battle plans for the siege were relatively simple; D'Estaing would cut off sea routes, while Sullivan, with assistance from French marines, cleared the nearby shoreline. Preparations completed, Sullivan

---

best account of Allied military cooperation, see Charles P. Whittemore, *A General of the Revolution: John Sullivan of New Hampshire* (New York, 1961), pp. 84–111.

[2] Mathews to Livingston, July 20, 1778, Livingston Papers, MHS, box I.

[3] *Providence Gazette*, Aug. 1, 1778.

would transport his army to Narragansett Island and attack in a southerly direction toward Newport. No problems would occur if D'Estaing protected the harbor while American troops were on Narragansett Island. Both commanders were eager for military laurels, and D'Estaing reminded Sullivan that the expedition "is the first occasion on which the Generals of the United States have it in their power to give an authentic proof of the value which they set upon the alliance of His Majesty and satisfaction with which they join their troops to his." [4]

Unfortunately, delays in organizing militia postponed Sullivan's attack and D'Estaing became restive, knowing that the British Fleet would soon try to relieve the Newport garrison. Paul Revere heard of D'Estaing's impatience, writing, "I find the Count Estang has expressed some uneasiness that he has been obliged to be Idle so long. I expect it wont be longer than Monday [August 10] if so long." [5] Action did occur on Monday, but it was of an unexpected and disastrous nature for the French-American assault on Newport. Richard Lord Howe, with reinforcements from Halifax, suddenly approached the numerically superior French squadron. D'Estaing set sail from Newport harbor on August 10 to meet the British, leaving word that he would definitely return to aid the Americans. The battle between the two fleets was indecisive, with each claiming victory. While at sea, a hurricane separated the fleets and inflicted heavy damage on the French.

The American forces on Narragansett Island could not attack Newport until D'Estaing returned to provide naval support. Eight days passed, and the Americans still did not know when D'Estaing would return. "The French Fleet has been some Days out of the harbour in pursuit of the English Fleet. Nothing has been heard of them since their departure. As soon as they return, they will, in cooperation with General Sullivan attend the main object of the expedition," an American officer wrote, "It appears to be an unlucky circumstance that the French Fleet left the port just at that time; tho I cannot say but in the event it will prove fortunate." [6]

When D'Estaing finally returned to Point Judith on August 20, he informed the Americans that he must immediately set out for Boston for refitting. He pointed out that five of the eleven ships of the line badly needed repairs, and that a council of officers unanimously recommended removing to Boston. The Americans, led by John Laurens and Nathanael Greene and supported by Lafayette, contended that the French could use Newport Harbor for refitting, thus enabling the offensive to con-

---

[4] D'Estaing to Sullivan, Aug. 7, 1778, Hammond, ed., *Sullivan*, Vol. II, p. 184.
[5] Revere to Heath, Aug. 7, 1778, Heath Papers, MHS, Vol. XI.
[6] Flint to Wadsworth, Aug. 18, 1778, Wadsworth Papers, CHS.

tinue. D'Estaing refused, leaving immediately for Boston. John Laurens protested to Washington, "He [D'Estaing] might have been furnished at this place with all the means of refitting which he can expect at Boston." Furthermore, dismantled vessels had a comparative advantage in the shallow water at Newport, Laurens argued. Although he failed to explain how D'Estaing could refit in Newport Harbor with both a British garrison and a British fleet nearby, Laurens had earlier noted important reasons for the French to remain at Newport:

> All the effects of a most dreadful storm which suddenly added to the expectation of Byron's arrival—for abandoning the American troops in the midst of a very important expedition—and reducing them to the necessity of making a desperate attack or a precipitate Retreat. The honor of the French Nation, the honor of the Admiral, the safety of the fleet, and a regard for the new alliance required a different conduct.[7]

In spite of D'Estaing's explanation, the French move to Boston outraged American officers, and D'Estaing should have considered the probable American reaction more carefully in reaching his decision. "If the French fleet has a right to fight when they please & Run when they please & leave Genl. Sullivan when they please & his Armey on a small island where a brittish fleet can surround it when they please which we expect every hour," one American officer complained, "I do not understand the Alliance made with France." [8] William Gordon, writing ten years later, summarized the immediate American reaction to D'Estaing's departure.

> Upon the fleet's sailing for Boston, it was said—"There never was a prospect so favorable blasted by such a shameful desertion." A universal clamor prevailed against the French nation: and letters were sent to Boston containing the most bitter invectives, tending to prejudice the inhabitants against D'Estaing and all his officers, to counteract which the cooler and more judicious part of the community employed their good services.[9]

Lafayette, while participating in American strategy conferences, became incensed at the caustic remarks being made about France. Although he too had urged D'Estaing to remain at Newport, Lafayette could not acquiesce in insults to French honor. One officer observed that

---

[7] Laurens to Washington, Aug. 22, 1778, Washington Papers, Vol. LXXXII.
[8] Eyre to Eyre, Aug. 22, 1778, "Original Letters and Documents," *PMHB*, Vol. V (1881), pp. 476–77.
[9] William Gordon, *The History of the Rise, Progress, and Establishment of the United States of America* (London, 1788), Vol. III, p. 163.

Lafayette was three-quarters American, but he could have added that the remaining quarter was thoroughly French. After one meeting it was reported, "one of the Genl. officers in the course of the Debates in Council took occasion from the Count's conduct to reflect on the Nation at large. The Marquis was very particular in inquiring his Name family & rank and determines to call him to an account for it." [10] Observing Lafayette's behavior, Nathanael Greene remarked, "The Marquis's great thirst for glory and national attachment often runs him into errors." [11]

Rather than dueling, as he first contemplated, Lafayette wrote a series of letters chastising American officers for their uncomplimentary remarks about France. "Would you believe that I, one who has the honor of belonging to the leading nation of the world, to a nation which can be envied, but which is respected and admired by all of Europe;" he raged to Alexander Hamilton, "that I have personally been put in the position of hearing the name of France spoken without respect, and perhaps with disdain, by a herd of Yankees from New England." [12]

Washington feared the very reactions that angered Lafayette and foreseeing the effect of D'Estaing's departure on American officers, he attempted to mollify General Sullivan. The French, he wrote, probably would not have stayed at Newport, even if Sullivan's opinion had reached D'Estaing before the decision to remove to Boston. Belatedly, Washington warned Sullivan about the consequences of criticizing the French. "Should the expedition fail through the abandonment of the French fleet the officers concerned will be apt to complain loudly," he advised Sullivan, "But prudence dictates that we should put the best face upon the matter, and to the world attribute the removal to Boston to necessity. The reasons are too obvious to need explaining." [13]

The French departure had indeed outraged Sullivan, who saw his prospects for military glory erased. In his daily orders on August 24, Sullivan charged the French with abandoning the United States. Two days later he had second thoughts about the statement, perhaps due to pro-

[10] Morton to James Bowdoin, Jr., Aug. 25, 1778, Bowdoin-Temple Papers, MHS, Vol. III.

[11] Greene to Washington, Aug. 28, 1778, George W. Greene, *The Life of Nathanael Greene* (New York, 1871), Vol. II, p. 127.

[12] Lafayette to Hamilton, Aug. 26, 1778, Harold C. Syrett, ed., *The Papers of Alexander Hamilton* (New York, 1961–), Vol. I, pp. 538–39; Lafayette to Henry Laurens, Aug. 25, 1778, "Letters from Marquis de Lafayette to the Honorable Henry Laurens, 1777–1780," *South Carolina Historical and Genealogical Magazine* (hereafter *SCHGM*), Vol. IX (1908), pp. 64–66; Lafayette to Clinton, Aug. 29, 1778, Sparks MSS, HU, Vol. XII, pp. 141–44.

[13] Washington to Sullivan, Aug. 28, 1778, Hammond, ed., *Sullivan*, Vol. II, pp. 270–71.

tests by Greene and Lafayette, and tried to make amends. Illiberal minds had distorted the true meaning of his orders, Sullivan claimed, insisting that he had not intended to speak disrespectfully of D'Estaing's motives or to cast aspersions on French honor.[14]

Sullivan, in an explanatory letter to Henry Laurens, revealed why he had committed such a thoughtless mistake, "I feel disgrace will attend this fatal expedition, though it gave at first the most pleasing prospects of success." Admitting his disappointment with failure, Sullivan denied that he had contributed to any animosity toward France—a disingenuous contention at the least.

> This movement has raised every voice against the French nation, revived all those ancient prejudices against the faith and sincerity of that people, and inclines them most heartily to curse the new alliance. These are the first sallies of passion, which will in a few days subside.
>
> I confess that I do most cordially resent the conduct of the Count, or rather the conduct of his officers, who have it seems, compelled him to go to Boston and leave us on an island without any certain means of retreat.[15]

Sullivan's retraction had come too late to check the torrent of invective encouraged by his original accusation. Frederick MacKenzie, fighting the Americans at Newport, heard that "They abuse the French for not having been more active in their co-operation, and blame them for the failure of the Expedition." [16]

Sullivan's blunder changed the American reaction to D'Estaing's abrupt departure. Instead of dwelling on the failure at Newport, American leaders now attempted to prevent a wider split between France and the United States; accusations against D'Estaing ceased, as the preservation of the alliance took precedence. Americans realized that the restoration of Allied harmony was imperative if they were to defeat Great Britain, and an effective alliance was more important than the disappointment suffered by both sides after Newport. As one Boston merchant commented, "I look upon it of the last importance to the United

---

[14] Rhode Island Headquarters Papers, Sparks MSS, Vol. XLVII, pp. 57–58, 60–61; Archives du Ministère des Affaires Étrangères, mémoires et documents (États-Unis), Paris, Vol. VII, folio no. 257. Luzerne states in a written report that Sullivan's protest was fortunately never made public; Gordon, *History*, Vol. III, p. 163; Cf., Whittemore, *Sullivan*, pp. 103–104.

[15] Sullivan to Laurens, Aug. 16 [*sic*, Aug. 26?], 1778, Hammond, ed., *Sullivan*, Vol. II, p. 219.

[16] *Diary of Frederick MacKenzie*, Vol. II, p. 387, Aug. 30, 1778.

States to keep good faith & treat her Allies with the greatest Candor & to pay the most sacred Regard to the Treaties they have entered into with them." [17]

Washington provided an official public explanation of the failure of the Newport expedition. He wrote General Heath, explaining that for public purposes the failure would be attributed to damage inflicted on the French Fleet by the storm. In a letter to Governor Clinton, Washington reiterated his position on the subject, adding, "Different opinions will be entertained on the propriety of the measure; but we ought all to concur in giving it the most favourable coloring to the people. It should be ascribed to necessity resulting from the injury sustained by the storm." [18]

D'Estaing, too, assisted the reconciliation of Allied differences. He ignored Sullivan's charge and refused to become involved in controversy. "I should have been distressed to know that you were in danger," D'Estaing tartly wrote Sullivan, "They told me that you had only two thousand men with you. I do not presume to weigh your motives. I have refrained from Criticism." [19] D'Estaing privately asked Nathanael Greene to support his policy of silence concerning Newport.[20] Greene saw that other staff officers at Newport read a copy of D'Estaing's expression of moderate policy.

John Laurens explained to Washington that, while D'Estaing was officially silent, he had offered to send all French troops under him to Newport to aid Sullivan's retreat. D'Estaing assured Laurens that French sensibilities could not be wounded by a moment of passion. Laurens concluded that D'Estaing's letter to Sullivan provided a foundation "for restoring harmony and good understanding—Genl. Sullivan's Answer I hope will improve it." [21] Washington accepted advice from Laurens and Greene rather than Sullivan, writing to D'Estaing, "the whole Continent sympathizes with you; it will be a consolation to you to reflect that the thinking part of mankind do not form their judgment from Events." Washington also told D'Estaing that he had worked, from the beginning of the campaign, to establish a good understanding between the officers of the Allied nations.[22]

---

[17] Cushing to John Adams, Oct. 21, 1778, Adams Papers, R. 349.

[18] Washington to Heath, Aug. 28, 1778; Washington to Clinton, Aug. 28, 1778, Fitzpatrick, ed., *Washington,* Vol. XII, pp. 364–65, 367.

[19] D'Estaing to Sullivan, Aug. 23, 1778, Hammond, ed., *Sullivan,* Vol. II, p. 238.

[20] D'Estaing to Greene, Oct. 1, 1778, Green Papers, WLC, Vol. II.

[21] Laurens to Washington, Aug. 2, 1778 [sic, Sept. 2, 1778?], Washington Papers, Vol. LXXXIII.

[22] Washington to D'Estaing, Sept. 11, 1778, Fitzpatrick, ed., *Washington,* Vol. XII, pp. 423–24.

In Philadelphia, Henry Laurens reported that the bad news from Newport had caused Gérard to succumb to an attack of fever which abated only after a four-ounce dosage of bark—apparently quinine. A better cure, Laurens suggested, would be a conciliatory letter from Sullivan praising the French for their assistance.[23] Recovered from his fever, Gérard responded to events at Newport in a deliberate manner, making it clear to Congress that there could be no condemnation of D'Estaing. He did not insist that D'Estaing was wise or correct, but simply contended that the alliance could not sustain attacks on French intentions similar to those made by Sullivan. Congress quickly passed a resolution thanking D'Estaing for his aid, which satisfied Gérard.[24] Hoping also to appease Sullivan and prevent further controversy, Congress passed a resolution commending Sullivan for leading the retreat from Narragansett Island with a minimum loss of men and supplies. Members of Congress, although disappointed with the French, wanted to prevent a public rupture at all costs.

Both sides understood that the failure at Newport did not warrant a break in the alliance. Vergennes reviewed the episode and complimented Gérard on his conduct. Congress, Vergennes believed, had also acted wisely in its measures to counteract bad feeling arising from the disagreeable affair. D'Estaing would not have left the Americans deliberately, Vergennes wrote, because he loved glory too much.[25] Each side agreed with Josiah Bartlett's reasoning, "The Rhode Island expedition though not successful, yet brought no disgrace to our arms, nor have the enemy any great cause for boasting." [26]

Although Congressional action did contribute to restoring Allied harmony, the Newport affair sounded a warning to some members of Congress, who revived their fear of depending on the alliance to achieve United States goals. Andrew Adams of Connecticut described Newport in a context which many Americans had forgotten in the euphoria caused by the arrival of D'Estaing and Gérard:

> I fully agree with you that we are not blindly to trust ye Justice: much less ye Generosity of any Nation unconnected with their Interest.
>
> An Instance of which to ground our caution I think we have before us in ye French fleet leaving R: Island in ye midst of an Expedition Jointly under taken and going to Boston when they

---

[23] Laurens to Washington, Aug. 29, 1779, Washington Papers, Vol. LXXXII.
[24] Gérard to D'Estaing, Sept. 12, 1778, AAE-cp-(EU), Vol. IV; Laurens to D'Estaing, Sept. 10, 1778, *LMCC,* Vol. III, pp. 405–406.
[25] Vergennes to Gérard, Nov. 18, 1778, Meng, ed., *Gérard,* pp. 374–75.
[26] Bartlett to Langdon, Sept. 21, 1778, Whipple Papers.

might as well refitted there and at the same time co-operated with our forces; & also in Carrying off their land as well as sea forces.[27]

James Lovell wrote, "As I always make the best of every Mishap, I think we ought to conclude that the Events at Newport will prevent too much of our Independence being attributed to the arrival of the allied Fleet on our Coasts." [28] After Newport, Americans realized that the alliance would not bring the quick decisive victory they had expected from it in May.

Knowing that the war would last at least another campaign, Americans began to worry that the Newport misfortune might prevent Allied cooperation in future endeavors. Joseph Reed expressed doubts that the United States and France could act in concert again.[29] Alexander Hamilton believed that the United States should reprimand Sullivan to assuage the insult to French honor and insure future cooperation. Calling Sullivan's indiscretion "the summit of Folly," Hamilton argued that "the stigmatizing an ally in public orders and one with whom we mean to continue in amity was certainly a piece of absurdity without parallel." [30]

American leaders, while not adopting Hamilton's suggestion, took measures to prevent material damaging to the alliance from being published in the press. The preservation of the alliance would be best served by as little press comment as possible, they thought. Nathanael Greene thus arranged to answer a Providence merchant's criticism of the Newport campaign through private channels rather than having either letter appear in the press.[31] James Lovell commented explicitly on the need to control discussion in the press. "Notwithstanding the most unpromising State of Things at this Moment let us nurse the new born Alliance, Stiffle the Sentiments of *Protest* however just they are in themselves," he wrote, "they should not be spoken at Noon Day without the most absolute and fatal Necessity. The Printers should be warned at the Eastward." [32]

The publishers showed admirable restraint. They, like members of Congress, realized that it was clearly in the interest of the United States not to reveal a schism in the alliance which the British could exploit. During the first part of August, the papers were filled with optimistic stories from Newport, but as soon as D'Estaing left for Boston there was no more mention of Newport. No stories appeared on the retreat of Sul-

27 Adams to Wolcott, Aug. 29, 1778, Wolcott Papers, Vol. I.
28 Lovell to Gates, Sept. 18, 1778, Gates Papers, box X.
29 Reed to ———, Sept. 2, 1778, Reed Papers, Vol. V.
30 Hamilton to Boudinot, Sept., 1778, Syrett, ed., *Hamilton*, Vol. I, p. 545.
31 Greene to Brown, Sept. 6, 1778, Greene, *Greene*, Vol. II, pp. 133–41.
32 Lovell to Gates, Aug. 29, 1778, *LMCC*, Vol. III, p. 392, italics in original.

livan's forces until early September. Only a Hartford paper expressed mild dismay at the results of the expedition.

> The French fleet returned to this harbour on the evening of the 20th, and the next morning set sail for Boston, to repair the injuries sustained in the late severe gale. This *disappointment* together with the prospect of the enemy's receiving speedy assistance by land and sea, make it necessary for this army to take measures for securing a retreat.[33]

Other newspapers limited themselves, apparently voluntarily, to reporting after the fact that Sullivan had made an orderly retreat and D'Estaing had arrived in Boston without the loss of any ships of the line.[34]

Nevertheless, some Americans still feared that D'Estaing would not be welcomed in Boston. Again the Massachusetts delegates requested that their fellow Bostonians work to restore harmony between the two nations. "In my opinion it would be in a great Degree impolitick at this Juncture to suffer an Odium to be cast on Count D'Estaing," Samuel Adams advised, "If there should be a disposition to do it I am perswaded Men of Discretion and Influence will check it." [35] The citizens of Boston needed no instruction from members of Congress. James Warren wrote, "if the Conduct of the French has been bad, Common discretion would dictate silence to us." [36] A merchant wrote John Adams about his efforts to make the French welcome in Boston: "Impressed with the importance of keeping up a good Understanding with our New Allies I exerted myself to the utmost to satisfy the People that the French were not to blame, that they had done everything in their Power to Cooperate with us in subduing the Enemy." [37]

D'Estaing and his battered fleet arrived in Boston on August 29, receiving a salute of welcome from nearby forts and ships.[38] On September 22, D'Estaing was greeted by the citizens of Boston at a breakfast with John Hancock.[39] Despite his reputed hostility to the alliance, Hancock was a gracious host throughout the French stay. The state government provided a dinner in honor of the French officers at Faneuil Hall with four hundred persons in attendance. By this time, Newport was ig-

---

[33] *Connecticut Courant,* Sept. 1, 1778, italics in original.

[34] *Packet,* Sept. 5, 1778; *Independent Chronicle,* Sept. 3, 1778; *New Jersey Gazette,* Sept. 9, 1778; *Providence Gazette,* Sept. 5, 1778.

[35] Adams to Warren, Sept. 12, 1778; also Adams to Savage, Sept. 14, 1778; and Adams to Bradford, Sept. 21, 1778, *LMCC,* Vol. III, pp. 409, 410, 418.

[36] Warren to Samuel Adams, Sept. 1, 1778, *Warren-Adams Letters,* Vol. II (Massachusetts Historical Society, *Collections,* Vol. LXXIII, Boston, 1925), p. 46.

[37] Cushing to Adams, Oct. 21, 1778, Adams Papers, R. 349.

[38] *Independent Chronicle,* Sept. 3, 1778.

[39] *Ibid.,* Sept. 24, 1778.

nored, and Americans again emphasized the mutual interests of the two allies:

> The genuine joy was never observed to rise higher upon any public occasion; and the toasts, and every circumstance thro' the day, express'd it in the most lively manner; the great and mutual pleasures diffused by the present happy Union between France and these States; which British tyranny has now rendered so important to the interest of both nations.[40]

D'Estaing and his officers contributed to the lessening of tension by their behavior while in Boston. Their discipline and manners impressed skeptical Bostonians, causing William Gordon to observe, "The behaviour of the French officers and sailors, the whole time that their fleet lay in port, was remarkably good, far beyond any thing of the kind ever before, when several men of war were present." [41] After D'Estaing had tea with Josiah Quincy, Quincy wrote Franklin, "The striking Contrast between French and English naval Civility was too remarked to pass unnoticed." [42] Abigail Adams, who earlier had called upon Americans "to Eradicate all those national prejudices" which England had "constantly instilld upon us," was undone by visits of the French officers. Social life in Braintree paled in comparison.

> Heaven continue to be propitious to our Friends & allies for whom I have contracted a most sincere regard. if chastity temperance industry frugality sobriety & purity of morals—added to politeness & compleasance can entitle any people to Friendship & respect, the behaviour of the whole Fleet whilst they lay in this harbour which was more than two months, demand from every unprejudiced person an acknowledgment of their merit, if I even had any [ir]rational prejudices they are done away and I am ashamed to own I was ever possessed of so narrow spirit. and I blush to find so many of my countrymen possessed with such low vulgar prejudices & capable of such mean reflections I have heard thrown out against the nation of our allies though the unblamable conduct of this Fleet left them not one personal reflection to cast.[43]

Abigail overlooked problems caused by the French Fleet, however. A riot between French and American sailors occurred on September 8, supposedly over the shortage of bread. This explanation is unconvinc-

---

[40] *Ibid.*, Oct. 1, 1778.
[41] Gordon, *History*, Vol. III, p. 200.
[42] Quincy to Franklin, Dec. 30, 1778, Franklin Papers, APS, Vol. XII.
[43] Adams to John Adams, May 18, 1778; Nov. 23, 1778, Adams Papers, R. 349.

ing, because there were three more riots in the following months when the bread shortage had lessened.[44] Both sides accused the Tories and sailors of British nationality on their ships of instigating the riots, which provided a convenient means of attributing trouble to their mutual enemy.[45] A Royalist paper later inquired if John Hancock would make another oration on the new Boston massacre.[46]

The riots did not indicate a deep discontent between the two nations. Rather, they reflected the nature of the clientele of the waterfront pleasure houses. The impressment procedures of all nations created mixed crews, which heightened the tension. A day after the first Boston riot, three persons were killed in a similar brawl between French and American sailors in Charleston, also attributed to the instigation of the Tories.[47] Conflict and distrust seemed to be endemic in the Navy. Abraham Whipple, an American naval captain serving in France, complained of trouble with mixed crews and port officials. He wrote, "the French here are a set of damned Deceitful Rasicals. They try to do us all the damages they can instead of their giving us all the protection in their power." Whipple concluded, "I hope to God we shall soon leave the Country [and] hope never more to return." [48] French officers in Boston probably expressed similar sentiments.

Contradictory evidence on the success of intermingling between the French and Americans can be explained by distinguishing the social levels involved. The compliments accorded the French Fleet in Boston were directed to officers, not enlisted men. Frenchmen who had contacts with American society during the Revolution were persons of high social rank in France. Military officers, French consuls in various cities, and merchants such as Holker deliberately tried to prevent conflicts between the two allies because of their official positions or commercial interests.

Americans rarely saw the average Frenchman. When they did, differences in manners and morals caused conflict; the few contacts between French and American sailors seemed to lead inevitably to a fracas. French officers, entertained by Samuel Cooper, John Hancock, Samuel Adams, and other prominent Boston leaders, saw little of the ordinary American. Relations between French and American leaders with

[44] Fritz-Henry Smith, Jr., "The French at Boston during the Revolution," *Bostonian Society Publications,* Vol. X (1913), pp. 43, 49. The dates of the riots were Sept. 8, 26, and 27, 1778, and Oct. 5, 1778.

[45] Heath to Washington, Sept. 28, 1778, Heath Papers, Vol. II; Boston Council to Heath, Oct. 6, 1778, *ibid.,* Vol. II; Washington to D'Estaing, Sept. 29, 1778, Fitzpatrick, ed., *Washington,* Vol. XII, pp. 516–17.

[46] *Royal Gazette* (Charleston), March 7, 1781.

[47] Gervais to Laurens, Sept. 9, 1778, Raymond Starr, ed., "Letters of John Lewis Gervais to Henry Laurens," *SCHGM,* Vol. LXVI (1965), p. 34.

[48] Abraham Whipple to Tucker, July 13, 1778, Whipple Papers, WLC, Vol. II.

education and social standing were amicable, and enabled people in both nations to insist that cooperation was possible despite their disparate cultures.[49]

D'Estaing remained at Boston until late December, when he sailed for the West Indies. His visit demonstrated the willingness of France to give immediate and large-scale military aid to the United States, although the first results of this aid were disappointing. D'Estaing had originally hoped to cooperate in a decisive blow against the British, bringing the war to an end in one season. The Newport expedition not only caused dissension, but also failed to challenge British sea superiority effectively. D'Estaing's visit, forcing the British only to delay the departure of one squadron, did not curtail any planned offensives in the Western Hemisphere.

Nevertheless, Americans claimed certain benefits from D'Estaing's arrival. Philadelphia had been evacuated, an important accomplishment since the Americans had not dislodged the British from any seaport after their success at Boston in 1776. Some Americans insisted that D'Estaing aided trade and commerce, although this was true only in a limited sense. The number of merchant ships arriving with D'Estaing was small, and D'Estaing did not remain in any port long enough to allow owners to plan a safe transatlantic voyage by merchantmen. Even Boston merchants first heard that D'Estaing would stay in their harbor only thirty days.

One visit of a French Fleet to the United States, with an unsuccessful military campaign, had failed to obliterate previous prejudices about France, however. John Laurens ended a letter to his father after the sailors' riots in Boston by writing, "I saw very plainly when I was at Boston, that our a[nc]ient hereditary prejudices were very far from being eradicated." [50] Boston citizens were not alone in their reserve toward the French. According to a French intelligence report, people in Laurens' home town reacted the same way. "Generally in Charlestown the French are not liked at all and in spite of the need that is felt for them they are subject to all sorts of unpleasantness; moreover a part of the city is royalist and they do what they can to incite distrust among others." [51]

Another Frenchman summarized the American attitude toward his countrymen: "the French are liked more than they are esteemed—an assertion the truth of which is recognized by all who have lived amongst

---

[49] On this point, see Echeverria, *Mirage in the West*, p. 104.
[50] Laurens to Laurens, Sept. 24, 1778, Simms, *John Laurens*, p. 228.
[51] Lee Kennett, ed., "Charlestown in 1778: A French Intelligence Report," *SCHGM*, Vol. LXVI (1965), p. 111.

them. They judge us to be like pedlers, very honest thieves. They are English as regards Frenchmen, but Americans towards the English." [52] The first year of the alliance lessened, but did not eliminate, old prejudices. Americans and Frenchmen were allies but not yet friends.

Although the first attempt at military cooperation was an unmitigated failure, it was not enough to disillusion Americans with their ally. Newport demonstrated to Congressmen that a narrow conception of personal honor would ruin harmony and cause recriminations, but Congressmen also realized that military cooperation needed only a victory to quell the lingering distrust of France. Even when unsuccessful, military cooperation did not pose the most critical problem of the alliance. More troublesome was the question of defining a mutually agreeable peace settlement, which by necessity would involve compromise by the radicals on their very conception of independence. The political settlements between allies which were to become the basis for peace ultimata were far more crucial than a temporary military setback. The determination of peace ultimata in 1779 was to cause Congressmen problems of significantly greater magnitude than Newport.

[52] "Mémoir by de Fleury," Nov. 16, 1779, Archives du Ministère des Affaires Étrangères, mémoires et documents (États-Unis), LC, Vol. II.

V. Limiting American Ambitions: The Peace Proposals of 1779

The conditions upon which the United States would agree to peace had not been determined during the first four years of the war except for universal agreement that Great Britain must acknowledge American independence. Few people agreed on the amount of territory needed to insure independence; the topic was endlessly discussed in Congress, but no formal decision had been reached. The radicals generally demanded that northern and western territory be added to the Thirteen States to make independence economically and militarily secure against European aggression. The moderates, however, reminded their colleagues that the struggle with Great Britain was for the independence of the Thirteen States, and that territorial goals beyond this would make the Revolution a war of conquest.

Debate over the meaning of independence became more involved after the alliance, because Article 8 of the defensive treaty stipulated that neither country could sign a separate peace treaty. Thus members of Congress were forced to agree among themselves and with their ally as well. Some Americans, notably Samuel Cooper, were not displeased with the restriction caused by the alliance. "I am pleased with what Congress has done respecting the Explanation of the 8th Article of the alliance; some, and among the Best [people] are for putting Britain on the compassionate List, and for inducing America from meer Pity to save her from becoming a Province of France." Cooper, referring to the publication of the defensive treaty with France, added, "I am glad we are held not to make a Separate Peace." [1] Cooper made his remarks at a time when diplomatic events in Europe made achieving peace more difficult.

Spain, under Floridablanca's guidance, was taking steps to end the war or to enter it allied with France. Despite Vergennes' efforts, Floridablanca had refused to become a party to the treaties signed between France and the United States, and on April 3, 1779, Spain offered to mediate the war on the basis of an immediate suspension of hostilities.

---

[1] Cooper to Adams, Jan. 5, 1779, Adams Papers, NYPL; the treaty was published in the *Independent Chronicle,* Dec. 10, 1778.

Floridablanca was confident that his proposals would be rejected by Great Britain, due to George III's contention that the conflict was a civil war. In addition, Floridablanca made it clear to Great Britain that Spain would expect the return of Gibraltar for its mediation efforts. Without waiting for Great Britain's answer to his thinly veiled ultimatum, Floridablanca agreed on April 6 to the Convention of Aranjuez, which stipulated that Spain would enter the war and France would support her demands for the Floridas, Minorca, and Gibraltar. Regardless of the British answer to the ultimatum, Floridablanca expected to achieve the long-desired return of Gibraltar, and if Spain entered the war he could be confident of gaining valuable territory in the Mediterranean and the New World.[2]

Long before the Convention of Aranjuez, Vergennes had instructed Gérard to prepare for the possibility that Spain would enter the war. Vergennes objected to the territorial ambitions of the radicals, or in his phrase, the "anti-Gallicans," and ordered Gérard to convince Congress to limit its demands in order to accommodate Spain and prepare for any mediation talks.[3] Vergennes did not change any of his previous instructions on Canada, the Mississippi, and the fishery, and thus the stage was set for the first serious diplomatic disagreement between the two allies. In later instructions Vergennes asked Gérard to speak to trusted members of Congress about the possibility of a truce, also a delicate subject. France would agree to a truce, Vergennes stated, only if Great Britain agreed to treat the United States as an independent nation and evacuate all territory within the confines of the Thirteen States.[4]

Gérard received his instructions in early February and revealed to select members of Congress that France wanted the United States to determine its peace ultimata.[5] Gérard's task was more difficult than either he or Vergennes first suspected. In introducing the topic of peace terms, Gérard would inevitably activate competing sectional interests and moderate-radical differences. But because his circle of friends was limited to a small number of moderate, pro-French, and pro-Deane delegates, Gérard did not foresee these conflicts and badly misjudged the temper of Congress. For example, after sounding out the opinions of members of Congress, he informed a probably incredulous Vergennes, "All the delegates whose conversations form the basis of this report have assured me that Congress is not planning to lay claim to New-

2 Bemis, *The Diplomacy of the Revolution,* pp. 81–85; Morris, *The Peacemakers,* pp. 15–21.

3 Vergennes to Gérard, Oct. 26, 1778, Meng, ed., *Gérard,* pp. 358–59.

4 Vergennes to Gérard, Dec. 25, 1778, *ibid.,* pp. 451–52.

5 Gérard to Vergennes, Feb. 15, 1779, *ibid.,* pp. 521–24.

foundland any more than to fishing rights on the [Grand] Banks." [6]

By May Gérard abandoned his reliance on private conferences with select members of Congress, concluding that more decisive steps were needed to compel that body to accept his plan for moderate peace ultimata. Gérard's new strategy emphasized newspaper articles in which Americans, paid by the French, publicly argued the merits of moderate peace proposals. Even this drastic step was not immediately successful, as Congress did not finish determining the ultimata until September. By the time Congress completed the peace proposals of 1779 Spain had declared war against Great Britain, so members of Congress understood that the first mediation effort had failed; they were preparing United States terms for any eventual peace negotiation.

During discussion of the ultimata, Gérard had two objectives in addition to limiting United States territorial ambitions. He asked Congress to appoint a single minister to negotiate the peace treaty, but the selection awaited completion of United States territorial demands. Gérard's remaining objective was to see that Congress determined what terms would be required for the United States to agree to a truce.[7]

Gérard broached the idea of a truce to three unidentified delegates who responded with *"avidité."* Gérard, however, believed that the majority in Congress was not receptive to the idea, so he requested trustworthy delegates to mention it at appropriate times during the debates. He suggested that discussion of a truce be introduced whenever members of Congress considered how the United States would respond if Great Britain proposed an armistice. Gérard's confidants stated that the evacuation of all United States territory would be the minimum requirement of any truce.[8] This position coincided with French policy outlined by Vergennes.

Congress rebuffed Gérard's suggestions concerning a truce and refused to take action on the question, since most delegates believed acceptance of truce terms would imply a break in the heretofore unanimous demand for complete independence. Furthermore, military conditions were not critical. The campaign of 1779 was at a virtual standstill, and the summer passed without a major battle taking place within the Thirteen States. Unable to execute French policy in this area, Gérard secretly hoped that France and Great Britain would agree to a truce while Congress was still debating. Congress, he implied, would be forced to accept the terms if independence were tacitly acknowledged. In June

[6] Gérard to Vergennes, March 1, 1779, *ibid.,* p. 547.

[7] Gérard to Vergennes, Feb. 15, 1779; May 7–8, 1779, *ibid.,* pp. 521–24, 628–29; Drayton, "Memorandum of Conference with Minister of France," Feb. 15, 1779, *LMCC,* Vol. IV, pp. 69–71.

[8] Gérard to Vergennes, May 7–8, 1779, Meng, ed., *Gérard,* pp. 628–29.

Gérard reported that Congress had still made no decision on a truce, and by August he admitted his defeat. Its proponents, according to Gérard, "simply decided that they would work toward the truce under consideration if circumstances required such action." [9]

Although bowing to American demands on the question of a truce, Gérard achieved limited success in persuading the United States to restrict its territorial objectives. Within three weeks after discussions began, one delegate predicted the eventual outcome. "I am afraid of the arts they are using to hurry us into a rash ultimatum, we are told that such is our first business, tho your letter and the observations of a blind man convince us to the contrary," James Lovell wrote. "But forsooth France & Spain are of that opinion fully as say the Lickspittles of the Plenip[otentiary]. There will be no puzzle about the south bounds, but neither shall canada nova scotia nor [the] Fishery be in the Ult[imatum for the peace treaty]." [10] In spite of Lovell's accurate prediction of the final terms, Congress was not to be hurried by French demands and in fact spent the better part of a year determining its peace ultimata.

Congress finally decided that the United States should claim all territory westward to the Mississippi and southward to the thirty-first parallel. The northern boundary west of New England was set on a line from below Montreal through Lake Nipissing to the conjectured source of the Mississippi river. Congress requested that Spain grant the United States permission to navigate the Mississippi south of the thirty-first parallel. Although American claims on the western boundaries were enormous and, in Gérard's opinion, spurious, he believed that he dare not intervene to prevent the United States from making an attempt to acquire the territory in peace negotiations.

Gérard continued the Janus-like French policy on Canada. He submitted a memorandum to Congress explaining the French position on territory outside the Thirteen Original States and again making it clear that France would not support any additional territorial demands unless the United States held possession at the beginning of peace talks. [11] But he advised Vergennes that it would be dangerous to try to convince Americans to renounce the conquest of Canada. Canada, Gérard emphasized, was so widely desired by Americans that it would endanger harmonious relations in the alliance if France summarily announced that it would not support United States aspirations to the area. [12]

[9] Gérard to Vergennes, May 21, 1779; June 11, 1779; Aug. 1–5, 1779, *ibid.*, pp. 658–59, 706, 822.

[10] Lovell to Gates, March 1, 1779, Gates Papers, box XI.

[11] Gérard to President of Congress, May 22, 1779, Wharton, ed., *Diplomatic Correspondence,* Vol. III, p. 177.

[12] Gérard to Vergennes, May 14, 1779, Meng, ed., *Gérard,* p. 639.

The issue which prolonged discussions of the peace terms was the fishery. Gérard made a tactical mistake when he combined the removal of Arthur Lee and reduction of American claims for the fishing rights.[13] Gérard wanted John Jay as United States Minister to the peace negotiations, and since the proposed site of the negotiations was Madrid, this necessitated dismissing Arthur Lee. Jay, in Gérard's opinion, was more amenable to French policy. Jay agreed that the fishery should not be included in the peace ultimata, while Arthur Lee, because of his close connections with the Massachusetts delegates, could be expected to insist on it. Gérard's strategy failed on May 3 when Congress refused to recall Lee.[14] Congress then postponed discussion of the peace ultimata indefinitely.

Massachusetts, Connecticut, and New Jersey had voted against the recall of Lee. This was sufficient to prevent the needed majority of seven, because four states did not have the two delegates in attendance required for their vote to be counted. An attendance problem seldom affected Massachusetts, which had the most sophisticated political organization of any state during the Revolution. Despite frequent changes of delegates, all Massachusetts delegates voted alike on the fishery question. The titular head of the Massachusetts delegation was Samuel Adams, but he had able assistants in Elbridge Gerry and James Lovell. Lovell served as an unofficial secretary to the delegation, keeping leaders in Massachusetts informed about upcoming political conflicts in Congress. Letters were constantly exchanged and discussed among leaders in Boston and Philadelphia. Massachusetts, due to its political organization, exercised more political influence in Congress than any other state.

James Lovell remained in Congress through the entire fishery debate, but Samuel Adams returned to Massachusetts after Elbridge Gerry arrived to replace him. Lovell viewed the French position on the fishery as an attempt to exclude the United States and not, as Gérard insisted, a necessary compromise to induce Great Britain to sign a peace treaty.

13 John Armstrong claimed that the "harmony of Congress rather grows than otherwise, there being but one point on the Carpet in which the House stand Martialed on every side (the retaining or [dismissing] of Arthur Lee) for the Fishery I think has gained a sufficient political base in effect amounting to an Ultimatum or *Sine qua non*." Armstrong to Gates, Aug. 16, 1779, Gates Papers, box XII.

14 Worthington B. Ford, ed., *Journals of the Continental Congress, 1774–1789* (Washington, 1904–1937), May 3, 1779, Vol. XIV, pp. 542–43. States which were divided or did not have enough delegates in attendance to have their vote counted were New Hampshire, Rhode Island, Pennsylvania, Delaware, South Carolina, and Georgia; states which voted to recall Lee were New York, Maryland, Virginia, and North Carolina. The number of delegates voting to recall Lee was twenty-one, while fourteen voted against his recall.

Two European Powers [France and Great Britain] have fancied that they could claim the Fishery of the Banks and Gulphs of America not only against their European Nations but ag[ain]st all *weaker* People even bordering on their Sease [*sic*]. A private Party [the anti-fishery group] pretend to know possitively that Gr[eat] Br[itain] will not be thought to set up a *strange* Claim if she persists to demand *all* that she has not given to France.[15]

Instead of realizing that Massachusetts had a highly developed political organization, Gérard believed that Samuel Adams was personally responsible for the state's opposition to French policy. He attempted to undercut Adams' influence by hiring Samuel Cooper to work for the French. Cooper promoted French policy by use of his extensive friendships with political leaders in Massachusetts. For example, when Samuel Adams asked Cooper for his opinion on the fishery, Cooper replied that the United States would acquire the fishery easily in the future, so there would be no need to insist on its inclusion in the peace ultimata.[16]

Gérard also hoped to induce John Hancock to oppose Adams on the fishery, but he was unsuccessful and had to rely solely on Cooper. In addition to advancing the French position to prominent Massachusetts friends, Cooper was supposed to devise plans for diminishing Adams' political influence. Cooper also argued against the fishery in private meetings and in articles for the Boston papers, but his efforts had no discernible effect in reducing the Massachusetts delegates' demand for the fishery.[17]

During the first few months of debate on the peace ultimata, the American press carried many articles advocating retention of the fisheries, and for the only time in the alliance a foreign policy issue, albeit an aspect of the Deane-Lee dispute, became a source of sustained public debate. A Boston paper opened public discussion of the fisheries with an essay by "An Inquirer":

The Newfoundland fishery is a source of wealth as valuable to us, as the hills of Potosi is to the Spaniards.

A temporary precarious peace, will not serve our purpose. I wish to see every spark extinguished—every seed of dissention eradicated. I hope these important objects will appear in a clear

[15] Lovell to Gates, April 5, 1779, *LMCC*, Vol. IV, p. 142, italics in original.
[16] Gérard to Vergennes, Jan. 17, 1779, Meng, ed., *Gérard*, pp. 481–82; Cooper to Adams, March 14, 1779, Adams Papers, NYPL.
[17] De Valnais to Holker, May, 1779; July 15, 1779; July 23, 1779, Holker Papers, Vol. IV; de Valnais to Holker, Aug. 12, 1779, *ibid.*, Vol. V.

point of light to the public eye. In such case, I am persuaded the people will chearfully support the Congress in the prosecution of the war, 'till peace, liberty and safety, the objects of our struggle, are secured beyond the fear of future violation.[18]

A number of similiar articles appeared in the first half of 1779, and almost none proposed that the United States renounce its claims to the fishery.[19]

Gérard decided to combat the overwhelming support given the New England position on the fishery by hiring writers to advocate French policy. In the spring of 1779 he hired Hugh Henry Brackenridge, who wrote articles for two years under the pseudonyms of "Anti-Anglican," "The Honest Politician," and "American." [20] Gérard also had dealings with another writer, known as "Americanus," whose articles reversed the public support for the fishery and put pro-fishery advocates on the defensive for the remainder of the summer.[21]

Two articles, "Americanus" and "O Tempora, O Mores," apparently written by the same author, charged that the New England delegates were primarily responsible for delaying final passage of the peace proposals. In the first article, "O Tempora, O Mores," the author, referring to the vote on the recall of Arthur Lee, maintained that Congress was ruled by a faction from New England, which allegedly advocated measures harmful to the best interests of the United States. In the second article, "Americanus" attacked a letter written by Francis Lee and published in an Annapolis paper. In the manuscript, but not in the published version, Lee stated that there was a French faction in Congress dedicated to defending Silas Deane and dismissing his brother, Arthur Lee. "Americanus" used Lee's letter as a pretext to dive into the riled waters of the peace proposals.

[18] *Independent Chronicle,* April 22, 1779.

[19] See *Independent Chronicle,* April 22, 1779 (two); *ibid.,* April 29, 1779; *Virginia Gazette* (Dixon and Nicolson), April 24, 1779, and June 12, 1779; *Packet,* May 20, 1779, June 24, 1779, and July 1, 1779. William Henry Drayton, writing under the pseudonym of "An American," *Packet,* Feb. 27, 1779, March 11, 1779, earlier advocated an immediate peace but wanted the United States to be awarded Nova Scotia and Bermuda. Drayton at this time was one of the closest followers of Gérard.

[20] Gérard to Vergennes, May 29, 1779, Meng, ed., *Gérard,* pp. 689–91; Brackenridge is identified by Luzerne as the author of these articles in Luzerne to Vergennes, April 1, 1780, Chevalier de la Luzerne Papers, Archives du Ministère des Affaires Étrangères, Paris.

[21] For the authorship of the "Americanus" articles, see the extended discussion by Burnett in *LMCC,* Vol. IV, pp. 276n–279n and 307n–308n. The citation for the "Americanus" and "O Tempora, O Mores" articles is from the *Pennsylvania Gazette* (Philadelphia), June 23, 1779.

It is not my intention to make any observation of this, or any other parts of the treaties: They are evidently expressed in clear, unequivocal terms, and appear to have been dictated by plain, sincere and sound policy. There can be no doubt as to what the contracting parties, by those treaties, guaranteed to each other; but it is reported, that the debates and delays in Congress, on the terms of the treaty proposed to be opened, have arisen from the desire and wishes of some men to include in it certain objects and rights, which were not in our possession, either at the time of the declaration of independence, or at the concluding of the treaties of Paris; In a word, that a right of fishing on the Banks of New-foundland shall be acknowledged and guaranteed to these States, and that such an article shall be made a *sine qua non* of the treaty.[22]

[22] *Ibid.* It is not clear what relationship Gérard had with the author of these articles. Gérard paid an author for these articles, but stated that he was not one of his regular writers. Gérard mentioned that he suggested to the author topics not currently being discussed, which is contrary to the facts. He also claimed that he had to moderate the zeal of the author. (Gérard to Vergennes, June 17, 1779, Meng, ed., *Gérard*, p. 733.) Gérard's identification of the author is puzzling. In "Minutes of the French Legation in the United States" (Vol. II, May 21, 1779), Gérard states that the author is a former member of Congress. In a dispatch to Vergennes on the same day he says that the author is currently a member of Congress. On May 29, 1779, Gérard reverted to his original statement, saying that the author was a former member of Congress. (Gérard to Vergennes, May 21, 1779; May 29, 1779, Meng, ed., *Gérard*, pp. 658, 690–91.) Gérard apparently had substantial control of the contents of the articles, because he sent Vergennes the original of an article which appeared in the *Pennsylvania Gazette,* June 2, 1779. (*Ibid.,* June 5, 1779, pp. 709–12.)

Thomas Paine charged that the author was one of three men, Gouverneur Morris, Silas Deane, or Edward Langworthy. (*Pennsylvania Gazette,* July 21, 1779.) Morris wrote Robert Livingston that the peace proposals should not be subject to public debate. He probably would not have made such a statement to a close associate if he were the author. (Morris to Livingston, July 22, 1779, Livingston Papers, N-YHS, box V.) There is no evidence in the printed works of Silas Deane to indicate that he was the author. Gérard would certainly have mentioned it in his dispatches if Deane were in any way connected. Edward Langworthy of Georgia must have been connected with the articles. James Lovell stated that he had no doubt that Langworthy at least copied the rough draft for the press, as Langworthy claimed. Lovell doubted, however, that Langworthy was the sole author. (Lovell to Samuel Adams, July 10, 1779; July 13, 1779, Adams Papers, NYPL.) Lovell's conclusion is not in contradiction with any evidence that Gérard sent back to Vergennes. Lovell noted that the publication of the treaties pleased Samuel Chase and others because the United States could not sign a treaty without France; this would put pressure on New England to give up its demand for the fishery. Lovell also noted that Langworthy was reputed to write under the pen name of Cato, which was also Samuel Chase's most frequent pseudonym. Chase and Langworthy's views on New England were almost identical to those expressed in the articles, and it is probable that they collaborated in writing them.

The pro-fishery advocates attempted unsuccessfully to rebut "Americanus'" charges of a junto. Thomas Paine denied that New England delegates were responsible for protracted discussion of the peace proposals. Oliver Ellsworth argued in his article, "A Friend to Fair Play," that the agreement of New England delegates on many issues resulted from independent decisions made by individual delegates rather than a prearranged plan.[23] Nevertheless, the pro-fishery group had been forced to justify their voting record publicly, and the initiative had passed to the opponents of the fishery. The anti-fishery articles were widely reprinted throughout the country.[24] One paper included an introduction to "Americanus" by a pro-fishery advocate:

> *Americanus* tries to persuade us, that all those who will not let Canada and Nova Scotia remain in the hands of Great Britain, and who will not consent to our being excluded from the fisheries, are members of an "execrable faction." *Americanus* may be an American, for we well know that America, as well as other countries, has produced patricides; and I remember *Joseph Galloway,* one of them, chose that indeterminate signature, when his *American zeal* inspired him to facilitate the execution of the stampact.[25]

Despite such protests, opponents of the fishery, supported by Gérard, pushed forward vigorously to destroy any hopes that New England delegates still held for including the fishery in the peace ultimata. Benjamin Rush admonished Congress, "And may the Members of the American Congress ever remember that *liberty*—not glory, and that *right*—not conquest, should be their only object in all their negotiations." [26] Although the direction of events was now favorable to the French position, Gérard found that he had instigated a campaign he could no longer control. The Silas Deane controversy became interwoven with the fishery debate. Generally, men divided into groups on three issues: either pro-Deane, anti-Arthur Lee, and anti-fishery; or anti-Deane, pro-Arthur Lee, and pro-fishery. A sectional split occurred in

[23] Paine's articles are in the *Pennsylvania Gazette,* June 30, 1779; July 14, 1779; July 21, 1779; "Timerius Graccus" answered "Americanus" in *ibid.,* June 30, 1779; "Americanus" continued the debate in *ibid.,* July 7, 1779; July 28, 1779; Ellsworth's article appeared in the *Connecticut Courant,* Sept. 1, 1779.

[24] For "O Tempora, O Mores," see *Virginia Gazette* (Dixon and Nicolson), July 17, 1779; *Maryland Gazette* (Annapolis), July 9, 1779; *Connecticut Courant,* Aug. 10, 1779; the "Americanus" article of June 23, 1779, is in *Providence Gazette,* July 10, 1779; *Maryland Gazette,* July 9, 1779.

[25] *Providence Gazette,* July 10, 1779, italics in original.

[26] *Packet,* Aug. 24, 1779, italics in original.

Congress, with the Middle and Southern States aligned against New England, and particularly Massachusetts.

The moderates' counterattack gained momentum as they convinced many Americans that New England delegates were prolonging the war. A correspondent of Thomas Burke reported from Williamsburg, "It is currently said that the Independence of the thirteen united States has been offered Congress by G. Britain, and that peace on those [terms] has been rejected by them, they demanding Canada & Nova Scotia." He continued, enunciating what became the standard refrain of moderates after 1779, "I can hardly think this possible when I consider the thousand urgent Reasons for accepting those terms: indeed the amazing Depreciation of our Paper Currency seems to threaten us with speedy Ruin." Southern delegates, aside from the few radicals in their ranks, reiterated the charges against New Englanders in letters to their governors. "I think we might have had Peace if our Eastern friends had not been so Sanguine in their demands respecting the Fishery," complained one North Carolina Congressman.[27]

The culmination of the press debate came at the end of the summer when a number of papers printed the Paca-Drayton memorandum. The memorandum, taken from the records of Congress, showed the vote to recall Arthur Lee, in which Lee was supported by seven of the eight New England delegates. The other part of the memorandum recorded William Paca and William Drayton's discussion of Arthur Lee with Gérard. Gérard had allowed Paca and Drayton, of Maryland and South Carolina respectively, to copy part of a dispatch from Vergennes in which he stated, "Besides, I confess to you that I fear Mr. Lee and those around him." [28]

The anti-fishery group did not consider the propriety of quoting the opinion of the French Foreign Minister against a fellow American. Gérard did not investigate the public use of the memorandum, nor did he protest the printing of his confidential correspondence. Gérard sent Vergennes a copy of the memorandum, implying that it was used only in Congress; he gave no indication that Vergennes' official opinion was

[27] Tazewell to Burke, June 4, 1779, Thomas Burke Papers, NCSA; Hewes to Caswell, July 27, 1779, Gratz Collection, HSP.

[28] *New Jersey Gazette*, Sept. 15, 1779, reprinted from *New York Journal*, Aug. 9, 1779; *Connecticut Courant*, Sept. 21, 1779; *Newport Gazette*, Oct. 6, 1779; *Packet*, Sept. 23, 1779. Apparently none of the Boston papers reprinted the memorandum. Thomas Cushing received a copy of it and wrote letters advocating an anti-Lee stand by Massachusetts Congressional delegates. Cushing to Holten, July 28, 1779, MSS, BPL. Cushing's pleading evidently had little effect on the delegates in Philadelphia. See Lovell to Samuel Adams, Aug. 12, 1779, Adams Papers, NYPL.

being reprinted in American papers to promote French foreign policy.[29]

The vitriolic press campaign was being conducted at the very time that Congress was negotiating a compromise acceptable to both France and New England. From the beginning, the moderate pro-French group included men who realized that it would be necessary to placate New England and still satisfy France. Robert Livingston expressed the position of this group, "I do not know upon the whole whether in our present tumoultrious [sic] situation it is not better that Congress sh[oul]d seem rather to *acqucess* [acquiesce] in the terms rather than *agree* to them." Thomas Jefferson retreated from his earlier pro-fishery position and urged acceptance of a limited program for peace, "It would surely be better to carry on a ten years war some time hence than to continue the present an unnecessary moment.".[30] After 1779, the moderates increasingly demanded steps which would bring about independence as quickly as possible, even if this meant renouncing territorial goals. But a radical New England delegate wrote, "I am very sensible of the present unhappy situation in our public affairs and ardently long for peace—but [I should ?] rather risk the continuance of the war than give up our rights to the fishery." [31]

After another postponement of the fishery question in June, Elbridge Gerry reopened congressional debate in early July.[32] In the following three weeks of intermittent argument, a final compromise was reached by making United States participation in the fishery an ultimatum for a commercial treaty with Great Britain rather than a part of the peace treaty. The peace treaty could be signed without a commercial treaty, so the fishery would not delay general peace.[33] As a result, the fishery could not be gained by strict adherence to the alliance unless Great Britain could be induced to include it in the general peace terms. Peace and independence could be achieved and the alliance fade into insignificance without New England's primary territorial demand being secured; thus it became critical for the radicals to have a trusted man to negotiate the peace treaty.

The compromise on the fishery ended the most prolonged dispute over the peace terms. Neither New England nor France gained its demands, but both agreed that they could abide by such an agreement. The controversy further diminished the enthusiasm for the alliance which

---

[29] Gérard to Vergennes, Aug. 8, 1779, Meng., ed., *Gérard*, pp. 844–45.

[30] Livingston to Jay, April 20, 1779, Livingston Papers, N-YHS, box IV, italics in original; Jefferson to Fleming, June 8, 1779, Boyd, ed., *Jefferson*, Vol. II, p. 288.

[31] Bartlett to Whipple, July 24, 1779, Whipple Papers.

[32] Henry Laurens, "Notes on Proceedings," June 19, 1779; July 1, 1779, *LMCC*, Vol. IV, pp. 274–76; 291–92.

[33] Lovell to S. Adams, July 20, 1779, *ibid.*, Vol. IV, p. 333; Ford, ed., *Journals of CC*, July 19, 1779, Vol. XIV, p. 851; "Minutes of the French Legation in the United States," Vol. II.

had existed the previous year. The fishery dispute had widened divisions left by the Deane controversy and the Newport expedition. After their conflict with Gérard over the fishery, radicals realized that the benefits of the alliance were not unqualified.

> I fear we place too much dependence on foreign alliances, which will tend to introduce a servility destructive to true Republicanism. we must expect all nations will be influenced by their own interest and so far as we may expect the Friendship of any power that inclines to form an alliance with us, if we expect more, we shall certainly be disappointed. it requires no great depth in Politics to discern that the alliance already entered into is as much for the interest of our ally as ourselves and there is every appearance of an increasing benefit on her part; it is not in the power of Great Britain to offer her [France] an adequate compensation for the surrender of those advantages, there therefore can be no danger from that quarter.[34]

Settlement of the fishery question left only the selection of the Minister to negotiate the peace treaty. Since Great Britain had rejected the mediation proposals, Americans waited for news that Spain had entered the war. Congressmen were not eager to take up the question of Arthur Lee again. Gérard asked only that the peace ultimata be determined and the Minister appointed before he left for France, so Congress waited until the end of September before selecting a new man.

In two unusual weekend sessions on September 26 and 27, Congress completed the peace proposals which had taken eight months to formulate. A number of intricate compromises were still needed to reach a final agreement. The New England delegates made one final try to retain Arthur Lee as commissioner to Spain; a procedural vote indicated that the delegates from the Middle and Southern States were adamant about a replacement for Lee.

Without voting on Lee's dismissal, Congress next considered the selection of a Minister to Spain who would be given additional powers to negotiate the peace treaty. John Adams was nominated and supported by New England delegates, while John Jay was nominated and supported by delegates from the Middle and Southern States. Neither Jay nor Adams received the seven votes required for election in three ballots taken on Saturday.[35] Overnight a compromise was arranged to divide the responsibility into two different positions, thus assuring each side of

---

[34] Whipple to Bartlett, July 27, 1779, Bartlett Papers, Vol. II. Bartlett agreed with Whipple's analysis, Bartlett to Whipple, Aug. 21, 1779, Whipple Papers.

[35] Ford, ed., *Journals of CC,* Sept. 26, 1779; Sept. 27, 1779, Vol. XIV, pp. 1109–14.

filling at least one post. On Sunday morning William Paca and Meriwether Smith moved, undoubtedly with Gérard's approval, that a Minister Plenipotentiary be nominated for Spain to supersede Arthur Lee, who held rank only as a commissioner. The results of the compromise were immediately apparent. "Lee will be, as tis intended and expected," Henry Laurens wrote, "superceded by Mr. Jay, an avowed and inveterate Enemy." Jay was elected to this post on the first ballot, and John Adams was then elected by a unanimous vote as sole Plenipotentiary to negotiate peace and commercial treaties with Great Britain.[36]

The compromise dividing the ministerial duties involved the abandonment of Arthur Lee for John Adams by the radicals. James Lovell had hoped that such a development could be avoided by Spain signing a treaty with the United States while Lee still held his post. This, Lovell believed, would enable Lee to resign with honor.[37] When forced with a choice, Lee's defenders sacrificed him in order that John Adams be appointed to negotiate peace. As Lovell explained to Richard Henry Lee, the moderates had turned against Arthur Lee, barring any possibility that he could be retained, so the Massachusetts delegates voted for the compromise which sent Jay to Spain. Lovell, never one to mince words, bluntly stated, "This is but one of the many Stains which we are liable to in this Sort of Business." [38] In a letter to John Adams, Lovell explained that the Massachusetts delegates wanted to prevent John Jay from being the Minister to negotiate the peace treaty; they were not trying to discard Lee, but to assure Adams' position as peace negotiator.

> Every restraining Motive must be *forgotton* or banished. Your Choice, was unanimous, save one Vote,[39] yet there are not a few, who wish you, being appointed, may refuse that the Election from another Quarter may take Place, & no other New England Man will be chosen, the Interest of America requires, blind as some People are to it, that a New England Man should negotiate a Peace.[40]

The appointment of Jay and Adams ended the prolonged conflict over the peace terms, and silenced the last outbursts in the Deane-Lee controversy. Neither faction had achieved a complete victory. Defenders

[36] *Ibid.;* Lovell to John Adams, Sept. 28, 1779 (two letters), Adams Papers, R. 350; Laurens to John Laurens, Sept. 27, 1779, Laurens Papers, R. 13.

[37] Lovell to John Adams, Aug. 24, 1779, *ibid.;* William Whipple made an identical suggestion to Richard Henry Lee, Whipple to Lee, Aug. 23, 1779, Lee Family Papers, R. 6.

[38] Lovell to Richard Henry Lee, Sept. 27, 1779, *LMCC,* Vol. IV, pp. 443–45.

[39] John Dickinson voted for Benjamin Franklin, but since he was not nominated the vote was declared to be unanimous.

[40] Lovell to Adams, Oct. 12, 1779, Adams Papers, R. 350, italics in original.

of Silas Deane rejoiced in the recall of Arthur Lee and his replacement by John Jay, who had been a consistent supporter of Deane. Deane himself believed that the New England junto had finally been broken, but not destroyed.[41] Although the radicals had gained a major victory in the election of John Adams as sole Plenipotentiary to negotiate peace, the achievement would fade unless there were serious peace negotiations within a year.

The peace ultimata of 1779 marked the high point of republican strength during the alliance. As the war progressed more delegates, including a great many radicals, became convinced of the absolute need for peace on the minimum terms of independence for the Thirteen States. Other radicals saw the peace demands as a capitulation to French pressure and grew discouraged with the performance of Congress. They slowly declined in strength in Congress, pleading illness or duty to their state governments. Most members of Congress, radicals included, attempted to mute conflicts after 1779 instead of bringing the critical issues of the day into the open as they had in the early years of the Revolution.

Gérard, surprisingly, never revealed disapproval of the compromise which allowed Adams and Jay to be appointed. He merely expressed dismay to Vergennes that Franklin had not even been considered as the Minister to negotiate the peace treaty. Gérard had lost touch with Congress by this time. On the day of the election he expected that Jay would be elected Minister for negotiating peace while Adams would be sent to Spain. After the election Gérard noted that Luzerne wished that Jay's and Adams' positions were reversed; Gérard himself made no comment.[42] Due to his illness, Gérard did not exert the same influence at the conclusion of the debates as he had earlier. The peace proposals which he had expected to be completed in three months had taken eight, during which Gérard became *persona non grata* to the supporters of Arthur Lee.[43]

The debate over the peace proposals in 1779 had revealed the confidence that Americans then had in their own resources and objectives. In the prolonged discussions and many compromises necessary to determine the final terms, it became apparent that there were definite limits on the French policy which Congress would accept. Although prodded by Gérard, members of Congress refused to be rushed into deciding United States terms. Nor would they indiscriminately accede to French

[41] Silas Deane to Simeon Deane, Sept. 28, 1779, Albert Bates, ed., *The Deane Papers, 1771–1795 (Collections of the Connecticut Historical Society,* Hartford, 1930, Vol. XXIII), p. 149.

[42] Gérard to Vergennes, Sept. 25–27, 1779, Meng, ed., *Gérard,* pp. 893–98.

[43] Burnett, ed., *LMCC,* Vol. IV, preface, xxvii.

preferences to satisfy their powerful ally. Congress declined to determine the terms of a truce, it would not totally renounce claims to the fishery, and it still insisted on vast claims to the undeveloped western area. But within a broad context, Gérard also accomplished French policy. The United States did not claim the Floridas, and it compromised on its demands for navigation rights on the Mississippi. Furthermore, Canada, Nova Scotia, and Newfoundland were omitted from the United States *sine qua non* for peace. The alliance, judged by the actions of Congress in 1779, was still in a negotiable stage, with each nation protecting its own interest. Yet a discernible trend was developing which augured little hope for the combative radicals of 1776.

Gérard had successfully supported a coalition which had moderated and refused some of the radicals' basic demands. This loosely organized and perpetually shifting coalition was able to win against the radicals in Congress and in the press. This group, which Gérard had organized by persuasion and payment, came to dominate foreign policy decisions for the remainder of the war. The coalition was not all-powerful and had to listen to radical demands, but in the future, foreign policy was guided by the primary consideration of ending the war as soon as possible. This policy, also dedicated to independence, entailed accepting French advice without the skepticism or reservations seen in the first eighteen months of the alliance.

Another change in foreign policy occurred almost unnoticed when the United States agreed that any peace negotiations must take place in Europe. The expression of American demands now rested in the hands of a few men serving in Europe, where they would be influenced as much by European diplomacy as by their instructions from Congress. Congressional control of peace-making became indirect in comparison with the response to Lord Howe's offer in 1776 and the Carlisle Commission in 1778. Congress still set broad policy, but the individual ministers in Europe made more policy decisions than before.

James Lovell understood this subtle change, but he believed that the appointment of John Adams insured the protection of United States rights, and particularly the fishery. Lovell warned Adams that France might try to evade its responsibilities under the alliance by informally agreeing to a merely tacit acknowledgment of United States independence by Great Britain. Undaunted by setbacks in Congress, he needlessly reminded his fellow Bostonian, "the way to insure the lasting Regard of France is by showing independent Virility instead of colonial Effeminacy." [44]

[44] Lovell to Adams, Nov. 1, 1779, Adams Papers, R. 350.

VI. The Chevalier de la Luzerne

At the close of Congressional debate on peace ultimata, Gérard's successor, Chevalier de la Luzerne, arrived in Philadelphia. The short, jovial Luzerne was an inexperienced diplomat, having spent only two years in the diplomatic service as Minister Plenipotentiary to the Bavarian Court at Munich. Luzerne had been recalled from this post in June, 1778, and was awaiting reassignment when Vergennes asked him to replace the ailing Gérard.

The new Minister, born and raised in Paris, came from a moderately wealthy noble family. One brother became a cardinal and the other a Minister of Marine, while Luzerne pursued a military career for eighteen years, rising to the rank of colonel. When his regiment was disbanded in 1775, he entered the diplomatic service. Of a higher social rank and receiving double the salary of Gérard, Luzerne came to his new calling with a knowledge of military affairs which served him in good stead in the United States.[1]

Luzerne's first secretary was François Barbé-Marbois, also his first secretary in Bavaria. Barbé-Marbois, who probably received the appointment at Luzerne's request, was an active and trusted assistant in the United States. The son of a bourgeois family, which had recently purchased a seat for him in the parliament of Metz, he had served in various diplomatic posts in Europe since 1768, generally either as first secretary or Chargé d'Affaires.[2] Barbé-Marbois was given more responsibility for dealing with Congress than Gérard had granted his assistants. At times it was difficult to determine whether Luzerne or Barbé-Marbois had the greater influence on decisions taken by Congress.

Luzerne operated under virtually the same instructions as Gérard. A change to Luzerne's advantage was the possibility that France might

[1] William E. O'Donnell, *The Chevalier de la Luzerne, French Minister to the United States, 1779–1784* (Louvain, 1938), pp. 39–42. The yearly stipend for Gérard was 36,000 livres a year, and Luzerne received 72,000 livres a year. The livre is worth approximately twenty cents. See Finances du Ministère, Archives du Ministère des Affaires Étrangères, Paris, Vol. VIII, pp. 63, 73.

[2] On Barbé-Marbois, see E. Wilson Lyon, *The Man Who Sold Louisiana: The Career of François Barbé-Marbois* (Norman, 1942), pp. 6–16. Eugene P. Chase, ed., *Our Revolutionary Forefathers: Letters of François Marquis de Barbé-Marbois* (New York, 1939) is not helpful, because Barbé-Marbois omitted all political opinions in letters to France.

send an expeditionary force to the United States. Luzerne carried out previous French policy on the navigation of the Mississippi, the conquest of Canada, and the subsidy of French agents in the United States. As a precautionary measure, Vergennes asked Luzerne to get each state to ratify the treaty in case the Articles of Confederation were not approved and Congress was stripped of its authority to conduct foreign affairs. Later, Vergennes also requested that Luzerne examine the possibilities of a truce without presenting the idea as a formal request to Congress.[3]

The political events of Luzerne's first few months in his new post foreshadowed the success he was to have in the United States. Luzerne was able to bring the long-awaited news that Spain had entered the war against Great Britain. This development postponed United States and French differences over peace terms for at least another campaign. The schism in Congress created by the Silas Deane affair had subsided after the decision to supplant Arthur Lee and grant Deane permission to return to Europe to collect his financial records. These steps allowed the controversy to remain quiescent until Arthur Lee returned from Europe.

The war in the United States had been at a stand-off with neither side making any spectacular gains. The Americans had achieved a minor victory by the capture of Stony Point, which discouraged the British from planning another attack on the Hudson Highlands. The British were preparing their long-expected southern offensive, but did not leave New York by sea until late December, 1779, for a spring attack on Charleston. The only ominous shadow fell when General Lincoln and Count D'Estaing failed to capture Savannah in the fall of 1779. But the failure at Savannah, unlike that at Newport, was accepted without mutual recriminations or widespread foreboding in the United States.[4] Thus Luzerne had a short period to become adjusted to his new position before having to make critical decisions.

Luzerne and his staff had sailed from L'Orient on June 17 aboard the frigate *Sensible*. John Adams, returning to the United States after the appointment of Franklin as the sole Minister to France, accompanied them. The pungent Adams recorded many conversations with Luzerne and Barbé-Marbois in his diary. Although Adams denied it, it appears that the Frenchmen got more information from him than he did from them. Adams gave freely of his unfavorable opinions of John Jay, John

[3] Vergennes to Luzerne, Sept. 25, 1779; Oct. 1, 1779, AAE-cp-(EU), Vol. X.

[4] Alexander A. Lawrence, *Storm over Savannah* (Athens, 1951), pp. 122–46, is an excellent account of the siege of Savannah. On press reaction, see *Packet*, Nov. 9, 1779; *Independent Chronicle*, Nov. 25, 1779; *Connecticut Courant*, Nov. 30, 1779. For French-inspired accounts of the failure at Savannah, see *Continental Journal*, Dec. 3, 1779; *Pennsylvania Gazette*, Nov. 10, and Dec. 1, 15, 22, 1779.

Dickinson, Gouverneur Morris, and Benjamin Franklin, and expressed his disappointment when Barbé-Marbois refused to return the favor by allowing him to read the dispatches of Gérard studied by the French staff during the voyage.[5]

Adams warned Barbé-Marbois that the alliance could not endure if a French Minister attached himself to a party in the United States. Barbé-Marbois, knowing that the remark reflected on Gérard, replied that this mistake would not be repeated. Adams then queried Luzerne to make sure that he agreed with his first secretary's pronouncement. Luzerne assured Adams that he would not interfere with the domestic affairs of the United States.[6]

The only valuable information that Adams elicited from Luzerne was the news of Spain's entry into the war against Great Britain. Despite their reserve, Adams formed a high opinion of both men. "Mr. Marbois is one of the best informed, and most reflecting Men I have Known in France," he wrote. A friend later reported, "Mr. John Adams seems much pleased with the new French Ambassador." [7]

Luzerne's arrival in Boston was marked by "a discharge of thirteen cannon, on his landing, from the fortress on Fort Hill, and every other mark of respect . . . which circumstances would admit." [8] Luzerne remained in Boston for a month, preparing his baggage and conferring with Massachusetts political leaders. During the month he was treated to the customary diplomatic reception, gave a speech in the State House, and visited Harvard College.[9]

Samuel Adams reported after several conversations with Luzerne that he had "communicated to him my Sentiments with Freedom and Candor." [10] By beginning his assignment with a six-week voyage with John Adams and a four-week stay in Boston talking to politicians, Luzerne developed a clear understanding of the most serious differences between France and the United States. He reported to Vergennes from Boston that Massachusetts was firm in its attachment to independence and the alliance, but would cause difficulties in peace negotiations. Luzerne predicted that Massachusetts would remain obdurate about attaining the fisheries and Canada despite Congressional instructions.[11] He

[5] Lyman Butterfield, ed., *Diary & Autobiography of John Adams* (New York, 1964), Vol. II, pp. 384, 385–86, 390, 399, diary entries June 18, 20, 22, 1779, and July 17, 1779.

[6] *Ibid.*, June 18, 1779, July 2, 1779, pp. 383, 397.

[7] *Ibid.*, June 21, 1779, pp. 387–88; Gordon to Gates, Aug. 21, 1779, Gates Papers, box 13A.

[8] *Independent Chronicle*, Aug. 5, 1779.

[9] *Ibid.*, Aug. 19, 1779; *New Jersey Gazette*, Sept. 15, 1779.

[10] Adams to Gates, Gates Papers, box 13A.

[11] Luzerne to Vergennes, Sept. 3, 1779, AAE-cp-(EU), Vol. X.

regretted the differences in objectives, but he was not surprised. Unlike Gérard, Luzerne believed that Americans could support the alliance and still advocate national interests contrary to French wishes.

Luzerne visited a number of prominent Americans on his way from Boston to Philadelphia. At Providence, he held lengthy conversations with Horatio Gates.[12] Later, Luzerne spent a day with Washington at West Point and, in the course of their discussions, inquired if the United States would be agreeable to France sending a squadron with a few regiments attached to it. Washington replied that "it would be very advancive of the common cause," which was obvious.[13] On June 21 Luzerne arrived in Philadelphia, heralded by the ringing of bells and firing of cannon. He did not officially assume his duties for another week and was not received by Congress until November 17.[14]

Luzerne brought to his position a more urbane view of the alliance than had Gérard. Although recognizing French-American disagreements, he consistently emphasized the common goals of the alliance which would benefit both countries equally. He did not expect Americans to follow the French position on important issues merely because France was the superior power. Instead, Luzerne emphasized that all France asked was adherence to the terms of the alliance and independence for the United States. He did not expect fundamental changes in American attitudes toward France. In one instance, he noted that the Massachusetts constitution of 1780 contained a Protestant oath for officeholders. But despite this intolerance toward Catholics, Luzerne informed Vergennes that Massachusetts respected the King of France.[15] Luzerne rarely forgot that the war effort, not French policy, was the most important ingredient for a successful alliance. Although New England and Pennsylvania frequently led the opposition to French policy, he observed that these states were the most prompt in fulfilling their quotas of men and money.[16]

Luzerne earnestly tried to convince Vergennes that members of the opposition were sincere in their attachment to the alliance. He reported that John Adams and Samuel Adams, although often disagreeing with French policy, publicly emphasized the United States need for the alliance and contributed substantially to the war effort.[17] Luzerne gave the

[12] Gates to ———, Sept., 1779, Gates Papers, box 19C.
[13] "Substance of a Conference between Chevalier de La Luzerne and General Washington," Sept. 16, 1779, Fitzpatrick, ed., *Washington,* Vol. XVI, pp. 294–99.
[14] *Packet,* Sept. 23, 1779; *ibid.,* Nov. 20, 1779.
[15] Luzerne to Vergennes, March 20, 1780, AAE-cp-(EU), Vol. XI.
[16] Luzerne to Vergennes, Jan. 25, 1780, *ibid.,* Vol. XI; Luzerne to Vergennes, July 15, 1780, *ibid.,* Vol. XIII.
[17] On John Adams, see Luzerne to Vergennes, Oct. 8, 1779, *ibid.,* Vol. X; Luzerne to Vergennes, March 3, 1780, *ibid.,* Vol. XI; Luzerne to Vergennes, Aug.

benefit of the doubt to delegates from other states as well. When Thomas Burke of North Carolina opposed relinquishing United States claims to the Mississippi, Luzerne characterized him as "a fiery and stubborn man, although a good citizen." [18] After the British offered John Sullivan a bribe, Luzerne studied Congress to determine if the British had successfully bribed any delegates before the offer to Sullivan. He concluded that there were only two members in Congress whose loyalty he suspected, but even here he admitted that he had no evidence of disloyalty.[19]

Luzerne rejected Gérard's practice of regarding the opposition as suspect. Refusing to describe any member of Congress as disloyal, he acted upon the assumption that virtually all Americans supported the alliance. He saw no need to arouse Vergennes with reports castigating the opposition to French proposals. There was one significant exception to Luzerne's policy, however. From the beginning, Luzerne suspected Henry Laurens. When Laurens was captured on his way to Holland, Luzerne speculated that his capture might have been prearranged, and he was aghast when Laurens was chosen as a peace commissioner in 1781 while still held prisoner by the British. Luzerne never gave any concrete reasons why he had singled out Laurens for distrust. He had heard that Laurens continued to have connections with George Johnstone, a member of the Carlisle Commission, but offered no evidence to support his suspicions.[20]

Vergennes, however, declined to accept Luzerne's basically moderate attitude toward political opposition. He continued to label all opposition as anti-French, describing Arthur Lee and Samuel Adams as "enemies of peace," who sought to prolong the war. Vergennes persisted in believing, against contrary evidence supplied by Luzerne, that the opposition wanted to negotiate with Great Britain without regard for article 8 of the alliance. He interpreted John Adams' desire to inform Great Britain of his powers to treat for peace as an attempt to negotiate separately from France.[21]

Luzerne's tolerance of dissent extended beyond the strictly political

---

6, 1780, *ibid.*, Vol. XII; Luzerne to Vergennes, Nov. 26, 1780, *ibid.*, Vol. XIV; on Samuel Adams, Luzerne to Vergennes, Jan. 28, 1781, *ibid.*, Vol. XV; Luzerne to Vergennes, Jan. 5, 1782, *ibid.*, Vol. XX.

[18] Luzerne to Vergennes, June 11, 1780, *ibid.*, Vol. XII.

[19] Luzerne to Vergennes, May 13, 1781, *ibid.*, Vol. XVI.

[20] Luzerne to Vergennes, Nov. 4, 1779, *ibid.*, Vol. X; Luzerne to Vergennes, Jan. 18, 1781, *ibid.*, Vol. XV; Luzerne to Vergennes, June 14, 1781, *ibid.*, Vol. XVII.

[21] Vergennes to Luzerne, Sept. 25, 1779, *ibid.*, Vol. X; Vergennes to Luzerne, June 3, 1780, *ibid.*, Vol. XII.

sphere. He perceived that Americans were fighting to protect and expand their own conception of liberty. Although disturbed by what he considered to be an excess of liberty in some cases, Luzerne did not argue that Americans should change their laws on freedom of the press and religion. At one time he suspected that the editor of the *Freeman's Journal* of Philadelphia, Francis Bailey, was receiving financial support from partisans of Great Britain. Rather than ask for an investigation, Luzerne informed Vergennes, he had worked out procedures so that the paper would not publish material harmful to the alliance. But he commented that he could not speak for the future, saying, "It is impossible to check this abuse of liberty which the Americans consider to be one of their most cherished rights." [22]

Religious freedom in the United States especially fascinated Luzerne, as it did many other French visitors. He believed that it was religious freedom which made the United States so attractive for prospective European emigrants, and he noted that due to freedom of religion, many members of the French Army serving in the United States planned to remain in the country after their term of duty had expired.[23] In 1784 he reported that the number of emigrants from "Europe, Germany, and Ireland is greater than one can imagine." [24] At another time Luzerne reminded Vergennes that "unlimited liberty" of religion prevented Pennsylvania from restricting or taxing the Quakers severely.[25] Luzerne's reservations about American liberties such as freedom of religion and the press were practical, not philosophical; he regarded the freedoms in the United States as sometimes detrimental to the war effort, because they restricted the powers of government.

By the time he left the United States, Luzerne understood the revolutionary implications of the American struggle better than any other Frenchman, including the observant Chastellux.[26] Although he sincerely believed that *"United States independence is the work of the King,"* he stated that the basis of American society and politics was complete equality and that all power derived from the people. He was optimistic about the future of republicanism in the United States:

> The basis of all political institutions of the American Republic, as that of Rome, is an excessive attachment to liberty and an extreme suspicion of anyone who might endanger it. Nothing is

[22] Luzerne to Vergennes, June 6, 1781, *ibid.,* Vol. XVII.

[23] Luzerne to Vergennes, Dec. 2, 1779, *ibid.,* Vol. X; Luzerne to Vergennes, April 20, 1782, *ibid.,* Vol. XXI.

[24] Luzerne to Vergennes, May 24, 1784, Luzerne Papers.

[25] Luzerne to Vergennes, May 4, 1781, AAE-cp-(EU), Vol. XVI.

[26] Howard Rice, Jr., ed., *Travels in North America in the Years 1780, 1781, and 1782 by the Marquis de Chastellux* (Chapel Hill, 1963), 2 vols.

more distinctive than the precautions they have taken to assure the preservation of liberty, and the Americans, in this regard, appear to me superior to Roman Legislators.[27]

His sympathy for the principle of equality having grown during his years in the United States, Luzerne wrote in 1784 that republican fears of the Society of the Cincinnati were "not altogether chimerical." [28] As a friend of humanity, he concluded in his final report, he was pleased that under the newly established government of the United States the citizen had greater political and social freedom than in any other nation in the world.[29]

Luzerne, with his understanding of the Revolution and his ingratiating manner, quickly gained the aceptance of American leaders. Socially, he became the lion of Philadelphia, and one delegate's wife described him as "one of the most amiable, politest, easiest behav'd Men I ever knew." [30] Luzerne's success was partly due to his ability to convince Americans that he was sincerely interested in the success of their cause. "I wish he [Luzerne] would tell you as a friend, a soldier, and a statesman, what he thinks we ought to do, as it is entirely in the interest of his Court to be sincere with us," Horatio Gates wrote, "I should not have the smallest doubt that what he says he firmly believes." [31] Luzerne convinced even Gérard's former critics. Phrases such as "common cause," "politeness," and "sincerity" appeared regularly in private letters describing him. The press, which generally saved encomiums for generals and Louis XVI, gave Luzerne more attention than Gérard had received.

> And the citizens under arms were particularly gratified with the presence of his Excellency the Chevalier de la Luzerne, Minister of France, who has on all occasions shewn the closest attention to the interest and honor of America, and on the present occasion expressed great pleasure at the martial appearance of the Militia.[32]

[27] Mémoire où le Chevalier de la Luzerne, Ministre de Sa Majesté auprès des États unis, rend compte de leur situation actuelle (hereafter Luzerne, "Final Report"), Paris, Aug. 4, 1784, Luzerne Papers, italics in original.

[28] Luzerne to Vergennes, April 12, 1784, *ibid.* Luzerne made this statement after he had concluded a visit to Washington at Mount Vernon.

[29] Luzerne, "Final Report," *ibid.*

[30] Bland to Tucker, March 30, 1781, Mary H. Coleman, ed., "Randolph and Tucker Letters," *Virginia Magazine of History & Biography,* Vol. XLIII (1935), p. 42.

[31] Gates to Reed, May 10, 1780, William Reed, *Life and Correspondence of Joseph Reed* (Philadelphia, 1847), Vol. II, p. 194.

[32] *Pennsylvania Gazette,* May 31, 1780.

Luzerne's enlightened attitudes soon produced results in his relations with Congress. Not one to underestimate himself, he reported his personal success with candor, if not modesty:

> Moreover, I have cause to be flattered by the esteem which the President has assured me that the delegates expressed in my behalf during the heat of a very lively debate. I feel that it is my duty not to leave you uninformed that the trust placed in me by Congress in general and by the individual members who compose it is all that I could possibly wish for at this point.[33]

James Lovell, always vigilant against excessive French influence, admitted, "The New Minister is much esteemed." [34]

Luzerne worked constantly to make Congress responsive to French policy. As the only national political institution in the United States, Congress was crucial to French objectives, he believed. After studying the informal blocs in Congress, Luzerne inaccurately concluded that the four New England states, Pennsylvania, and Delaware consistently voted together. He noted that this coalition did not constitute an absolute majority, but since the Georgia delegates were frequently absent, it could prevent Congress from considering business contrary to its interests. Having studied Gérard's dispatches, Luzerne originally expected that the coalition would be hostile to French policy, and he wished to see its power in Congress reduced.

Luzerne conferred with Robert R Livingston, who recommended that New York, New Jersey, Maryland, Pennsylvania, and Delaware form a coalition and serve as a broker between the northern and southern blocs.[35] Since Luzerne did not want three different blocs in Congress, he discounted Livingston's advice and instead attempted to build a stable pro-French coalition in Congress. Luzerne's task was facilitated when the Southern States started voting consistently in favor of French policy after the British occupied most of North and South Carolina and Georgia. With southern votes added to the consistent support of the Middle States, Luzerne had a working majority against New England after 1780. The new majority owed its genesis to the peace proposals of

---

[33] Luzerne to Vergennes, March 16, 1780, AAE-cp-(EU), Vol. XI.

[34] Lovell to Abigail Adams, March 7, 1780, Adams Papers, R. 351.

[35] Luzerne to Vergennes, Jan. 16, 1780; Jan. 25, 1780, AAE-cp-(EU), Vol. XI. William Livingston thought New Jersey voted too often with Massachusetts and Virginia. He proposed to a New Jersey delegate that a coalition similar to the one suggested by Robert Livingston be created with New York, New Jersey, Pennsylvania, and Maryland. Livingston to Fell, Dec. 14, 1779, Livingston Papers, MHS, Vol. II.

1779, but Luzerne worked to make it an effective controlling coalition on all questions.

Barbé-Marbois also devoted a major portion of his time to working with Congress. He, too, attributed exaggerated solidarity and influence to New England. But, unlike Luzerne, Barbé-Marbois believed that Congressional voting patterns reflected religion, and he chose "Presbyterianism" as the influence which had created a stable New England majority during Gérard's tenure.[36] Religion, however, did not provide an adequate explanation of Congressional alignments. Barbé-Marbois contradicted his own thesis when he observed that New Jersey, linked by religion to New England, voted against her much of the time, while Pennsylvania and Delaware supported New England without having religious ties.[37]

Fortunately for France, Barbé-Marbois worked under Luzerne, who quickly realized that French efforts must focus on building a coalition within a political context. This coalition, cemented by regionalism rather than religion, had to be strong enough to defeat Massachusetts, and often all of New England. Luzerne wanted to prevent a recurrence of the radical coalition which had compelled Gérard and a majority in Congress to compromise on the fishery question.

Included in Luzerne's political strategy was an effort to enhance the prestige of Congress. A coalition favorable to France would signify little if the powers of Congress were not strengthened against the centrifugal tendencies of the states. Congress, Luzerne realized, was the stronghold of French influence in the United States and the only national institution, besides the Army, which could provide a semblance of unity in the country. Thus he argued that it was "equally essential for France and for the United States to conserve the influence and authority of this body." Another Frenchman, although simplifying the argument, succinctly stated the rationale for bolstering Congress: "The power of Congress heretofore weak and wavering, will be consolidated, and the prejudices against our nation will vanish." [38]

The relation between Congress and the states often frustrated Luzerne. Initially he had protested to Congress about delays in organizing the 1780 campaign.[39] Luzerne decided to put the full authority of the

[36] "Presbyterianism" for Barbé-Marbois and Luzerne did not denote any one sect. Almost all Protestants except Quakers and Anglicans were included in their definition.

[37] Barbé-Marbois to Vergennes, July 11, 1781; July 14, 1781, AAE-cp-(EU), Vol. XVII.

[38] Luzerne to Vergennes, Feb. 6, 1783, Luzerne Papers; C. C. Robin [actually Abbé Robin], *Travels in North America*, translated by Philip Freneau (Philadelphia, 1783), p. 79.

[39] Gerry to Washington, Jan. 12, 1780, *LMCC*, Vol. V, p. 7.

alliance behind Congressional efforts for the campaign by asking permission to write the state legislatures directly to exhort them to fulfill their quotas. He received approval from Congress to write the states, but not without Congressional misgivings:

> The Cheval'r De la Luzerne, from the purest Motives and a most cordial anxious Concern about the Affairs of America and the Alliance, was writing a circular letter to the Gov[ernor]s and Presid[en]ts of the respective States by way of a friendly Stimulus, but his Delicacy led him to inclose his Sentiments to the Presid[en]t [of Congress] That the Opinion of the Delegates might be had. . . . I own that I felt no Zeal of Jealousy on this Occasion. But since the matter has been agitated and delicately quashed, I hope there will not hereafter be any Room to say Congress have not Influence with the States nor chuse to let the Minister of France try his.[40]

Luzerne explained to Vergennes that he dropped his plan after President Huntington said that he believed it would set a bad precedent.[41] After this attempt, Luzerne communicated with states by asking their delegates in Congress to make French policy known to their state legislative bodies.

Dipping into the murky waters of state politics at least once more, Luzerne protected the legal position of Congress by cajoling Daniel Jenifer to achieve Maryland's acceptance of the Articles of Confederation in 1781. Jenifer was present and voting "no" when the Maryland senate refused ratification. When the motion was reconsidered later the same day, Jenifer was absent, begging illness, and the motion passed by one vote.[42] One scholar states, "The evidence . . . does show . . . that the last push, the influence which determined the action of Maryland *at this time,* came from the minister plenipotentiary of Louis XVI." [43] Luzerne apparently offered Jenifer the inducements of a French fleet conducting operations in the Chesapeake and a loan for Maryland to purchase arms, if the state would accede to the Articles of Confederation.[44] Whatever else Luzerne may have offered is not revealed in his regular dispatches.

[40] Lovell to Samuel Adams, Feb. 28, 1780, *ibid.,* Vol. V, p. 53.

[41] Luzerne to Vergennes, March 16, 1780, AAE-cp-(EU), Vol. XI.

[42] St. George L. Sioussat, "The Chevalier de la Luzerne and the Ratification of the Articles of Confederation by Maryland: With Accompanying Documents," *PMHB,* Vol. LX (1936), pp. 391–418.

[43] *Ibid.,* p. 407, italics in original.

[44] Jenifer to Luzerne, Jan. 5, 1781; Luzerne to Jenifer, Jan. 10, 1781, AAE-cp-(EU), Vol. XV, copies included as one document.

An American officer in Philadelphia expected that Maryland would receive additional consideration for its action, "Mons. Marbois [starts] out this Morning for Annapolis with two other French Gent[le]m[en] Colonels in that Service. They will tell you how much credit your State has acquired by their Timely consideration." [45] Luzerne indicated in his final report in 1784 that he, and probably Barbé-Marbois, had a more active role in Jenifer's illness than was generally recognized.

> Thus by means of a tactic known only to myself and one other person, this great venture was brought to a favorable conclusion and the confederation was consummated at a time when it was infinitely important, for the alliance and the dealings of the United States, to put the finishing touches on this important piece of work.[46]

Luzerne's concern for confederation reflected his confidence in Congress and the support it gave the alliance. Congress, he wrote, "will take no measure against the general interest of confederation and against its commitments with the King." [47] Luzerne believed that his policy of supporting Congress had been successful; after the election of the sympathetic Robert R Livingston as Secretary of Foreign Affairs, he had even greater cause for satisfaction.

> What I have just given you an account of, My Lord, is furthermore a proof of the influence which His Majesty has over the Congress: this assembly is, in fact, in the most favorable disposition toward the alliance. I hope it will be lasting, for this body is subject to too many changes for me to be in a position to be responsible for its actions.[48]

When news of peace talks arrived in 1782, Luzerne again emphasized that Congress was the backbone of French support in the United States and there need be no fear of defection from the alliance by Congress.[49]

Luzerne won the confidence of Congress even without the financial powers he wanted. Despite repeated requests, he lacked authority to announce subsidies to the United States. Constantly besieged by the antiwar party in the French Cabinet, led first by Turgot and then by Necker, for the exorbitant costs of the American effort, Vergennes could not

---

[45] Forrest to Lee, Feb. 12, 1781, J. Hall Peasants, ed., *Archives of Maryland, Journal and Correspondence of the State Council of Maryland* (Baltimore, 1930), Vol. XLVII, p. 68.
[46] Luzerne, "Final Report," Luzerne Papers.
[47] Luzerne to Vergennes, June 24, 1780, AAE-cp-(EU), Vol. XII.
[48] Luzerne to Vergennes, Aug. 11, 1781, *ibid.*, Vol. XVIII.
[49] Luzerne to Vergennes, Sept. 9, 1782, *ibid.*, Vol. XXII.

afford to grant Luzerne this opportunity. Although Necker announced publicly in 1781 that the budget had been balanced, it actually ran a deficit of 46 million livres.[50] Each campaign cost the French government approximately 150 million livres, but Americans could generate little sympathy for their ally's precarious financial position at a time when French aid was critical to the continuation of the war effort in the United States.[51]

Although Vergennes had refused to grant an annual subsidy in the original treaty, by 1780 France had made the American government a gift of 6 million livres, guaranteed a loan of 8 million, and agreed to pay the interest charges on the loan during the war. In 1780, 1781, and 1782, France gave the American government a subsidy of 6 million livres each year in addition to spending 16 million for financing the French Army in the United States for two years.[52] The total expenditures, excluding naval costs, reached 48 million livres or about 9.6 million dollars; this aid, amounting to about one-third of the total French expenditure for a single campaign, was indispensable for the American cause. Through her subsidies and purchases, France provided the only hard currency and reliable credit in the United States after 1780.

Yet when Luzerne sought the additional leverage he could gain if allowed to announce the subsidy to Congress, Vergennes insisted that he inform Congress that the year's subsidy would definitely be the last. Franklin received credit from Congress for negotiating the subsidies in Paris, as Luzerne protested in vain that this procedure damaged his influence in Congress. Congress ignored Luzerne's admonitions and repeatedly appropriated the expected subsidies.[53]

Luzerne privately regarded a subsidy as essential for the preservation of the army and the continuation of the American war effort.[54] He became one of the strongest advocates of a French subsidy—if it were

[50] Jacques Godechot, *France and the Atlantic Revolution of the Eighteenth Century, 1770–1799,* translated by Herbert H. Rowen (New York, 1965), p. 70.

[51] Vergennes to Luzerne, Feb. 19, 1781, AAE-cp-(EU), Vol. XV; Vergennes to Luzerne, Jan. 31, 1782, *ibid.,* Vol. XX.

[52] Vergennes to Luzerne, March 9, 1781, *ibid.,* Vol. XV; Vergennes to Luzerne, Dec. 24, 1781, *ibid.,* Vol. XIX; Vergennes to Luzerne, Oct. 14, 1782; Dec. 21, 1782, *ibid.,* Vol. XXII. For an estimate on army expenses, see Luzerne to Vergennes, Feb. 10, 1782, *ibid.,* Vol. XX. For the American side, see E. James Ferguson, *The Power of the Purse* (Chapel Hill, 1961), pp. 127, 333. Ferguson arrives at slightly, but not significantly, higher figures on French aid than those mentioned above. He estimates that the total of French loans and gifts amounted to about 5 per cent of the total cost of the Revolution.

[53] Luzerne to Vergennes, July 9, 1782, AAE-cp-(EU), Vol. XXI; Luzerne to Vergennes, March 25, 1781, *ibid.,* Vol. XVI; O'Donnell, *Luzerne,* pp. 161, 189–91.

[54] Luzerne to Vergennes, Dec. 28, 1780, AAE-cp-(EU), Vol. XIV; Luzerne to Vergennes, Feb. 7, 1781, *ibid.,* Vol. XV; Luzerne to Vergennes, Nov. 11, 1781, *ibid.,* Vol. XIX.

properly handled through him. When peace appeared imminent, Luzerne argued that France should continue the subsidy after the peace treaty to preserve Congress and the Army; by strengthening the only two national institutions in the United States, French influence could be maintained against the natural American inclination toward Great Britain, he believed.[55] This, like all other requests to change the allocation of the subsidy, was ignored by Vergennes, even though it would have immeasurably strengthened French influence after independence.

Although Congress was the political institution which Luzerne emphasized in the United States, he gradually started to accentuate the role of Washington and the Army. Luzerne considered Washington to be a skillful leader who could contribute more than any other person to the success of the alliance. Moreover, military success was the fastest, most efficient method to achieve the aims of the alliance. There were other reasons as well for the added emphasis on Washington and the Army. The diplomatic struggle had moved to Europe after Congress passed the peace instructions of 1779, and revenue for maintaining the Army and national credit had to come from Europe after 1780. Congress, having only indirect control over foreign relations and no control of revenue, became ineffective in devising joint military strategy.

Contrary to his interest in strengthening Congress, Luzerne actually contributed to a weakening of Congressional powers by his active intervention in military planning. He withheld military information about French plans from Congress while at the same time imparting the information to Washington. In one instance Luzerne failed to inform Congress that he had rejected Count de Grasse's offer to bring his fleet to the American coast in August and September, 1780. He explained to Vergennes that the style of war had so changed that there was no need to tell Congress of the offer.[56] Luzerne may have had second thoughts about his wisdom as a military strategist when the French Fleet and Army were bottled up in Newport in August, 1780. In 1781 Luzerne reported that Washington had been informed of de Grasse's expected arrival, but, as for Congress, "I have kept completely quiet with respect to Congress and the Committee about the eventual arrival of Monsieur Count de Grasse off the coast of this continent with all or part of his squadron." [57]

Luzerne may have started to emphasize the American Army because of his own military background, but his action can be more easily explained by French self-interest than by a personal preference for the

[55] Luzerne to Vergennes, Jan. 15, 1783; Feb. 6, 1783, *ibid.*, Vol. XXIII.
[56] Luzerne to Vergennes, Dec. 26, 1779, *ibid.*, Vol. X.
[57] Luzerne to Vergennes, June 1, 1781, *ibid.*, Vol. XVII.

Army over Congress. Luzerne had to defend the American Army against French detractors. After the expeditionary force under Rochambeau landed, Luzerne complained that French officers had been badly informed about the degree of weakness in the American forces. He claimed that French officers had exaggerated the Army's deficiencies in their official and private letters back to France.[58] Luzerne realized that no matter how weak the Army appeared, the Americans would still have to carry the major burden of the war in both the northern and southern theaters. The most realistic policy, as Luzerne saw it, was to assign the Americans primary responsibility for defeating the British in the United States. A French-British war in the United States, with the Americans playing only a token role, was to be avoided.

A common denominator ran through all of Luzerne's actions. In the building of Congressional coalitions, treatment of the opposition, support of Congress as a political institution, and enhancement of the role of the Continental Army and Washington, Luzerne's actions reflected his estimate of the quickest way to achieve the primary goal of the alliance—United States independence. The policies of Gérard and Luzerne were the same, although events were assuredly kinder to Luzerne. But Luzerne, unlike Gérard, used diplomatic skills, personal sincerity, and an understanding of the Revolution to gain the respect of an overwhelming number of Americans.

Luzerne was a diplomat who understood that each country would pursue what it believed to be its own self-interest. He, more than any other Frenchman, convinced Americans that the interests of both countries coincided closely enough for them to work together harmoniously. Near the end of the war Luzerne commented on his service to the King and the alliance, "I admit that I have found fewer difficulties than I had feared." [59]

[58] Luzerne to Vergennes, July 23, 1780, *ibid.,* Vol. XIII.
[59] Luzerne to Vergennes, Dec. 27, 1782, *ibid.,* Vol. XXII.

VII. The Pulpit and the Alliance

"Christendom would never have roused, with firmness, to have attempted to free themselves from the *hierarchy of Rome,* had not the oppressions of that power put them upon the expedient," Jonas Clarke expounded in an election sermon. Clarke's assertion seemed self-evident to a majority of American clergymen and their parishioners. Later in the sermon he took up the subject of the French alliance as if it had no relation to the problem of Catholicism. The King of France had finally taken "a decided part, and made our cause their own, by a *public treaty,* both *generous* and *just,* and nobly founded on principles of *equality* and *independence.*" The significance of this "happy alliance" was "too important to have escaped notice, and too well known to need a mention." [1] Like most of his fellow clergymen, Clarke considered the oppression of Great Britain comparable to that of Rome, but expressed no second thoughts about an alliance with France.

Clarke, a close associate of Samuel Cooper, found it unnecessary to enumerate the advantages of the alliance, for independence was synonymous with civil and religious freedom and hence required no justification. The embarrassing dependence of American goals on a Catholic power was frequently glossed over or ignored by clergymen during the alliance, a fact eagerly noted by the Loyalist press. Shortly after the signing of the alliance, the *Royal Gazette* contrasted Samuel Cooper's remarks at the victory of Wolfe over Montcalm during the Seven Years' War and his new-found enthusiasm for France in 1778.

> The same Dr. Cooper, in his public prayers every Sunday, calls for vengeance upon the whole English nation, and for the best of his blessings upon their *"most potent and magnanimous ally Lewis 16th King of France."* Upon their new brethren [,] this *"perfidious, restless, politic and enterprizing nation."*
>
> If there is as much stability in the Doctor's religion as there is in his politics, and as ardent desire for independence with regard

[1] Jonas Clarke, *A Sermon Preached before His Excellency John Hancock, Esq; Governor; His Honor Thomas Cushing, Esq; Lieutenant-Governor; The Honorable Council and the Honorable Senate and House of Representatives of the Commonwealth of Massachusetts, May 30, 1781* (Boston, 1781), pp. 42, 49, italics in original.

91

for the former as the latter, we may expect to see him, in less than twenty years, embrace the scarlet whore, and adorn the first Papal chair in America.[2]

The overwhelming majority of clergymen, ignoring both Loyalist attacks and their own past statements, exhorted parishioners to live by the laws of God. In Revolutionary times this directive was interpreted to mean that the public should support the American cause by fulfilling local quotas and paying taxes. In commemorative sermons, election sermons, and thanksgiving addresses the clergy justified the conduct of the war by the United States and reiterated the dangers of British rule. Often they cited Locke in defending the right of rebellion when human authorities, notably George III and Lord North, defied the laws of God. Montesquieu, too, found service in theological arguments supporting the United States position. The clergy argued that the United States was obeying the higher law of God in resisting British tyranny; the Revolution was consistent with the dictates of both religion and rationality.

The liberating spirit of the Enlightenment helped clergymen avoid the religious problem posed by the alliance. Many now believed that reason, as well as faith, must play a critical part in religion, and they were more concerned than before with the earthly context of man's life. As earlier seen in the Seven Years' War, the clergy's zeal for quasicrusades against Catholicism had slackened. The emphasis had shifted to the natural rights of freedom for mankind, not hegemony for one creed. John Murray, a Presbyterian, expressed a typical combination of the Enlightenment and religion when he said, "The Cause of Liberty is the cause of God; reason, truth, justice, religion mutually support and are supported by it." [3] Support for the French alliance was easily defensible in this context.

Partly freed from the rigid dogmas of the past, clergymen were willing to allow foreign policy decisions to remain the province of the State, yet they did not ignore their duty to inform parishioners which contestant was more righteous. The clergy, especially the evangelical Calvinists, repeatedly aimed their denunciations at Great Britain.[4] Thus they affirmed and convinced themselves anew that Great Britain presented a greater danger to religious liberty than France ever had while it held possession of Canada.

Clergymen, like all other groups, had divided into opposite camps at the outbreak of the Revolution. A great many who remained loyal were

[2] Rivington's *Royal Gazette*, July 1, 1778, italics in original.
[3] John Murray, *A Discourse delivered at the Presbyterian Church in Newbury-Port* (Newburyport, 1779), Nov. 4, 1779, p. 17.
[4] Heimert, *Religion and the American Mind*, p. 391.

Anglicans like Jonathan Boucher and Jacob Duché, but most of the Dissenting clergy cast their fate with the United States. Peter Oliver, although embittered, correctly claimed that the "black regiments" of rebellious clergymen held control of the New England pulpits.[5]

Loyalists constantly charged that mob rule in rebel territory had forced the Loyalist ministers to flee. This was partly true in 1775 and 1776, when Anglican and Methodist ministers virtually disappeared from New England and were greatly weakened in the South and Middle States.[6] In North Carolina, the Committee of Public Safety delayed the pay of a Loyalist-inclined minister after he refused to honor a day of fast declared by Congress. By early 1778 only the Baptist church remained open in Charleston; two other churches closed, both ministers "being drove off on account of Tory principles."[7]

Loyalists also charged that the clergy who supported the Revolution were all Dissenters, but the evidence is far from clear on this point. The Loyalist clergymen, almost all of them Anglicans who received protection from the Crown, were those who had fled by 1776 or came from areas which the British occupied for long periods. In New York City at least nine Loyalist ministers, all from the New York or Philadelphia areas, were appointed chaplains in the British Army.[8] When Charleston was evacuated in 1782, 31 clergymen left with a group of 500 refugees.[9] In New York, however, there were 22 other clergymen, but only one "sinner" who received Loyalist allowances.[10] In a survey of Loyalist claimants one scholar concluded that 20 clergymen asked for compensation after the war out of a total of 138 mentioned; of the total group at least 33 supported the Revolution. How many of the remainder, many of whom are unaccounted for, maintained neutrality or shifted to other professions during the Revolution is not known; nevertheless, a sizable percentage of the Anglican clergy did not seek refuge or emigrate.[11]

British military commanders fully recognized that the Dissenters

[5] Douglass Adair and John Schutz, eds., *Peter Oliver's Origin & Progress of the American Rebellion* (San Marino, 1961), pp. 41–45.

[6] Emory S. Buckle, ed., *The History of American Methodism* (New York, 1964), Vol. I, pp. 158, 175.

[7] Robert DeMond, *The Loyalists in North Carolina during the Revolution* (Durham, 1940), p. 67; the quote is from Smith to Ray, March 7, 1778, Josiah Smith Papers.

[8] Inglis to Tyron, April 25, 1778, Henry Clinton Papers, WCL.

[9] DeMond, *Loyalists in North Carolina*, p. 186.

[10] "List of Royalist Allowances," The Earl of Shelburne Papers, WCL, Vol. LXVII; the total list includes 307 persons—48 merchants, 20 businessmen other than merchants, 21 planters and gentlemen, 29 widows, 19 lawyers, 74 officeholders, 7 physicians, and 14 in armed services in the occupations identifiable from the list.

[11] Brown, *The King's Friends*, pp. 27, 70, 165, 188.

generally supported the Revolution. Regarding the entire group as disloyal, they systematically replaced them if the British occupied a city for
any length of time. In New York City many of the Dissenting pulpits
were taken over and presumably filled by adherents of the King.[12] In
Charleston, according to one scholar, "The Board of Police secured
Loyalist ministers for the churches after the British occupied the city." [13]
In Georgia, John Zubly claimed in 1780 that he was the only Dis-
senter allowed to preach in the state by the British authorities.[14]

Zubly's case was exceptional. A native of Switzerland and former
member of the Continental Congress, he consistently opposed independence and declared his support for reconciliation after 1776. His philosophy explained his position, "I had rather have no home than sit uppermost in the Congregation of the Violent." He castigated other ministers
for agreeing to serve as chaplains in the British Army.[15] After the news
of the rebels' defeat at Camden by Cornwallis, he recorded in his diary
that it was pleasing news "since nothing will do with an unhappy deluded obstinate People but shedding of Blood." [16]

The alliance made Zubly even more adamant in his opposition to independence. He attacked the alliance in private letters and in articles
written for the *Georgia Gazette* after his expulsion by the rebels.[17]
Americans, Zubly believed, were a people who had "rejected neglected
and sin[n]ed away the Gospel, & who in my opinion would still rather
have Independancy & papist Con[nections] than the Gospel & their
former acknowledged happy Con[nections] with G[reat] B[ritain]." [18]
Although banished and accused of treason, Zubly understood the rebels'
treatment of him, "I can forgive them the more freely as I really was a
thorn in their side as long as I was suffered among them." [19]

The American clergymen who supported the Revolution, and with it
the alliance, were fully as suspicious of Catholicism as Zubly. Samuel

[12] Buckle, ed., *The History of American Methodism*, Vol. I, p. 174.

[13] Richard Walsh, *Charleston's Sons of Liberty* (Columbia, 1959), p. 91. It
should be added that the Presbyterian clergy in Virginia and North Carolina
were apparently attacked by Loyalists during the Revolution. See Alice M. Baldwin, "Sowers of Sedition: The Political Theories of Some of the New Light
Presbyterian Clergy in Virginia and North Carolina," *William and Mary Quarterly,*
third series, Vol. V (1948), pp. 53, 63.

[14] Zubly Diary, GHS, diary entries Dec. 6, 30, 1780. Mrs. Lilla M. Hawes,
Director of the Georgia Historical Society, kindly allowed me to use her type-
script copy of the diary. I have relied on her translations.

[15] *Ibid.,* April 3, 1779; Dec. 6, 1780.

[16] *Ibid.,* March 26, 1781.

[17] Smith to Zubly, July 13, 1781; for an account of Zubly's banishment and
subsequent public criticism of the alliance, see Smith to Roger, Oct. 10, 1779,
Josiah Smith Papers.

[18] Zubly Diary, Dec. 15, 1780.

[19] Zubly to ———, April 9, 1780, Zubly Papers, GHS.

Cooper, later a French agent, exhibited the virulent anti-Catholicism characteristic of many clergymen before the Revolution in the Dudleian lecture of 1773. Paul Dudley, a Boston businessman in the early eighteenth century, had endowed a series of four lectures at Harvard, with the third topic in the series to be a sermon on

> . . . detecting and exposing the idolatry of the Romish church; their tyranny, usurpation, fatal errors, abominable superstitions, and other crying wickednesses in their high places; and finally to prove that the Church of *Rome* is that mystical *Babylon,* that MAN OF SIN, that apostate church, spoken of in the *New Testament.*[20]

Paul Dudley would have been pleased with Cooper's literal interpretation of the terms of the endowment:

> Nor can we take even a cursory view of the Papal system of religion; it's direct opposition to the honour of God and the one mediator; it's gross superstition and idolatries; it's tendency to debase and enslave the human mind; the indulgence it grants to vice in every form; and the pleas it allows for crimes, at which the untutored breast immediately revolts; without acknowledging, that the contrivers of such a system, with the gospel in their hands, must have had an heart, to an uncommon degree insensible and depraved.[21]

Although Cooper obviously had strong reservations about Catholicism, a shift at the conclusion of his sermon revealed the tension of the growing conflict with Great Britain. He charged Great Britain with establishing a "Popish" colony in Quebec, and warned that "Popery is incompatible with the safety of free government." [22] Great Britain, not Catholicism, was becoming the principal adversary of the politically minded ministers.

After the alliance was signed, there were almost no public objections by clergy of any Dissenting sect, although it must have troubled them privately. Some, notably Samuel Cooper, went to extremes to support the alliance. Others, such as James Dana, pastor of the First Church in Wallingford, Connecticut, saw no inherent evil in the alliance, but continued to fear popery as inconsistent with free government. Probably a majority of the patriotic clergy agreed with the continued anti-Catholi-

---

[20] Samuel Cooper, *A Discourse on the Man of Sin* (Boston, 1774), p. 12, italics in original.
[21] *Ibid.*, pp. 40–41.
[22] *Ibid.*, pp. 65–66.

cism but with support of the alliance like that which Dana enunciated in his election sermon to the Connecticut legislature.

> Whether civil or religious usurpation hath been greatest, is difficult to say. Tyrannical rulers have generally favored the views of tyrannical ecclesiasticks, in return for the services they rendered them. Together they have deluged the earth in blood. A better reason cannot, probably be given for the late establishment of popery by a British parliament [Quebec Act], while the protestant religion, founded on principles of liberty, is barely tolerated. Popery can prevail only by an arbitrary government, implying a general ignorance of civil rights. Hence the preservation of our religion depends on the continuance of a free government. Let our allies have their eyes open on the blessings of such a government, and they will at once renounce their superstition. On the other hand, should we lose our freedom this will prepare the way to the introduction of popery.[23]

Dana reflected a cautious view of the alliance and Catholicism, but the connection he drew between independence and freedom of religion was widely accepted. Differing opinions over the alliance did not follow denominational lines, with the exception of the Quakers. Many clergymen of all sects did not feel obligated to reconcile anti-Catholicism and the alliance. Others who tried to justify the alliance went beyond Dana's reasoning, emphasizing the common bond of all men. Christians everywhere have a common fellowship with one another, they argued. God, for purposes of the alliance, became non-denominational; universals came to be emphasized rather than the particular tenets of any one faith. Religious and political liberty were intertwined, with the attainment of both being the universal aspiration of all Christians.

John Murray believed that Christians should make a positive affirmation of the alliance rather than accept Dana's negative approach. The alliance, for Murray, was sanctioned by a benign, watchful, and all-knowing God

> . . . whilst the rest of the world stood aloof and looked on—and Protestant powers, once in the same case, like the priest and Levite shunned our cries—behold the Samaritan hastes to our help—our wounds are softened by his wine and ayl, whilst his treasure is lavished to finish our cure: does the bigot give credit to the Tory's tale—and dream it unlawful to accept such aid? so might Israel

[23] James Dana, *A Sermon Preached before the General Assembly of the State of Connecticut at Hartford on the Day of the Anniversary Election, May 13, 1779* (Hartford, 1779), p. 15.

have spurned the Persian's offer and the temple of God still remained rubbish! gratitude and piety will not stand and gaze—both will unite to improve the favor—while the example of each prompts the other to cry "this is the Lord's doing and wonderous in our eyes." [24]

The wisdom and forethought of the Deity in arranging the alliance once praised, few of the clergy ever ignored the religious injustices which they perceived in France. Like James Dana, they hoped that the alliance would enable France to see the error of its ways and follow the example of the United States. After condemning the repeal of the Edict of Nantes, each minister expressed the pious hope that France would again tolerate Protestants, but clergymen refrained from the usual atrocity stories which before the war accompanied the condemnation of the repeal of the Edict of Nantes.[25]

Instead, pastors turned to the Book of Ezra to invoke an allegorical description of the King of France. Louis XVI was often compared to Cyrus, King of Persia, who aided the Israelites in rebuilding the House of God in Jerusalem. Phillips Payson exclaimed in an election sermon, "How wonderful that God, who in ancient times 'girded Cyrus with his might' should dispose his most Christian Majesty the King of France to enter into the most open and generous alliance with these independent states." [26]

Allegorical symbols might aid clergymen when they supported the alliance, but it was more difficult to convince parishioners that the alliance would benefit Protestantism. This question raised the problem of the relation of church and state, and few clergymen of any denomination elaborated on this subject. The Loyalists were clear on this point. Wholly opposed to Catholicism and its influence through both church and state, they offered a defense of Protestantism through the establishment of the Anglican Church. In public celebrations they toasted "CHURCH AND STATE." [27] Seizing upon the fear of Catholicism, Loyalists made the issue the principal thrust of their attack on the clergy and the alliance. Charles Inglis cleverly needled the patriots on this point:

[24] Murray, *A Discourse*, p. 17.

[25] Zabdiel Adams, *The Evil Designs of Men made subservient by God to the Public Good; particularly illustrated in the rise, progress, and conclusion of the American War* (Boston, 1783), April 19, 1783, p. 25.

[26] Phillips Payson, "A Sermon preached before the Honorable Council of Boston and Honorable House of Representatives at Boston, May 27, 1778," John Thornton, ed., *The Pulpit in the American Revolution* (Boston, 1860), p. 347; also Murray, *A Discourse*, p. 50.

[27] *Royal Gazette*, June 5, 1779.

Supposing then that the Independency of America could be established, this must be done by the assistance of your French alliance, as is acknowledged on all hands. Do you really imagine that the liberties of America, or the Protestant religion, would not thereby be endangered? If you do not think so, you must be utter strangers to the genius of Popery, to the ambitious, enterprising spirit of that insidious monarchy.[28]

David Rowland, a graduate of Yale and a New Light minister in Connecticut, was one of the few who attempted to answer the charges made by Loyalists such as Inglis.

It has been a matter of speculation with some, that the Americans should be fond of forming an alliance with France, on account of her religious sentiments, being in general Roman Catholics; and doubtless everyone that is an enemy to this alliance will make this the ground of their objections, even though they were Catholics themselves, or equally superstitious, and not a whit better.

Upon which I would observe, that such an alliance is not unexampled; England has been in alliance with Portugal, the inhabitants of which are almost if not wholly Roman Catholics; and France with Holland, yet the Hollanders are chiefly Presbyterians. . . . Differences in religion have no operation in the political system, and commercial interest of nations and people. . . . Now the alliance may have a good tendency to cure the nation [France] of their bigotry, root out their sanguinary notions, and introduce a universal toleration.[29]

Rowland was one of the few who asserted that religion had no role in the political system or commerce, but Loyalist attacks probably impelled a good many clergymen to adopt a more radical concept of church and state. Some came to conceive of freedom of religion as requiring the separation of the state not only from Catholicism but from all denominations; no longer would the state intervene in religion, or the church seek special powers and privileges within or through the state. Joseph Willard ably expressed the doctrine of mutual suspicion which would separate the civil and ecclesiastical realms, "any denomination of Christians who would endeavor to bring the Civil Authority of the State to grant any peculiar privileges to their church, and to give it a pre-

---

[28] [Charles Inglis], *Letters of Papinian* (New York, 1779), p. 67.
[29] David S. Rowland, *A Sermon Preached at Providence, June 6, 1779* (Providence, 1779), pp. 31–32.

eminence over others, ought to be watched over and guarded against." [30]

The more analytical views of the clergy found expression through the colleges and universities, the majority of which were under church control and the presidency of a minister. Although most colleges could not maintain a regular schedule of classes during the war, they attempted to give students an education which included support of the alliance. After attending the 1781 graduation exercises at the University of Pennsylvania, Barbé-Marbois wrote Vergennes that the colleges and professors were eradicating old American prejudices toward France, a comment perhaps premature.[31] Ezra Stiles, acting on the suggestion of Silas Deane, asked the Yale Corporation to hire a professor of French. Deane had recommended that it would be more discreet to hire a Frenchman from Geneva, thus avoiding religious conflicts, but even so the provincialism of the Yale Corporation remained too powerful to permit such a dangerous precedent.

> You are sensible, Sir, that Great Delicacy is requisite in conducting any public Matters, that require a Reconciliation of the minds of the People at large to new proposals which however safe and salutary, may yet be apprehended to involve the most distant Idea of a tendency to bring them under a foreign influence to affect their internal state as to Policy or religion.[32]

Nevertheless, Barbé-Marbois' belief in the liberal influence of the colleges and universities found confirmation in the Dudleian lectures at Harvard. Although the third lecture on the Catholic Church represented one of the ugliest aspects of Protestant bigotry, the wartime lecturers enunciated a more liberal concept of religion. The anti-papal orthodoxy never disappeared, but was softened enough not to offend the French.[33] During the Revolution, the lecturers concentrated their hostility on Great Britain instead of fully venting their more deeply ingrained animosity to Catholicism. They nonetheless continued to express their distaste for Catholic doctrines and practices, although in more measured tones than formerly. The Catholic Church, they argued, had grievously

[30] Joseph Willard, "Persecution opposite to the genius of the Gospel," Sept. 7, 1785, HU Archives, pp. 48–49.

[31] Barbé-Marbois to Vergennes, July 5, 1781, AAE-cp-(EU), Vol. XVII.

[32] Stiles to Deane, Sept. 9, 1778, quoted in Edmund Morgan, *The Gentle Puritan: A Life of Ezra Stiles* (New Haven, 1962), pp. 338–39. Harvard hired Albert Gallatin with no apparent controversy.

[33] The anti-papal lecture was given once every four years. Edward Wigglesworth, *The Authority of Tradition Considered* (Boston, 1778), Nov. 5, 1777; William Gordon, "The Doctrine of Transubstantiation considered and refuted," Sept. 5, 1781, HU Archives; Joseph Willard, "Persecution opposite to the Genius of the Gospel," Sept. 7, 1785.

erred in its violation of the separation of church and state.[34] Underlying many other criticisms was the high value the lecturers placed on the role of reason in religion. They took offense at what they considered the nonsensical and mystical rites of Catholicism.

In the Dudleian lecture of 1777, Edward Wigglesworth criticized Catholicism while addressing himself to a more subtle religious question than Cooper had in the 1773 lecture. Wigglesworth attempted to refute the Papacy's use of tradition, a topic which restricted him from commenting on France or a prospective French alliance. In temper and tone, however, his address was much milder than Cooper's.

In 1781 William Gordon presented the only Dudleian lecture on the Papacy given during the alliance. The apparent conflict between the alliance and the topic of the lecture aroused the interest of other clergymen. "Perhaps we may meet at Cambridge, for the Dudlean [sic] Lecture sermon is to be preached by Dr. Gordon," John Eliot wrote, "& upon a subject I wish to hear at this time, Popery being a delicate point to handle, where people boast of their alliance with Roman Catholic powers." [35]

Gordon, who rarely mixed his theology and his politics, was well suited to handle this dilemma. He opposed the Quebec Act not because it established Catholicism in Canada, but because it restricted United States expansion. "The reduction of Canada is a favorite topick with many. I could wish it was attempted," he wrote Arthur Lee, "that we might be assured of their joining the united States, of their not choosing a form of government inconsistent [with?] their birth, of their not giving the preference to a royal one, & of their not inclining to have a French Sovereign. I want also to have the boundaries of Canada settled, lest the Canadians should claim [western lands] according to the Quebec Act, or what was done before it was conquered by Britain." [36] Gordon advocated support of the alliance and held a good opinion of the French, "The French are the most disinterested people in the world. They are everything, but Protestants: & their being otherwise is a matter of no great importance." [37]

---

[34] Belief in the separation of church and state was common in American religious thought at this time, although it was not as well defined as it later became. Sidney Mead, *The Lively Experiment* (New York, 1963), p. 52; Bridenbaugh, *Mitre & Sceptre*, pp. 3–22; William G. McLoughlin, "Isaac Backus and the Separation of Church and State in America," *AHR*, Vol. LXXIII (1968), pp. 1392–1413.

[35] Eliot to Belknap, Sept. 5, 1781, *Belknap Papers*, part I (Massachusetts Historical Society, *Collections*, fifth series, Vol. II, Boston, 1877), pp. 215–216.

[36] Gordon to Lee, March 2, 1782, Misc. MSS, HU; also Gordon to Gerry, March 15, 1780, Gerry-Knight Papers, MHS.

[37] Gordon to John Adams, Sept. 7 & 19, [1782?], Adams Papers, R. 361 (one letter).

In his lecture Gordon discussed the doctrine of transubstantiation, which enabled him to avoid commenting on political and religious history of recent centuries. But Gordon was too honest a clergyman and too much a politician to avoid mentioning the alliance. He concluded with a brief mention of the alliance and Protestant responsibilities under it.

> While we are politically allied to *Popish* powers, & admit the right of all to judge for themselves in matters of religion, & to follow the dictates of their own consciences, they conducting [themselves] as good members of civil society; let us not thro' a false complaisance decline opposing the erroneous tenets of *Popery,* & become indifferent to *Protestant* truths. Such conduct instead of recommending us to our allies, must sink us in the opinion of the sensible among them; & they will be jealous, that they, who for present interest, will set lightly their own religion, & be inattentive to their solemn compacts with their God, will never make conscience of being true to their engagements with men, when future interest may dictate the contrary.[38]

Gordon's tolerant views were quickly forgotten after the war, and in the 1785 Dudleian lecture Joseph Willard returned to the more jaundiced interpretation of Catholicism. "And what shall we say of this Church, which when persuasion will not answer the end, propagates her tenets by racks and tortures, or by gibbets, fire and faggots; and by the same means endeavors to exterminate those whom she deems obstinate heretics?" he asked.[39] Willard's sermon is similar to Cooper's in the use of the old rallying cries.

> The time would fail me should I mention but a small proportion of the persecutions which have been raised by this cruel Church against other Christians, merely for their differing from her in some doctrines and forms of worship. France had been witness to many shocking scenes. The Edict of Nantes had granted security to the Protestants in that kingdom: But the Revocation filled it with bloodshed. We cannot read the account of the massacre in Paris, which was the consequence of this Revocation, without being filled with horror; though this perfidious and cruel action was so grateful at Rome that a Jubilee was appointed "That thanks might be given to God for the slaughter of the enemies of the Church in France." How often have the dragoons

[38] Gordon, "The Doctrine of Transubstantiation," unpaginated, italics in original.
[39] Willard, "Persecution opposite to the Genius of the Gospel," p. 40.

been let loose upon the Protestants in that kingdom to force them into the bosom of what the Papists call the Mother Church! The most wanton cruelties and murders have been the consequence of such proceedings, and many thousands of families have been ruined.[40]

By 1785 it seemed that the United States had never signed the alliance; the softening of anti-Catholicism had proved ephemeral.

In wartime many clergymen had been content to say that the alliance was beneficial simply because of the aid provided the United States. Phillips Payson, near the close of the Revolution, went further than most in discussing its favorable effects.

> But our greatest human friend and supporter is, His Most Christian Majesty, the King of France, whom that God has the hearts of kings in his hands, disposed to enter into a most generous alliance with these States; and he has given us the strongest evidences of his sincerity and friendship. . . . We well know our absolute need of this foreign aid, and the many ways we have felt the benefit of it; but I fear we are not in general so mindful of the hand of Divine Providence, in this particular, as we ought in justice to be.

Payson stressed the new attitude to be taken toward France, "We are now induced to view and esteem the French by far the most polished, humane, and generous people in the world." He concluded his remarks by reminding his listeners that to forget the kindness of France would "expose us to be reproached with base ingratitude; and not to acknowledge the hand of Providence in this alliance, must bring us the guilt of great impiety." [41] At the successful end of the war, few clergymen or their parishioners were inclined to heed this admonition.

The clergy had faced difficulties in supporting the alliance, but as a group they managed quite skillfully. They were in advance of many members of their congregations in their belief in religious freedom and separation of church and state. Yet, like their parishioners, they had to overcome or control an abiding prejudice toward Catholicism in order to support the French alliance. Most patriotic clergymen found a satisfactory solution by making independence synonymous with religious freedom. Thus the alliance was understood as a necessary step to achieve independence, and God as wise, if mysterious, in achieving His will. The

[40] *Ibid.*, pp. 35–36.
[41] Phillips Payson, *A Sermon preached at Lexington, on the Nineteenth of April, 1782* (Boston, 1782), pp. 13–15.

clergy further fortified their position by invoking the rights of man and depicting opponents of the alliance as misguided, narrow-minded men. Within this context, an overwhelming majority could rationalize their personal support of an alliance with a Catholic power.

Although clergymen frequently thanked God for the intervention of France, and detected the inscrutable work of Divine Providence in arranging an alliance with Catholics, they did not believe that the United States was, or should be, obligated to aid France in the future, nor tolerate the establishment of Catholicism in the United States. The residents of Northampton, Massachusetts, expressed feelings prevalent among the clergy and their countrymen in a toast during the celebration of the peace treaty, "May the protestant religion prevail & flourish through all nations." [42]

[42] *Maryland Gazette,* June 12, 1783.

VIII. The Press and the Alliance

> Firm the alliance made with France,
> Nor was it made by fate or chance,
> Such skill and wisdom shine:
> And such it never rose from man,
> Such the contrivance of the plan,
> But from Some hand divine.[1]

During the Revolution the press actively supported American policy even more than the clergy. Like the clergy, the press had local loyalties and few previous national concerns, but it was nevertheless in the forefront in supporting the action of Congress in ratifying an alliance with France. In pre-Revolutionary times the press had contested both the wisdom and the constitutionality of many acts of Parliament. After initiating the opposition to the Stamp Act, the press considered itself to be the keystone of American resistance.

Strongly Protestant in mentality, publishers as well as clergymen had to adjust to new circumstances if they were to remain loyal to the Revolution. The three years between the outbreak of fighting and the signing of the alliance allowed them to establish a pattern of loyalty to which they adhered for the remainder of the war. The pattern took the form of a virulent anti-British stance expressed in frequent exhortations to the people to resist Great Britain, enlist in the militia, and pay taxes to defeat the diabolical enemy of American freedom. The press accepted the alliance with the rationalization that any aid was justifiable in the fight against British tyranny. To accept French aid implied no sympathy for Catholicism, however.[2]

The transition from militant anti-Catholicism and pre-war hostility to France was not easily accomplished by the press. It took considerable restraint to avoid past shibboleths about the King of France, let alone praise him without offending the Protestant sensibilities of the populace. Yet the press handled this delicate problem with sophistication and even some finesse.

At the time of the Revolution, newspapers were not evenly dis-

---

[1] *Connecticut Courant,* Jan. 19, 1779.
[2] Charles Metzger, *Catholics and the American Revolution* (Chicago, 1962), p. 52.

tributed in the United States. The northern and middle states, with the exception of New York City and Newport, had regular patriot presses which operated continuously even under wartime conditions of financial and paper shortages. After 1780 Philadelphia had four papers, including the *Pennsylvania Packet,* which published twice a week. In the more rural South only Maryland had a paper which published without fail after 1779. The British occupation and paper shortages restricted the press in Virginia, South Carolina, and Georgia; North Carolina had no newspaper between 1779 and 1783.[3] One Virginian complained that it was "hardly possible to get any paper of consequence published here. The printers have advertised they will not publish any Controversial pieces but for a very high Price. . . . I wish a Printer could be procured from the Northward, for ours have got to such a pass as to neglect everything." [4]

Residents of the Southern States depended on mail delivery, often from congressional delegates, of the Maryland or Philadelphia papers for the latest news. The Philadelphia papers, especially the *Pennsylvania Packet,* had the widest circulation due to their central location and their coverage of war news, Congressional actions, and foreign dispatches.

A newspaper needed some sort of government support to supplement subscriptions. The *New Jersey Gazette,* published by Isaac Collins, was founded with the active encouragement and support of the New Jersey legislature.[5] The Philadelphia papers vied with one another in seeking state or Congressional printing contracts.[6] This informal but indispensable subsidy was widespread; it provided a ready financial weapon which a government could use to insure loyalty to the Patriot cause.

[3] Charles Crittenden, *North Carolina Newspapers Before 1790* (Chapel Hill, 1928), pp. 60–62. Most studies of the press concentrate on the pre-war era, and very few comment on the French alliance and its treatment in American newspapers. The best over-all treatment is Philip Davidson, *Propaganda and the American Revolution, 1763–1783* (Chapel Hill, 1941), but Davidson is concerned with propaganda between the British and Americans, and he argues that the alliance put the Patriots on the defensive, a conclusion that is far too sweeping, p. 363. For the pre-war period, Schlesinger, *Prelude to Independence,* is the best work. Other studies which are helpful, but contain very little on the French alliance are Joseph T. Wheeler, *The Maryland Press, 1777–1790* (Baltimore, 1938); Clifford K. Shipton, *Isaiah Thomas* (Rochester, 1948); and Sidney Pomerantz, "The Patriot Newspaper and the American Revolution," *The Era of the American Revolution,* ed., Richard Morris (New York, 1939), pp. 305–31, for a discussion of the press in New York and New Jersey.

[4] Parker to Richard Henry Lee, March 26, 1779, Lee Family Papers, R. 5.

[5] Richard McCormick, *Experiment in Independence: New Jersey in the Critical Period, 1781–1789* (New Brunswick, 1950), p. 59.

[6] Peter J. Parker, "The Philadelphia Printer: A Study of an Eighteenth Century Businessman," *Business History Review,* Vol. XL (1966), pp. 32, 37.

A publisher's patriotism, however, was usually not open to doubt, and officials seldom had to use their financial leverage to prevent a publisher from printing items unfavorable to the Revolution. The publishers early proved their loyalty by "ceaselessly fueling the martial spirit and sustaining civilian morale." [7] Significantly, only one publisher, Morton Draper of Boston, received a Loyalist subsidy from the British in New York City. [8]

Patriot papers had to devote considerable attention to reporting American reverses, since they faced the prospect of conflicting stories from the authorized Loyalist press in New York City. The Tory and Patriot papers circulated widely in each other's territory, thus giving readers some check on the accuracy and completeness of each side's accounts. For instance, Christopher Marshall, a staunch Patriot, read about the British victory at Charleston from Rivington's *Royal Gazette* in his Philadelphia coffeehouse. [9] Alexander Hamilton arranged with the British for a weekly exchange of New York and Philadelphia newspapers at the request of the French Legation in Philadelphia. [10]

The rebel papers displayed considerable uniformity in the kind of news they printed, or more often reprinted from other papers. American publishers faced severe problems in obtaining current and accurate news, particularly from France. Their difficulties are evident in the news coverage of the peace negotiations by the *Maryland Gazette,* which was typical of other Patriot newspapers. A strongly pro-French paper, the *Maryland Gazette* carried no dispatches from Paris between January and August, 1782. The ousting of the North Cabinet, the replacement of Sir Henry Clinton by Sir Guy Carleton, and Parliament's resolution prohibiting offensive warfare in the United States by British forces were reported via British sources with no news of French plans or reactions to rapidly changing circumstances. [11] None of the five dispatches from Paris in the fall of 1782 carried news of peace talks or prospects of peace. [12]

As the news coverage of the *Maryland Gazette* indicates, American publishers often had no choice but to rely on British sources for the latest news from Europe. French dispatches were generally outdated by the time they reached publishers in the United States. News from Great Britain was more easily available, because Great Britain had more regu-

[7] Schlesinger, *Prelude to Independence,* p. 235.

[8] "List of Royalist Allowances," Shelburne Papers, Vol. LXVII.

[9] Christopher Marshall Diary, diary entry June 12, 1780.

[10] Hamilton to Barbé-Marbois, May 18, 1780, Syrett, ed., *Hamilton,* Vol. II, p. 325.

[11] *Maryland Gazette,* March 21, May 9, 16, 1782.

[12] *Ibid.,* Aug. 15, Sept. 5, 19, Oct. 3, Nov. 21, 1782.

lar supply and packet ships traveling between Europe and America than did France. After the Loyalist press in New York published the news from Parliament and the London newspapers, American publishers would reprint from the British sources. But Americans were highly selective in the items they reprinted, tending to exaggerate opposition to the war in Great Britain and rumors of peace.

In addition to standard news coverage from Europe, American newspapers also printed and reprinted many of the same essays. Thomas Paine's essays were widely used, no matter what the topic. A majority of the other essays dealt with state politics, currency, and taxation, while orders and proclamations by Congress were reprinted without fail. Publishers made an independent decision on the extent to which their papers would extoll the French and the alliance; their choices involved whether or not to reprint an essay lauding their ally, not whether to publish one denigrating her. In general, publishers made a random selection among the pro-alliance articles they printed. About the same number of pro-alliance essays was printed in all papers, except for the *Pennsylvania Gazette* and the *Maryland Gazette,* both of which were strongly pro-French.

The Loyalist press, on the other hand, attacked the alliance without inhibition. The significant Loyalist papers, James Rivington's *Royal Gazette* and Hugh Gaine's *New York Gazette,* were located in New York City, but Newport, Charleston, and Savannah also published Loyalist papers for short periods during the British occupation. All of these were under the control of the British military commander, and published only with his permission. Thus Rivington's *Royal Gazette,* although the best newspaper during the Revolution in news coverage, was a closer indication of the policy of the British military government than the rebel papers were of any policy or government.

The underlying theme of Loyalist attacks on the alliance was the Catholicism of France and what the writers saw as the ultimate dependence of the United States on France. Arguments against the alliance varied little in tone and substance in five years, a rigidity that often prevented the Loyalist press from being effective. Due to restrictions of military policy—or more accurately, military censorship—the Tories failed to concentrate on domestic politics as it influenced the alliance. Only in 1778 during the abortive negotiations by the Carlisle Commission, and in 1782 with the attempt for a separate peace negotiated by General Carleton and Admiral Digby, did the Loyalist press seek to persuade people in rebel-held territory to reject the legitimacy of Congress and the alliance. Generally, it simply attempted to provoke dissatisfaction behind rebel lines or dissension between the French and Americans. Like the Patriot press, although with different intentions, Tory papers often dealt with the desperate currency situation in the United States.

When the alliance was announced the lesson was clear to Loyalists. Congress had betrayed the people by such a policy and ought to be emphatically repudiated.

> On this side, you are invited to a safe constitutional re-union with your *Mother-Country,* to whom the ties of kindred, language, and laws ought to bind you for ever;—on the other side, the Congress would draw you into a league with France and Spain, the natural-restless, and enterprizing enemies of all civil and religious freedom, and who wish you to renounce any kind of accommodations with Britain, only with a view of making you the convenient dupes of their unbounded ambition! Judge for yourselves: and whatever may be the wish of *Congress,* you cannot be at a loss on which side to fix *your* choice.[13]

Loyalist critics revised their argument after it became clear that the Carlisle Commission would not succeed. "Britannicus" charged that Congress could not negotiate because of restrictions in the still secret provisions of the defensive treaty. Actually the complete treaties had been widely published in the rebel press, with the exception of the clause which allowed Spain to join the alliance on the same terms as France. But because Congress had not revealed all the terms of the treaty immediately, Loyalist writers effectively exploited its secretive nature. "While therefore, this treaty is concealed from you, you have all the reason in the world to suppose you are *sold,* from being *free* and *equal* subjects of Britain; [you] are made the *vassals* and *slaves* of *France.*" On the other hand, Britannicus continued, under "the terms lately offered you by Great Britain, you might have been the *freest* and *happiest* people in the universe." [14]

The Loyalists' most constant charge was that the alliance caused a critical dependence on France, an argument given ever more emphasis after 1779. After Congress passed a resolution that the United States would not negotiate separately from France, a provision of the published treaty, Charles Inglis felt confident that the American people would never support such a policy. "The people grow more and more disaffected to the Congress's alliance with a Popish King, and their disgust has greatly encreased since the publication of a resolution of that

---

[13] *Royal Gazette,* June 6, 1778; also *ibid.,* Oct. 10, 14, 1778, italics in original. All references to the *Royal Gazette* are to the New York edition unless otherwise specified.

[14] *Ibid.,* Jan. 2, 1779, italics in original.

body, published in our last Gazette, which implies the most abject DE-PENDENCE upon the will and pleasure of their *great* and *good* ally, Louis the 16th," he wrote.[15] Interspersed with such attacks the Loyalist press printed spurious information from within rebel lines, "the People in general are very discontented with the French Alliance, and are justly Apprehensive that it will certainly lead to the Subordination of their Country to France, the Loss of their Liberties, and the certain introduction of Popery." [16]

The arrival of Rochambeau's troops in Newport in 1780 confirmed Loyalist suspicions of the sinister purpose of the alliance. "Actuated by this sound policy, France with avidity, seized the first pretext to make a lodgement to one of the gates of America, and she will not speedily lose sight of the finer provinces of the country; from which she never can be expelled, save by Great Britain, the natural guardian of America." [17] Immediately after the arrival of the French troops the Loyalist papers in New York neglected no opportunity to report any conflict between the French and Americans.[18] After Yorktown the attacks subsided, probably because the Tories shared the rebels' surprise at Rochambeau's cooperation. When the Army departed from Boston in December, 1782, the Loyalist press neither commented on the performance of the French troops nor expressed relief that they had left the continent.

In 1782, when the British government opened negotiations and again attempted to break American adherence to the alliance, the Loyalist papers sought to reassure those who feared American independence to be imminent.

> It is earnestly recommended to the Loyalists, everywhere, to suspend their opinion on the *present* important occasion, and, each in his *place,* to continue firm to the professions he has made of loyalty and zeal for the re-union of the Empire. The independency of the Thirteen Provinces has indeed been *proposed* at a conference in Paris, . . . In the mean time, therefore, we are bound by every consideration of prudence and duty, to wait the issue, with that manly steadiness, and cheerful reliance on the abilities and attention of our Commanders in Chief, which are at present our surest pledges of safety. By such conduct we shall *preserve* a claim to *national regard* and *protection,* which it would be madness to forfeit; since, by giving way to suggestions of impa-

---

[15] *Ibid.,* Feb. 17, 1779, italics in original.
[16] *New York Gazette,* Sept. 14, 1778.
[17] *Royal Gazette,* Aug. 5, 1780.
[18] *Ibid.,* Aug. 2, 23, Sept. 27, Oct. 25, 1780, Feb. 24, June 23, July 18, Dec. 5, 1781; *New York Gazette,* Sept. 18, Oct. 23, 1780, July 16, 1781, May 27, 1782.

tience, we can only disgrace ourselves in the eyes of our enemies without a show of advantage.[19]

Hugh Gaine, the publisher, perhaps should have borrowed a line from his old adversary Thomas Paine and started his editorial, "These are the times that try men's souls."

In the summer of 1782 the Loyalist press made a concerted effort to woo Americans from the alliance and the Revolution, pointing to the desperate condition of the currency and the failure to pay taxes as indications of fast-diminishing support for the war. The papers emphasized the deprivation of the rebels rather than the Loyalists' even more precarious position. "The Independants are at Their Wits End in all Parts of the Continent," was the start of one article, and another reported, "We learn that the general voice of the country is, *no taxes* and a *speedy reunion with Great Britain.*" [20] Despite repeated articles urging reconciliation, time favored the Patriots, and the important question of the terms of independence went undiscussed in the Loyalist press.[21]

In the fall of 1782, however, the tone of the Loyalist papers changed as they prepared for the inevitable acknowledgment of United States independence. This change took many forms, but as the rumors of peace multiplied, more articles were reprinted from the rebel papers and the news of the preliminary treaty was reprinted from a Philadelphia paper.[22] By April, 1783, Rivington had started referring to George Clinton as the governor of New York.[23]

Rivington and Gaine, both sound businessmen, began to adapt to independence immediately. Gaine, soon to emigrate to Nova Scotia with other Loyalists, carried the following advertisement, "A New Map of the UNITED STATES OF AMERICA, laid down from the best Authority, agreeable to the Peace of 1783: an allegorical Print of the Independence of America, and Portraits of Gen. Washington, Dr. Franklin, and Mr. Laurens, sold by the Printer." [24] James Rivington, who remained in New York and merely changed the name of his paper after the American occupation, reminded departing Loyalists, "Mr. Rivington entreats those Gentlemen who are in Arrears for this Gazette, &c. to favor him with Payment, before their Embarkation; this is suggested, with great Deference, on a presumption that some, perfectly willing to satisfy him, may leave the City without recollecting Trifles." [25]

[19] *Ibid.,* Aug. 12, 1782, italics in original.
[20] *Ibid.,* June 17, 1782; *Royal Gazette,* May 29, 1782, italics in original.
[21] See "A New York Freeholder" articles in *ibid.,* June 15, 22, 29, July 6, 13, 24, 27, Aug. 3, 1782.
[22] *Ibid.,* March 19, 26, 1783.
[23] *Ibid.,* April 23, 1783.
[24] *New York Gazette,* June 23, 1783.
[25] *Royal Gazette,* Nov. 8, 1783.

The Loyalist press served the British command competently but without success in attacking the alliance. The failure of efforts to break the alliance lay not with the press but with the British military. The Americans and the French won the war, and Rivington and Gaine could not alter the fact. By any measurement a majority of Americans backed the Revolution, and attacks by the Loyalist press had to rely on the ability of the British military to convince the population that the United States could not win.

Moreover, the Loyalist papers suffered from a weakness of imagination. Rarely did they dip into domestic issues relevant to the alliance. They reprinted very few articles in the Silas Deane-Arthur Lee controversy, and during the debate over peace ultimata in 1779, they remained silent on the issues which split Congress and caused deep antagonism toward France. When the combined attack on Newport failed, Gaine ran an insipid article stating that both countries were equally to blame.[26] The first accounts of the allied defeat at Savannah were reprinted verbatim from a rebel paper.[27] After Yorktown the Loyalist press, in its most pointed attack, could only appeal to Protestant Americans to castigate Congress for attending a Mass to celebrate the victory.[28]

By ignoring existing controversies, described and available to them in rebel papers, Loyalist publishers failed to exploit divisions within Congress and between France and the United States. They regularly emphasized only American dependence on France and fear of Catholicism, and there was simply not enough evidence of French control or Catholic inroads to bring a majority of Americans back into the protective custody of Protestant Britain. In ideology, the British-controlled press fought the Seven Years' War with little acknowledgment that a revolution had occurred in the United States. The Revolution, a republican war for independence, remained to the Loyalists an imperial struggle between Protestant and Catholic monarchies.

Patriot publishers kept a watchful eye on their opposite numbers, eager to rebut any and all charges. Much of the controversy between the two groups took the tone of a vendetta, with taste and truth often ignored. The surest method to induce a Patriot publisher to comment on the alliance was for a Loyalist paper to allege that the French had excessive influence in American politics. James Rivington, after the news of Yorktown, asserted that a French loan to the United States was given to Washington at his discretion "so that every soldier of this alliance is now become in every sense a Frenchman." [29] This insult whetted a

26 *Ibid.*, April 21, 1779.
27 *New York Gazette,* Nov. 22, 1779.
28 *Royal Gazette,* Dec. 5, 1781.
29 *Ibid.*, Nov. 7, 1781.

Yankee publisher's appetite, and he replied in a manner typical of the running controversy between the Tories and the rebel press.

> We can also assure the public from past observation, that Sir Henry Clinton, and his Aide de Camp Mr. Rivington, have long been in the actual service of his most diabolical Majesty, Satan the First. Formerly the fraternity at New York reproached us for paying our army with paper rags. They now fret and are displeased that we pay them with a loan from France, which they rationally suppose will metamorphose our army into Frenchmen and catholics. Surely we ought to thank these gentlemen for their benevolence, brotherly care, and officious concern for the welfare and morals of the American Army: Many People, however, are of the opinion, that it would become them better to provide for the safety of the remnant of their own.[30]

In addition to contradicting Loyalist allegations, the Patriot press controlled its criticism of Catholicism, just as it had restrained its remarks on the Allied military failures at Newport and Savannah. The almost perfect performance of the rebel press in discussing Catholicism is difficult to explain except within the context of repeated Loyalist attacks. One scholar noted, "Papers which before the Revolution were loud in their denunciations of the old faith either ignored the religious affiliations of France or noticed them only to affirm their harmlessness. On the other hand they consistently supported the alliance." [31]

Patriot publishers believed that it was in the best interests of the United States to disregard the religious affiliation of their allies. They perceived the disservice which an anti-Catholic article would do to the American cause; the British were not as remote as the Pope and infinitely more dangerous. Americans were fighting a Protestant country for control of North America, and the papacy issue had become not only irrelevant but harmful.

Yet the press did not have an easy task in explaining France in a favorable light. After the signing of the alliance, newspaper articles often cited the example of Switzerland to allay American fears. The authors observed that Switzerland, a republic, had maintained a diplomatic alliance with France for two centuries, although they failed to elaborate on the terms of this alliance or the Swiss role in maintaining it. A Boston paper provided the reassuring information that the three most celebrated financiers of France—Sully, Colbert, and Necker—were all Protes-

---

[30] *Connecticut Courant*, Dec. 4, 1781.
[31] Sister Mary Augustina Ray, *American Opinion of Roman Catholicism in the Eighteenth Century* (New York, 1936), p. 338.

tants.[32] Samuel Cooper probably planted an item in the same paper to show the generosity of France at the peace table. "Louis XIV gave back almost everything he had conquered for the sake of an advantageous settlement in favour of those powers with which he was in alliance," the article declared.[33] Despite these efforts, the image of France remained almost as mysterious as it had been before the Revolution. American publishers, knowing little of French traditions or government, emphasized French personages rather than politics.

Thus Louis XVI was commonly depicted as a protector of the rights of mankind, a description which conveniently ignored religion. The Queen of France rarely received attention unless pregnant.[34] Americans had little evidence to prove that Louis XVI was the protector of mankind, but one paper did note that he had abolished slavery in France, an item that appeared when Pennsylvania was considering the abolition of slavery.[35] In another publisher's judgment, the safe-conduct pass which the French gave to explorer Captain Cook demonstrated the humanitarian instincts of the King. It is notable that the paper did not report that Benjamin Franklin had also issued a safe-conduct pass to Cook, probably because Franklin was suspect to the radicals from New England.[36]

A Newport paper carried a poem dedicated to the King of France on his birthday.

> When injur'd freedom in distress,
> To LOUIS did himself address,
> And claim'd her gen'rous aid,
> Her hapless States his pity mov'd,
> Her righteous cause, by all approv'd,
> His own he nobly made.
>
> Great COLUMBIA shall revere,
> The MONARCH to his country dear,
> And to mankind a friend;
> All nations shall in this combine,
> Their praises and applause to join,
> Till nature has an end.[37]

[32] *Independent Chronicle*, July 12, 1781.

[33] *Ibid.*, Oct. 17, 1782.

[34] For one account when she was not pregnant, see *Providence Gazette*, April 22, 1780.

[35] *Packet*, Feb. 19, 1780.

[36] *Connecticut Courant*, Dec. 14, 1779.

[37] "Crito," "An ODE on the Anniversary of the Birth of the King of France, Navarre &c.," *Newport Mercury*, Aug. 30, 1782.

In addition to praising the King, the Patriot press proclaimed the munificence of France in sending the expeditionary force headed by Rochambeau in 1780. Rochambeau's arrival gave publishers their first opportunity to print enthusiastic praise of French armed forces in the two years since the signing of the alliance and Americans eagerly anticipated offensive action to drive the British from New York. The Newport paper advised its readers that the French could not immediately take the field, but reassured them that there was no danger of smallpox or yellow fever from the nearby French forces.[38] The Loyalist press offered its own opinion on the schedule of French activity, "We trust this naval armament will not depart from the Continent without a Permit first obtained from the BRITISH ADMIRAL." [39]

Press coverage of the French Army concentrated on the officer corps, revealing an ambivalence in the American attitude toward rank and nobility. Few articles extolled enlisted men or their dedication to the American struggle for freedom.[40] The publishers' concern over rank was symptomatic of a curious inconsistency in American thought during the Revolution. The drive for equality of status, which the Revolution accelerated, was accompanied by a desire for distinction to signify merit and more probably stability in revolutionary times. For example, an item from the *Pennsylvania Packet* was widely reprinted despite its dubious validity.

> It is observed of the army at Newport, that in proportion to its numbers, it has more principals of distinguished character and family, than any army that ever was sent to such a distance from France; a demonstration that the leading men in that nation are warmly engaged in the American cause.[41]

The press awarded Rochambeau the usual number of accolades as commander of the army, but Chastellux quickly became the most widely acclaimed officer in the expeditionary force. Chastellux, a member of the French Academy, arrived in the United States bearing an introduction to Washington from Franklin, in which the Frenchman was commended as "particularly a Friend to our Cause." [42] Chastellux won further esteem by advocating decisive action to aid the Americans, while Rochambeau insisted on remaining in Newport. But even the adulation

---

[38] *Ibid.*, July 22, 1780.

[39] *Royal Gazette*, July 22, 1780.

[40] John Shy noted the same ambivalence by Americans toward the British Army around Boston before the Revolution. John Shy, *Toward Lexington* (Princeton, 1965), p. 393.

[41] *Packet*, Jan. 9, 1781.

[42] Franklin to Washington, March 19, 1780, Washington Papers, Vol. CXXX.

of Chastellux did not match the outpourings for Lafayette, who had eagerly supported the American cause since 1777 and held an independent command in the American Army. As Luzerne once noted, "it is impossible to be more generally loved than M. and Mme. de la Fayette are in all parts of the United States." [43] The press, although fascinated with personages and status, rather shrewdly gave the best coverage to those Frenchmen most dedicated to American interests.[44]

The inactivity of the French Army, and the consequent dearth of favorable military news, contributed to the attention accorded rank and social position. But after the French and Americans joined forces in 1781, the press changed its emphasis from personal items to panegyrics on the behavior of the entire army. An article in a Connecticut paper praising its conduct was reprinted in almost every area where the French forces marched for the following two years.

> A Finer body of men were never in arms, and no army was ever better furnished with every thing necessary for a campaign. The exact discipline of the troops, and the attention of the officers to prevent any injury to individuals, have made the march of this army through the country very agreeable to the inhabitants, and it is with pleasure we assure our readers that not a single disagreeable circumstance has taken place.[45]

The Patriot press in its most critical role provided a continuous justification of the alliance. Published explanations of the alliance were not sweetened with essays on the generosity of nations or the friendship of man, but emphasized the obvious political ties of mutual interest requiring each nation to maintain the alliance. As one writer expressed it, "National friendship is but a creature of the imagination. National interest is the only object of our alliance." [46] In another article, "A Republican" asked his readers not to become sentimental about France or the French, because "Whatever motives may ostensibly connect an alliance between two nations, the real cause of union lies not so much in principles of generosity, as in a reciprocal interest. This foundation is real, this [is] the firmest bond of national friendship." [47] Although most Americans believed that mutual interest had dictated the alliance and would perpetuate it, the press continued to remind them to expect nothing more from it.

43 Luzerne to Vergennes, Oct. 2, 1783, Luzerne Papers.
44 See, for example, *Maryland Gazette,* Dec. 29, 1780.
45 *Connecticut Courant,* July 3, 1781.
46 *Newport Mercury,* March 3, 1781.
47 *Maryland Gazette,* Oct. 25, 1781.

The alliance itself caused little domestic political conflict in the United States, if press coverage is any indication. One minor exception might be the *Freeman's Journal* of Philadelphia, which printed a number of essays implying criticism of French officials. It published a letter protesting James Wilson's holding a seat in the Pennsylvania legislature while reputedly serving as the Advocate-General of France in the United States. The thrust of the charge was anti-Wilson, not anti-French, however, and the controversy died soon after it was announced that Wilson no longer held any post for the French.[48] The *Freeman's Journal* also carried two attacks on the French consul, John Holker, after he entertained a former business associate of Benedict Arnold. The guest was probably James Duane, also a business associate of Holker. The article criticized Holker's private business transactions rather than his use of his office as consul general of France.[49] Unknown to the public, Luzerne was then completing steps to remove Holker from office because of his private business activities.

Despite the delicate treatment of France and Catholicism, the alliance did not interfere with public discussion of the church-state question in the press. All writers assumed that Catholicism would never become a possibility in the United States; the Protestant character of American society was taken for granted. Religious discussion in the press focused on the wisdom of an established church and the degree of religious freedom desired in the United States. No state considered whether the Catholic Church should be recognized or whether any special consideration should be given to Catholicism because the United States was allied to France.

The majority of writers discussing the church-state issue advocated complete religious freedom. Baptists in Massachusetts complained that they had not received a fair hearing from members of the state constitutional convention when it established the Independent Church. But they were less vehement in their protest against an established church than the Protestants of pre-war times had been over the question of an Anglican bishop for America or the Quebec Act.[50] "Philanthropos" supported the Baptists in Massachusetts, and "A Social Christian" advocated complete religious freedom in Virginia.[51] Commentators on religious freedom refrained from disparaging France for having a state-supported church. One of the rare American authors to support an estab-

---

[48] *Freeman's Journal* (Philadelphia), Jan. 25, Feb. 15, 1783.
[49] *Ibid.,* June 9, 1781.
[50] *Independent Chronicle,* Dec. 2, 1779; Bridenbaugh, *Mitre & Sceptre,* chs. VII–XII; Charles Metzger, *The Quebec Act* (New York, 1936), pp. 39–40, 83–84.
[51] *Independent Chronicle,* March 2, 9, 23, April 6, 1780; *Virginia Gazette* (Dixon and Nicolson), Sept. 11, 18, 1779.

lished church noted that France suffered no ill effects from this arrange-
ment—a minority interpretation in the United States. The writer did not
advocate the establishment of Catholicism, but he attempted to invoke
the favorable predisposition of Americans toward France by calling himself "A Gallican." [52]

Patriot papers in all sections of the country supported the Revolution and with it the alliance, but they were constantly challenged by the
widely circulated Loyalist press. The conflicting interpretations offered
by the Loyalist papers checked wildly inaccurate coverage, but also
made Patriot publishers more selective in their criticism of American actions. Nevertheless, the Patriot press operated without governmental editorial restraint in contrast to the military control of the Loyalist papers.
Any restraint exercised by Patriot publishers was self-imposed by an individual's judgment of what would serve the best interest of the American cause.

The Patriot press, with its more numerous newspapers, reached
wider geographical areas and more people than did the Loyalist press.
Furthermore, much of the American population strongly supported the
Revolution and distrusted the British, and were thus disposed to favor
accounts in the Patriot press. Patriot publishers nonetheless sought to
destroy all vestiges of credence accorded the Loyalist press, especially
the key New York papers, in order to diminish whatever influence the
Loyalist cause had in rebel-held territory. In this, as in its news coverage, the Patriot press consistently sought to maintain public support for
the Revolution and the alliance.

The freedom of Patriot publishers to determine what to publish was
greater than that of their Loyalist counterparts, but this freedom was not
absolute. No restrictions were enacted by the states or Congress, but it
was assumed that each publisher would make an active commitment to
American independence. Freedom of the press remained untrammeled if
the press supported the Revolution and the alliance. As the American
military situation worsened in 1780 and 1781, patriotic publishers felt a
desperate need for material to bolster public morale. One expedient was
to accept pro-French articles emphasizing eventual victory through the
aid and friendship of France. The commitment of Patriot publishers to
victory with independence and to facilitating the alliance gave the
French ministers and their agents a unique opportunity to saturate
American newspapers with their own propaganda.

[52] *Maryland Gazette,* Jan. 18, 1781.

IX. French Propaganda in the United States

The unwavering loyalty of the American press to the Revolution enabled the French ministers to exploit it for their own purposes. Due to the paucity of news, publishers gladly printed articles submitted to them about France. The French ministers fulfilled the demand for news about France by hiring at least three agents—Samuel Cooper, Thomas Paine, and Hugh Brackenridge—to write stories, and by planting items favorable to the alliance in American newspapers.[1]

French propaganda sought to strengthen American loyalty to the alliance. When the articles concerned the French, they emphasized the close cooperation of the Allied forces at Savannah, the merits of the French Army at Newport, and French dedication to United States independence. They also dealt with such topics as paying taxes, filling quotas, and cooperating with other states and the Continental Army. The articles, in themselves, intended no injury to the American cause. The mutual interest of both France and the United States required that the Americans be as militarily powerful and prepared as possible, and only the British and Loyalists could be shaken by reports of cooperation at Savannah or the friendship of the Allied armies under Rochambeau and Washington.

American freedom of the press initially disturbed the French ministers. After a letter in a Philadelphia paper threatened action to restrict the power of big merchants, including John Holker, French consul general, Gérard protested to Vergennes, "Nothing proves more conclusively, it seems to me, the abuses of unlimited freedom of the press." [2] Gérard

---

[1] There are no studies of French propaganda in the United States during the alliance. For a general treatment of Revolutionary propaganda, see Davidson, *Propaganda and the American Revolution;* Carl Berger, *Broadsides and Bayonets: The Propaganda War of the American Revolution* (Philadelphia, 1961); and Homer L. Calkin, "Pamphlets and Public Opinion During the American Revolution," *PMHB,* Vol. LXIV (1940), pp. 22–44. The French apparently hired only Americans because French journalists were so rare in the United States. See Allen J. Barthold, "French Journalists in the United States, 1780–1800," *Franco-American Review,* Vol. I (1936), pp. 215–30.

[2] Gérard to Vergennes, Dec. 12–14, 1778, Meng, ed., *Gérard,* pp. 425–26.

could see no advantage in a free press, and Luzerne frequently admitted that the press created added difficulties for him. Nevertheless, the French were quick to exploit the freedom of the press to further their own policy. They improvised, and reached an accommodation with the American press by which the French ministers paid agents and planted articles favorable to France. The writers employed by France became, at least when writing about foreign affairs, the most productive and successful political group in utilizing the press during the last four years of the Revolution.

Gérard developed the French propaganda policy without advice from Vergennes, and Luzerne continued Gérard's policy, but made the arguments in the articles more abstract. Vergennes approved any request to pay for articles in the press, allowing each Minister latitude in determining the content of the articles. The Silas Deane controversy had served as the catalyst which induced Gérard to subsidize writers. During this conflict, Gérard concluded that it was necessary to attack Samuel Adams and the anti-Deane forces without waiting for permission from Vergennes.[3]

The French position, in Gérard's judgment, had suffered distortion and neglect in the press. To counteract this problem he hired Hugh Henry Brackenridge of Philadelphia, "I congratulate myself, Monseigneur," Gérard wrote, "for having found the means for putting an end to the disgraceful silence which reigned in the newspapers of this country over France and the alliance," [4] thereby exaggerating press abuse and neglect to justify his unauthorized actions to Vergennes. Even before Gérard hired anyone, press coverage was one-sided and favorable to the alliance; after Gérard devised his system of paid writers, the press became overwhelmingly pro-French.

Vergennes authorized Luzerne to continue Gérard's policy without change. Luzerne continued with the same group of writers, but supervised them more closely. Gérard had allowed each author to select his own topic, but Luzerne recommended themes and at times wrote a synopsis of the story he wished to have printed. After Luzerne assumed his position in September, 1779, the articles closely reflected the official French position.[5]

The most important French agent, both for Gérard and Luzerne, was the Reverend Samuel Cooper, who worked for the French longer than any other agent. Serving from 1779 until his death in December,

---

[3] Gérard to Vergennes, Jan. 17, 1779, *ibid.*, pp. 480–82.

[4] Gérard to Vergennes, May 29, 1779, *ibid.*, p. 691.

[5] Vergennes to Luzerne, Sept. 25, 1779, AAE-cp-(EU), Vol. X; Luzerne to Vergennes, Aug. 14, 1780, *ibid.*, Vol. XIII; Luzerne to Cooper, Nov. 1, 1779, Cooper Papers, HL, quoted by permission of the Huntington Library.

1783, Cooper received nearly a thousand dollars a year for his services.[6] Joseph de Valnais, French consul at Boston, speculated that Cooper accepted the post because of his "inclination for gold," but this is too simple an explanation.[7]

Although he was an unquestioned patriot, Cooper's politics were influenced by friendship as much as ideology. An early advocate of resistance to Great Britain, he frequently used the pulpit to expound his political outlook.[8] After independence, Massachusetts politicians divided into two major groups, both of which supported the Revolution. Cooper aligned himself with the faction led by John Hancock, Thomas Cushing, and his brother, William Cooper. The other faction, the more powerful in national politics, was led by John and Samuel Adams, James Warren, and Elbridge Gerry. The second group was more republican in ideology, more suspicious of French programs, and more passionate in advocating additional United States acquisitions, including the fishery. Cooper originally had strong personal ties with Samuel Adams, but these ended with the fishery dispute of 1779. After 1779 Cooper rarely had influence within the radical Adams faction.

For many years Cooper was a close friend of Benjamin Franklin. After 1779, the Massachusetts faction led by John Adams became critical of Franklin's performance as minister to France, believing him to be a willing tool of Vergennes and French policy. Cooper broke with the Adams faction on this issue as well as the fishery question. He constantly supplied Franklin with information which Franklin used to influence the French against John Adams. Cooper became an outspoken advocate of policies and personages opposed by the Adams faction, and he came to believe that the radicals of this bloc were undermining the French alliance by their intransigent policies.

When Cooper heard of the alliance, he accepted it with no reservations. He immediately wrote Franklin requesting information for the Boston papers in order to "strengthen the Friendship between France & America." [9] Cooper allowed his enthusiasm for the alliance to leap out of rational control after he met a few Frenchmen. "The more I am acquainted with Gentlemen of character of that nation, the more I am convinced of their thorough attachment to the Independence of the

---

[6] Luzerne to Vergennes, March, 1780, Dec. 31, 1780; March 31, June 30, Oct. 8, Dec. 30, 1781; July 7, Oct. 1, Dec. 31, 1782; April 1, July 1, Oct. 1, 1783; Jan. 1, March 30, 1784, Luzerne Papers.

[7] De Valnais to Holker, Jan. 11, 1779, Holker Papers, Vol. II.

[8] Alice Baldwin, *The New England Clergy and the American Revolution* (Durham, 1928), pp. 93–94, 156–57.

[9] Cooper to Franklin, June 1, 1778, Franklin Papers, UP, Vol. II; another copy in Franklin Papers, APS, Vol. X.

States," he wrote, "How happy is it for us that the Interest of France is so closely combin'd with ours in the glorious Revolution." [10]

Nevertheless, Cooper demanded that France relinquish all claims to Canada. "France must give the most unequivocal assurances that she means not to resume the government of Canada, but to incorporate it with the United States," he advised. "This is her true Interest, and is so agreeable to the Principles and Basis of the alliance, that I have not the least doubt she intends it; and it will only be needful to make known her Intentions in the most explicit manner, at least to us." [11] In the following months, after he started to work for the French, Cooper modified his views, "Should we have Peace on the cession of Independence and the Fishery, Canada, Nova Scotia, and Florida would in time naturally unite with us." [12] Samuel Adams was in no mood to compromise on the fishery, and his friendship with Cooper cooled rapidly after this letter.

Cooper's fondness for Frenchmen increased when the French Fleet was in Boston in 1778. After Cooper and D'Estaing had become close friends, Cooper wrote a long article in defense of D'Estaing's actions at Newport. He based the article on a memorandum received from a Frenchman, probably D'Estaing. Although Cooper did not publish the article in the United States, he sent it to Franklin in 1781 and asked him to have it published in Europe. Cooper explained that he did not publish it in the United States because he feared that it would offend General John Sullivan and incite a public controversy. He requested that Franklin conceal the authorship except from D'Estaing. Franklin arranged to have the article published in the *Leiden Gazette,* but he did not give the French Foreign Office a copy as he usually did with pro-French articles written by Americans.[13] D'Estaing recalled Cooper fondly and once asked William Carmichael to remember him to "his Boston acquaintances & particularly Dr. Cooper." [14]

After Gérard had read Cooper's defense of the French at Newport, he asked Joseph de Valnais to offer Cooper the opportunity to write more often for the benefit of the alliance. Gérard failed to explain to

[10] Cooper to Samuel Adams, Dec. 1, 1778, Adams Papers, NYPL.

[11] Cooper to Franklin, [Jan. 4, 1779?], Franklin Papers, APS, Vol. XIII.

[12] Cooper to Samuel Adams, March 14, 1779, Adams Papers, NYPL.

[13] "Précis de La Campagne de 1778," Cooper Papers; the title of the panegyric is "A Letter from a Gentleman in America to his Friend in France," April, [1779?], Franklin Papers, LC, Vol. II; Cooper to Franklin, Feb. 1, 1781, Franklin Papers, APS, Vol. XXI; Franklin to Cooper, May 25, 1781, Franklin Papers, LC, Vol. IV. There is an article in praise of D'Estaing by Cooper, but a totally different one, in AAE-cp-(EU), Vol. VII; this is an extract from Cooper to Franklin, [Jan. 4, 1779?], Franklin Papers, APS, Vol. XIII. This is the article which inspired Gérard to ask Cooper to work for the French.

[14] Carmichael to Harrison, Oct. 6, 1780, Misc. MSS, WLC.

Vergennes what Cooper could do for the French, but he described him as the best orator in Massachusetts and an influential figure in Whig circles.[15] Although Gérard did not admit it, he hired Cooper in an effort to diminish the influence of Samuel Adams in his home state.

Joseph de Valnois reported on Cooper's activities, identifying him as "our reverend friend." Cooper convinced de Valnais of his devotion to the French, and de Valnais prematurely reported that Cooper had succeeded in destroying Samuel Adams' reputation in the campaign to retain the fishery. After he had obviously failed, Cooper devised another plan to defeat the "obstinate partisans of the fishery," but by this time de Valnais admitted that Cooper could only diminish Adams' influence, not destroy it.[16] Cooper's opposition to Adams did not go unnoticed. James Lovell asked Adams, "Is yr. Name, your Fame still the object of the malice of 'your friend?' " [17]

Luzerne visited Cooper when he arrived in Boston and later sent him some wine. Thanking Luzerne for the gift, Cooper informed him that he was ready to continue his work for the French.

> No one can exceed myself in ardent Wishes for your Health and Happiness, and for the Success of your Negotiations in the Establishment of the great object of that happy Alliance which that wise and generous Monarch whom you represent has entered into with these States, and which I have ever regarded as the Honour and Security of my Country. It will be the Pleasure of my Life in every way within my small Compass of my abilities to promote this object, and to fulfill every Direction respecting this, or any other Matter with which you shall please to favor me.[18]

Luzerne wasted no time putting Cooper to work on an article about Allied harmony at Savannah.[19] Although Luzerne assigned Cooper the task of writing on special events such as Savannah, he seldom asked him to do more than exhort his countrymen to greater efforts to sustain the war. Luzerne requested that Cooper write stories explaining the defeat at Charleston, citing the advantages of having Rochambeau's expeditionary force in the United States, minimizing De Grasse's defeat in the

---

[15] Gérard to Vergennes, Jan. 17, 1779, Meng, ed., *Gérard*, pp. 481–82.

[16] De Valnais to Gérard, Feb. 5, 1779, Holker Papers, Vol. II; de Valnais to Holker, Feb. 23, 1779, *ibid.*, Vol. III; de Valnais to Holker, June 3, July 23, 1779, *ibid.*, Vol. IV.

[17] Lovell to Adams, July 13, 1779, Adams Papers, NYPL.

[18] Cooper to Luzerne, Oct. 6, 1779, Cooper Papers.

[19] Luzerne to Cooper, Nov. 1, 1779, *ibid.; Connecticut Courant*, Nov. 30, 1779, carried the article.

West Indies in 1782, and lauding the behavior of the French while waiting to embark at Boston in 1782.[20]

Cooper wrote a number of articles in addition to those assigned to
him. He explained to Luzerne that he signed one letter "A Farmer," because the farmer "has the chief influence in our public affairs and [farm-
ers] attend particularly to [letters which] appear to come from their
own Order." After Benedict Arnold defected to the British, Cooper
wrote that Arnold was guilty of treason, avarice, barbarity, speculation,
and robbery, and thus qualified to be a general in the British Army.[21]

Cooper made sure that Franklin was not slighted in the press. He
persuaded some New England papers to correct themselves after they
attributed a new French subsidy to John Laurens' mission to France in
1781 instead of to Franklin.[22] After the peace treaty, Cooper informed
Franklin that John Adams was turning the people against the French
and taking personal credit for the advantageous terms. Franklin supplied
the French with a copy of the letter.[23]

Cooper, who had always devoted as much attention to his high social standing as to the pulpit, provided a Boston variant of a Parisian
salon for visiting French officers. He impressed many officers with his
devotion to the alliance, but Vergennes, who knew Cooper was working
for Luzerne, must have smiled when Lafayette wrote, "We must especially put Doctor Cooper at the head of the list of our Friends." [24]
Baron Von Closen thought highly of Cooper, and the Marquis de
Chastellux was even more entranced. He wrote that Cooper was "a man
justly celebrated, and no less distinguished by the graces of his mind and
the amenity of his character, than by his uncommon eloquence and patriotic zeal." Chastellux continued in a perhaps deliberately ambiguous
passage, "Among the Americans attached by political interest to France
none has displayed a more marked attention to the French, and none
has received from Nature a character more analogous to theirs." [25]
Other French officers were less impressed. Claude Blanchard, compli-

[20] Cooper to Luzerne, June 21, Aug. 17, 1780, June 13, 1782, Cooper Papers;
Luzerne to Vergennes, Nov. 11, 1782, AAE-cp-(EU), Vol. XXII. Some of the
Cooper articles are in *Independent Chronicle,* Aug. 17, 1780; *Packet,* June 13,
1782.

[21] Cooper to Luzerne, Aug. 3, Dec. 8, 1780, Cooper Papers; *Independent Chronicle,* Aug. 3, 1780; *Pennsylvania Journal* (Philadelphia), Dec. 27, 1780.

[22] Franklin to Cooper, May 25, 1781, Franklin Papers, LC, Vol. IV; the cor-
rection is in *Newport Mercury,* Sept. 8, 1781.

[23] "Extract of Dr. Cooper to B. Franklin," May 5, 1783, AAE-cp-(EU), Vol.
XXIV.

[24] Lafayette to Vergennes, May 1, 1780, *ibid.,* Vol. XII.

[25] Evelyn Acomb, ed., *The Revolutionary Journal of Baron Ludwig Von Closen,
1780–1783* (Chapel Hill, 1958), pp. 65, 66; Rice, ed., *Travels in North America
in the Years 1780, 1781, and 1782 by the Marquis de Chastellux,* Vol. II, p. 505.

mentary at first, later called Cooper "a pompous protestant clergyman." Vicomte de Rochambeau, son of Count de Rochambeau, alleged that Cooper told Frenchmen only what they desired him to say.[26]

The attention Cooper received from the French was duly noted by William Gordon, who warned John Adams to "guard what you write to Dr. ——— for he is Franklified & Frenchified." Earlier in the letter Gordon commented, "Silver-Tongue Sam is the pink of complaisance to the French Admirals, Generals, & Officers. You would never have believed him to have been the author of a Sermon upon the Conquest of Canada, & preacher of such contents: but *tempora mutantur*." [27]

Despite discontent with Cooper in some Massachusetts circles, Luzerne came to depend on him, and formed a high opinion of Cooper's ability to handle delicate situations such as the occasional fights between French and American sailors.[28] After Cooper's death, Luzerne wrote Vergennes that Cooper "was an excellent citizen, a man with a great deal of merit and adroitness," who had "served his country well." [29] Luzerne's understanding of American loyalty allowed him to overlook the fact that Cooper had informed him of the contents of letters from Arthur Lee and John Adams to Samuel Adams.[30]

Another agent was Hugh Henry Brackenridge. Two unidentified members of Congress suggested Brackenridge to Gérard and recruited him to work for the French. Writing under the pseudonyms of "The Honest Politician," "Anti-Anglican," and "American," Brackenridge worked for the French from April, 1779, to April, 1781, when he moved to Pittsburgh to start a law career.[31]

A Princeton graduate of 1771, Brackenridge was a Presbyterian minister and attorney as well as a novice editor in Philadelphia. In 1779 he edited the *United States Magazine*. The magazine, issued bimonthly, collapsed after only one year of publication. Brackenridge did not print any of the articles he had written for the French in the magazine, but probably used money from the French to finance it.[32]

[26] Thomas Balch, ed., *Journal of Claude Blanchard, 1780–1783* (Albany, 1876), pp. 50, 182; Jean Edmond Wheelen, ed., *Rochambeau Father and Son,* translated by Lawrence Lee (New York, 1936), pp. 266–68.

[27] Gordon to Adams, Sept. 7 & 19, [1782], Adams Papers, R. 361.

[28] Luzerne to Vergennes, Jan. 26, 1781, AAE-cp-(EU), Vol. XV; an account of the affair is in Tudor to John Adams, Feb. 5, 1781, Adams Papers, R. 354.

[29] Luzerne to Vergennes, March 30, 1784, Luzerne Papers.

[30] Cooper to Luzerne, May 1, 1780, Cooper Papers.

[31] Gérard to Vergennes, May 29, 1779, Meng, ed., *Gérard,* pp. 689–91; Luzerne to Vergennes, April 1, 1780; April 1, 1781, Luzerne Papers. Claude Newlin, *The Life and Writings of Hugh Henry Brackenridge* (Princeton, 1932), does not cover Brackenridge's work for the French.

[32] *United States Magazine,* Vol. I, WLC; Lyon N. Richardson in *A History of*

Although Gérard checked the contents of each article before publication, Brackenridge selected the themes for "The Honest Politician." In his first five articles, "The Honest Politician" argued for the permanent separation of the United States from Great Britain, primarily stressing the commercial advantages of independence. In the following ten articles Brackenridge emphasized the advantages of the alliance with France. France, he contended, had no territorial aspirations in North America and had actually neglected her own self-interest in the West Indies by sending D'Estaing to aid the United States in 1778. Brackenridge noted that although the Allied forces failed at Newport, the arrival of the French Fleet forced Great Britain to evacuate Philadelphia.[33]

Luzerne assumed direction of "The Honest Politician" starting with number fifteen, which summarized Gérard's role in drafting the treaty of alliance.[34] Brackenridge then began writing articles on the role of France in maintaining a European balance of power during the previous two centuries. France, he wrote, had waged only defensive wars, while Great Britain and her allies had repeatedly tried to dominate Europe and upset the precarious balance of power. Brackenridge cited France's role in supporting small Protestant countries in the Treaty of Westphalia and in tacitly assuring Holland her independence in the Treaty of Munster. The wars of the Spanish and Austrian successions and the Bourbon alliance were explained as French efforts to thwart the insatiable ambitions of Great Britain. Rarely did the Loyalist press ever attack the work of what, unknown to it, were French agents, but in this case the *Royal Gazette* challenged Brackenridge's interpretation of Louis XIV and his renunciation of the Spanish throne in the seventeenth century in an article entitled, "A curious Instance of French Perfidy." [35]

Luzerne asked Brackenridge to interrupt his historical analysis to

---

Early American Magazines (New York, 1931), pp. 202–203, notes that a softening in Brackenridge's attitude toward the French is apparent in the magazine.

[33] "The Honest Politician" appeared in the *Pennsylvania Gazette* in 29 articles on May 26, June 9, 16, 23, 30, Aug. 11, 18, Oct. 6, 13, 20, 27, Nov. 3, 10, Dec. 1, 15, 22, 1779, Jan. 5, 12, 26 (two), Feb. 2, 16, 23, May 10, 24, 1780. The series ended March 10, 1780, in the *Maryland Gazette,* which corresponds with the time that paper started publishing "Anti-Anglican" in 1780, beginning with March 17, 24, 31, April 7, 14 (two), 21 (two), July 14, 21, 28, Aug. 11, Sept. 8, 1780. I have not found any article in Philadelphia papers which could reasonably be attributed to Brackenridge writing under the pseudonym of "American." However, "The Honest Politician" series was interrupted when the "Americanus" articles appeared. According to Gérard, Brackenridge worked with two men in Congress, perhaps Chase and Langworthy, and he may well have contributed articles in the "Americanus" controversy in Gérard's defense.

[34] *Pennsylvania Gazette,* Oct. 27, 1779.

[35] *Royal Gazette, Supplement,* Nov. 10, 1779.

explain the contributions of D'Estaing at Savannah.[36] Brackenridge responded by writing that D'Estaing had contributed, even in failure, to the Allied cause by upsetting British planning for the year and forcing the British to evacuate Newport.[37] He then returned to his distorted description of the British balance of power until completing "The Honest Politician" in March, 1780.

Brackenridge, now writing under the pseudonym "Anti-Anglican," again emphasized the need for American independence. The "Anti-Anglican" articles contained denunciations of Great Britain intermixed with pleas for the states to support the defense of Charleston, to raise taxes and to allow Congress revenue power, and to fill quotas for the critical 1780 campaign. Although Brackenridge emphasized the need to pay taxes and strengthen financial support for the war, Luzerne considered these articles futile.[38] Brackenridge then wrote a number of articles urging the incipient Catholic protest movement in Ireland to join the American struggle against British tyranny, but the imminent defeat at Charleston caused him to return to the theme of supporting the campaign in the South.[39]

Luzerne appreciated Brackenridge's work and believed that it aided the alliance. When Brackenridge left Philadelphia for Pittsburgh, Luzerne wrote, "I hope to replace him with some other person to fill in equally well the outlines I have furnished him." [40] Herein lay the weakness of the productive but shallow Brackenridge; although he wrote what was requested, his articles lacked the revolutionary fervor often seen in the Patriot press. His essays presented gentlemanly instruction on the history of European rivalries and the debt owed to France for her intervention. The topics were timely and the arguments sometimes well founded, but the articles must have seemed inconsequential to many Americans. A sure indication of this is the infrequency with which other papers reprinted Brackenridge's essays in comparison to Cooper's, not to mention those by the influential Thomas Paine.

In addition to Brackenridge and Cooper, Paine was the only other known author who wrote for the French. As the most widely read author during the Revolution, he held a different position from the other two agents. After Paine was dismissed, at Gérard's insistence, as secretary to the Committee on Foreign Affairs, Gérard offered him a job and

[36] Luzerne to Vergennes, Nov. 30, 1779, AAE-cp-(EU), Vol. X.

[37] *Pennsylvania Gazette,* Nov. 10, Dec. 1, 15, 22, 1779.

[38] Luzerne to Vergennes, Nov. 3, 1780, AAE-cp-(EU), Vol. XIV.

[39] Luzerne to Vergennes, Aug. 14, 1780, *ibid.,* Vol. XIII; *Maryland Gazette,* July 14, 21, Aug. 11, 1780. For the discontent in Ireland, see Godechot, *France and the Atlantic Revolution,* pp. 46–48.

[40] Luzerne to Vergennes, April 1, 1781, Luzerne Papers.

reported that Paine had accepted the offer.[41] Paine, however, denied accepting the offer, and Gérard later stated that Paine was not working for the French.[42]

After Luzerne assumed office, he reported that he was deliberately keeping Paine at a distance, but noted that he would be valuable in writing articles or a history of the Revolution. Barbé-Marbois wrote that Paine was seeking to gain Luzerne's confidence and submitted all his work to Luzerne before publication.[43] Apparently Paine's careful cultivation of Luzerne was successful, because in December, 1781, Luzerne asked him to "refute in an indirect manner the public letters [published in the Loyalist press] under the name of Mr. Deane." [44] Paine, fired from his post in 1779—at the insistence of Gérard—for his attacks on Silas Deane, was asked by Luzerne in 1781 to counter the charges of the apostate Deane.

Paine continued to write for Luzerne throughout 1782, opposing the Carleton-Digby peace offer, urging a 5 per cent impost, and refuting the writings of Abbé Raynal.[45] Paine's new restraint, and particularly his advocacy of the impost, did not go unnoticed by the Loyalist press.

[41] Gérard to Vergennes, Jan. 17, 1779, Meng, ed., *Gérard*, pp. 480–81.

[42] Paine to Committee of Continental Congress, [Oct., 1783], Philip Foner, ed., *The Complete Writings of Thomas Paine* (New York, 1945), Vol. II, p. 1230; Gérard to Vergennes, May 29, 1779, Meng, ed., *Gérard*, pp. 690–91.

[43] Luzerne to Vergennes, Dec. 16, 1780, AAE-cp-(EU), Vol. XIV; Barbé-Marbois to Vergennes, April 7, 1782, *ibid.,* Vol. XXII.

[44] Luzerne to Vergennes, Dec. 14, 1781, *ibid.,* Vol. XIX. There is some confusion as to whether Paine was paid for his articles attacking Deane or whether this task represented Luzerne's last test of Paine's reliability. Luzerne's personal copy of this dispatch asserts that he hired Paine, but in the official dispatch it is unclear. Luzerne did not record any expenses for Paine for this period in his extraordinary expense account, where all other payments to American agents were listed. (Luzerne to Vergennes, Dec. 14, 1781; Luzerne to Vergennes, Dec. 30, 1781, Luzerne Papers.) However, Paine did accept money from Luzerne in 1782 and 1783 for his articles. (Luzerne to Vergennes, Oct. 1, 1782; Luzerne to Vergennes, Jan. 1, 1784, *ibid.*) A payment of fifty guineas to Paine is mentioned in the regular dispatches. (Luzerne to Vergennes, Aug. 27, 1782, AAE-cp-(EU), Vol. XXIII.) Probably this is an additional payment, because Luzerne mentioned it in a regular dispatch and did not convert it into French currency in his extraordinary expense account of Oct. 1, 1782, as he customarily did for secret expenses. In the Aug. 27, 1782, regular dispatch, Luzerne claimed that this was the first time he had given any money to Paine, which probably means on a systematic basis. Luzerne had stated in a regular dispatch in May that he had hired Paine. (Luzerne to Vergennes, May 14, 1782, *ibid.,* Vol. XXIII.)

[45] *Ibid.;* Luzerne to Vergennes, Aug. 27, 1782, *ibid.* Paine's writings which probably were submitted to Luzerne included the following: "To the Public," March 13, 1782; "On the Present State of the News," May 22, 1782; "A Supernumerary Crisis to Lord Carleton," May 31, 1782; "Letter to Abbé Raynal," 1782; "Six Letters to Rhode Island," 1782, all in Foner, ed., *Paine,* Vol. I, pp. 186–88, 208–17, 217–21, 221–63, 333–66.

The condescension of the French Minister and his hirelings, is not however very grateful to the *majesty of the people,* and especially in the Eastern Quarter of the Colonies, where the *frenchified* politics of *Master Payne,* begin to peep through the threadbare disguise they have hitherto worn, under the name of *Common Sense.*[46]

At the same time that he received a subsidy from the French, Paine also received a Secret Service allowance from the American government, apparently for the same articles. Joseph Reed observed, "Your old Acquaintance Paine is a hireling Writer pensioned at £300 p[er] ann[um] payable by genl. Washington out of the Secret Service money. In short the Changes of this nature have been so many, and so great that they would greatly surprize you." [47] Reed's statement was perhaps uncharitable, but it seems clear that the talents of the most popular writer in the United States were for sale, and Luzerne readily purchased his services for France.

Each person who worked for the French did so for purely personal reasons. Of the three, Cooper demonstrated the greatest commitment to the French. All three were active Patriots long before the alliance, so no one had to change his loyalties drastically. Cooper and Paine were able to convince themselves that French and American interests were identical, although Paine did not believe this until 1781. They probably did not conceive of their actions as being disloyal to the United States, but they were both very discreet about accepting money from the French. Paine believed that authors like himself were entitled to a subsidy by the government. He never indicated that he felt any twinges of conscience in accepting Secret Service money from both the United States and France for his work in 1782. Significantly, Paine admitted taking money from Washington, Robert Morris, and Robert R Livingston, but did not reveal that he received any aid from the French.

Cooper went far beyond the other agents in his work for the French. He admitted his devotion to the French, but not his employment, to all of his regular correspondents. Yet fondness for France cannot explain his disclosure to the French of the contents of Arthur Lee's and John Adams' letters. As William Gordon pointed out, Cooper suffered from a lack of moderation. When Cooper attacked Catholicism in the Dudleian lecture, he advocated taking Canada by force if necessary. When he decided that French and American interests were identical and Amer-

---

[46] *Royal Gazette,* May 29, 1782, italics in original.
[47] Reed to Greene, March 14, 1783, Reed Papers, Vol. X. Paine did not deny his subsidy from Washington. Paine to Committee of Continental Congress, [Oct., 1783], Foner, ed., *Paine,* Vol. II, pp. 1236–37.

ican success depended on French aid, he was willing to betray some of his oldest political associates to assist French policy. Cooper's temperament, not gold, led him to work for the French. The differences between Cooper and the Adamses were actually small, but Cooper believed them to be absolute.

The French Ministers enjoyed easy access to the press whenever they wanted a particular article published. Gérard reported a number of times that a Philadelphia paper had carried an item at his urging.[48] Luzerne hired an unknown translator to prepare articles for the press and once explained this expense as "a sum I annually pay to a Translator of French pieces which I have had inserted in the public papers." [49] Luzerne took care to make it appear that all the letters or articles he wanted printed did not originate in Philadelphia. On one occasion he instructed Cooper to write on a particular topic and then had the article carried in a Philadelphia paper as a reprint from Boston.[50] Another time Luzerne directed Cooper to translate an article from French, and at the same time had his translator in Philadelphia prepare a second copy for southern consumption. The articles appeared in Philadelphia and Boston within a day of each other.[51]

The facility with which the French published stories depended on the personal status of the Americans cooperating with them. Luzerne mentioned that one unidentified member of Congress submitted his writing for prior approval before it was published.[52] A member of Congress was the most suitable person to submit an article to the press. James Madison, for example, often cooperated in planting French-inspired articles in the papers.

> The letter on the first page of the Gazette [sic, Packet] of this morning was written by Mr. Marbois. In an evening of promiscuous conversation I suggested to him my opinion that the insidiousness of the British Court, and the good faith of my ally, displayed in the late abortive attempt of the former to seduce the latter, might with advantage be made known in some form or other to the public at large. He said he would think of the matter, and the next day sent me the letter in question, with a request that I would revise and translate it for the press, the latter of which was

[48] Gérard to Vergennes, Sept. 20–21, 1778; Jan. 21, 1779; March 18, 1779, Meng, ed., *Gérard*, pp. 304–305, 389–90, 586–87.

[49] Luzerne to Vergennes, April 1, 1783, Luzerne Papers.

[50] *Packet*, Nov. 27, 1781.

[51] Luzerne to Cooper, July 30, 1780; Cooper to Luzerne, Aug. 17, 1780, Cooper Papers; *Independent Chronicle*, Aug. 17, 1780; *Pennsylvania Gazette*, Aug. 16, 1780.

[52] Luzerne to Vergennes, Aug. 30, 1780, AAE-cp-(EU), Vol. XIII.

done. I mention this that you may duly appreciate the facts and sentiments contained in this publication.[53]

In addition to having their own agents and ready assistance in securing publication for articles, the French also benefited from occasional unpaid writers. The productivity of the unpaid writers was quite low in comparison with that of the agents, but when favorable articles by unpaid writers appeared, the French Ministers exploited them fully; they tried to have them reprinted as often as possible and sent copies to Vergennes.[54] These writers, unlike the agents, addressed themselves to the question of religion and the alliance. Benajmin Rush and John Adams attacked the belief that a Protestant country should not have an alliance with a Catholic monarchy.

The individualistic Rush refused to accept money for his articles, and John Adams was never offered payment for his work.[55] Rush, using the pseudonym "Leonidas," wrote many articles advocating support for the alliance. Gérard reported that he hoped to convince Rush to publish more articles, calling him a "great schemer" for the alliance.[56] Luzerne thought so highly of his work that he arranged to have most of his articles reprinted in 1782.[57] Rush was apparently impelled to defend the alliance, with no encouragement from the French, when his old adversary Joseph Galloway accused Americans of selling their birthrights:

> Speaking of the strange alliance with France, I am naturally led to express my astonishment, at the supineness, the shameful negligence, with which the people of America have suffered themselves, without their consent or approbation, to be linked, bound,

---

[53] Madison to Randolph, June 11, 1782, *LMCC*, Vol. VI, p. 370.

[54] *Packet,* March 31, 1781, the article by "Janus"; Luzerne sent this to Vergennes, but possibly it was Brackenridge's last article for the French. Luzerne to Vergennes, March 31, 1781, AAE-cp-(EU), Vol. XVI; Luzerne to Vergennes, April 1, 1781, Luzerne Papers.

[55] On Rush, see O'Donnell, *Luzerne,* pp. 58n–59n, who surmises that Rush was offered money but refused to accept it; also Luzerne to Vergennes, Jan. 4, 1780, Luzerne Papers. One example of Adams' work was an extract from Adams to Genêt, May 17, 1780, Wharton, ed., *Diplomatic Correspondence,* Vol. II, pp. 685–87. In addition to being printed in Europe, it was published in *Newport Mercury,* April 21, 1781; and *Packet,* March 27, 1781.

[56] Gérard to Vergennes, Aug. 3, 1778; July 6, 1779, Meng, ed., *Gérard,* pp. 196–97, 749–50.

[57] Some "Leonidas" articles are in *Packet,* July 3 and Aug. 24, 1779; *Pennsylvania Journal,* May 29, June 19, July 3, 10, 17, 31, and Aug. 14, 1782. For the authorship of the articles, see Rush to John Adams, Oct. 12, 1779, Butterfield, ed., *Letters of Benjamin Rush,* Vol. I, pp. 240–41; Rush to Greene, Sept. 16, 1782, *ibid.,* Vol. I, pp. 285–86. For Luzerne reprinting Rush's articles, see Luzerne to Vergennes, Aug. 9, 1782, AAE-cp-(EU), Vol. XXII.

chained to a nation, which from souls, they abhor! a nation, which, in manners, customs, policy, religion, every thing differs from America, as light from darkness.[58]

Rush tried to counter Galloway's argument with the rather original contention that the alliance with France gave the United States a unique opportunity to develop her own national character. "The wisest civilians and legislators lay it down as a maxim, that when nations form alliances with each other," Rush stated, "they should be with those that are as *unlike* themselves as possible in religion, laws, manners, and government." [59] Later in the article Rush returned to the question of religion.

> We have nothing to fear for *our* religion, laws, manners, and government from our alliance with the Court of France, so as we have been educated in prejudices against the religion, laws, and government of France, the most intimate union with that Court cannot alter our opinion of them. Even their manners (so wholly unlike our own) will never find a footing among us, as to be dangerous to the simple manners of our republics.
>
> You speak in your letter with some dread of the consequences to Protestantism from our alliance with France. But what have we to fear from an alliance *only* with a Catholic power? a power too which has lately distinguished itself for its moderation towards Protestants. How infinitely better is our situation in this equal *alliance* than in a mean *dependence* upon a protestant power that has lately distinguished itself by *establishing* the Popish religion throughout a province the largest in America.[60]

Rush cooperated closely with Gérard and Luzerne, but still distinguished between the different interests of France and the United States. He remained committed to the alliance while advocating a separate policy and dignity for the United States.[61] Unfortunately, some of his countrymen lost sight of these distinctions. When France and the United States had policy conflicts in 1781 and 1782, many Americans saw no

---

[58] [Joseph Galloway], *A Letter to the People of America* (New York, 1778), pp. 22–23.

[59] *Packet*, Aug. 1, 1778, signed "Gallo-Americanus." Rush is not generally identified as the author of this article, but I am quite sure that he wrote it. The evidence from Gérard clearly indicates this, and in his "Leonidas" letter of Aug. 24, 1779, in the *Packet*, Rush makes the same points and some of the passages are identical in wording. Rush emphasized simplicity and republicanism in his public and private letters. Both letters use the same wording on these two points. Italics in original.

[60] *Ibid.*, Aug. 1, 1778, italics in original.

[61] Rush to John Adams, Jan. 21, 1781, Butterfield, ed., *Rush*, Vol. I, pp. 260–61.

alternative but to adhere to the French position. Rush and Adams, at least, felt no contradiction between backing the alliance and refusing to grant France all her requests.

The French Ministers exploited the blurring of the distinction between common and separate interests to French advantage in the press. The French had no difficulty either in hiring writers or in achieving publication of articles they wanted available to the public. Moreover, Paine, even before his employment, and an unknown number of Congressmen, considered it to be in the best interest of the alliance to submit articles to Luzerne prior to publication.

Obviously no Patriot publisher would intentionally offend the French, but voluntary cooperation gradually made Luzerne the most influential figure in controlling news published about France in the American press.[62] The number of articles by paid writers cannot be determined precisely, but it was very substantial. In one six-month period Cooper contributed at least twelve pieces to the Boston papers. Brackenridge published a minimum of forty-two articles and probably more in an eighteen-month period. If these two examples are indicative of the whole period, and there is no reason not to consider this the case, then the paid French agents contributed a sizable percentage of the articles on France and foreign policy after 1779. The primary source of news for a majority of the public was the Patriot press, and they read, much of the time, what the French Minister wanted them to read.

---

[62] But there were limits to what he could accomplish. In Massachusetts demands for all of Canada and of course the fishery continued to be published throughout 1782 and 1783. See *Salem Gazette,* Nov. 21, Dec. 26, 1782, Jan. 2, 9, 1783.

X. French Military Aid, 1780–1782

At the close of the campaign of 1779, Americans were frustrated and depressed about the prospects for independence. They had finished their fifth exhausting campaign of the war and the second under the alliance, with victory apparently farther away than at the end of 1777. After the 1779 campaign Great Britain changed her strategy, and Sir Henry Clinton headed south to lay siege to Charleston. Although the Americans had achieved a minor victory when Anthony Wayne captured Stony Point, the failure to regain Savannah left North and South Carolina vulnerable to invasion.

Great Britain, on the other hand, had gained no allies, and Spain had joined the United States and France. But the Spanish entrance meant little, because her resources were concentrated on retaking Gibraltar; even the minimal efforts of Spain in North America diminished the chances for the coveted western lands and the Floridas. And one southern observer speculated, "Spain's declaration against Britain may as you Conjecture prolong the war." [1]

American attitudes toward the alliance had grown jaded as the vision of victory became more distant. Although writing ten years later, David Ramsay accurately expressed the gloomy outlook of early 1780:

> The flattering prospects inspired by the alliance with France in 1778 banished all fears of success of the revolution, but the failure of every scheme of co-operation produced a despondency of mind unfavourable to great exertions. Instead of driving the British out of the country, as the Americans vainly presumed, the campaigns of 1778 and 1779 terminated without any direct advantage from the French fleet sent to their aid. Expecting too much from their allies, and then failing in these expectations, they were less prepared to prosecute the war from their own resources

[1] Harnett to Burke, Oct. 9, 1779, Burke Papers, SHC. Although this chapter is not concerned with the total military situation from 1780–1782, several general accounts are valuable. For the over-all military picture, see Theodore Thayer, *Nathanael Greene* (New York, 1960), pp. 282–420; for the situation in Virginia before Yorktown, see Louis R. Gottschalk, *Lafayette and the Close of the American Revolution* (Chicago, 1942), pp. 189–306. Washington was the only military leader who had extensive contacts with the French. Freeman, *Washington,* Vol. V, pp. 223–427.

than they would have been had D'Estaing not touched on their coast.[2]

The desperate military situation combined with a catastrophic currency deterioration impelled many leaders to turn to France for provision of the men and material essential to victory. The alliance changed in 1778 from a relation of partnership, although assuredly not on an equal basis, to one of dependence by 1780. The moderate demand for a quick end to the war gained converts, especially in the South, as Americans increasingly believed the alliance crucial to independence. The growing reliance on France was accepted and eagerly sought by many. Alexander Hamilton concluded in 1780 that his "countrymen have all the folly of the ass and all the passiveness of the sheep in their compositions. They are determined not to be free and they can neither be frightened, discouraged nor persuaded to change their resolution. If we are saved France and Spain must save us." [3]

The more optimistic Americans hoped that France would send D'Estaing or De Grasse from the West Indies to operate off the American coast. Lafayette, however, arriving from France after the proposed invasion of Great Britain had failed to take place, reported the unexpected news of the impending arrival of a French fleet with fifteen thousand soldiers to operate in the American theater permanently. Appointed liaison officer between the French and Americans, Lafayette carried the news to Washington, who wrote to Luzerne via Lafayette, "He announces a fresh and striking instance of the friendship of your Court and which cannot fail to contribute greatly to perpetuate the gratitude of this country." [4]

The magnitude of French aid caught Americans by surprise. They had never discussed publicly whether France should send an army to the United States, although Luzerne had asked Washington if he had any objections to it almost a year before.[5] Vergennes did not indicate that he had consulted any Americans about sending troops, but he had undoubtedly mentioned it to Franklin. "The King has decided to send a squadron with a troop corps to North America," Vergennes informed Luzerne, requesting that he tell only Washington, the President of Con-

[2] David Ramsay, *The History of the American Revolution* (London, 1793), Vol. II, p. 124.

[3] Hamilton to John Laurens, June 30, 1780, Syrett, ed., *Hamilton,* Vol. II, pp. 347–48.

[4] Washington to Luzerne, May 11, 1780, Fitzpatrick, ed., *Washington,* Vol. XVIII, p. 348.

[5] "Substance of a Conference between Chevalier De La Luzerne and General Washington," Sept. 16, 1779, *ibid.,* Vol. XVI, p. 298.

gress, and patriots who had discretion.[6] Luzerne reported that he had difficulty convincing members of Congress that the troops were not being sent to conquer Canada for France, but concluded that "Most of the people from these states desire nothing more intensely than the arrival of a French squadron." [7]

Members of Congress were reserved in their response to news of the French troops, since they probably wanted to see the reaction of the public before committing themselves. Although urgently needed, a French army in America would, they realized, signify a major change in tactics; no one could predict how the public might react to having foreign troops in their midst. Philip Schuyler, for one, had no fears about the consequences of a French army in the United States. "The [dispatches] evince the most decided determination on the part of France to Support us thro the Contest," he wrote, "and an event will soon take place which will announce to all Europe and America that his most Christian Majesty will not confine himself to mere professions of amity to us or to pecuniary aids." [8] Although Schuyler was one of the few to greet the news with enthusiasm, no one voiced any dissent. The newspapers carried the news almost routinely, perhaps waiting for public reaction: "We are happy in being able to inform the Publick from the best Authority, that a French fleet, with a large body of troops, are hourly expected on the American coast." [9] The imminent defeat at Charleston forestalled second thoughts about the inherent danger of having French soldiers on American soil, or the increased dependence on France accelerated by such an action.

The French Fleet under Chevalier de Ternay and the troops commanded by Count de Rochambeau headed for Newport, after learning en route that the fall of Charleston had eliminated the possibility of a base in the Southern States. The fleet arrived off Newport on July 11, and Rochambeau went ashore with a small party the following day. Rochambeau was disappointed with the reception at Newport; he complained that no one was on the streets and no official came to greet him. Luzerne reported that Newport citizens were cold in their response until they learned that Rochambeau led only the first part of a larger body of troops to be sent.[10]

---

[6] Vergennes to Luzerne, Feb. 5, 1780, AAE-cp-(EU), Vol. XI.

[7] Luzerne to Vergennes, May 20, 1780, *ibid.,* Vol. XII.

[8] Schuyler to Clinton, May 15, 1780, *LMCC,* Vol. V, p. 142. James Bowdoin also welcomed the news with no reservations. Bowdoin to Franklin, May 1, 1780, Franklin Papers, APS, Vol. XV.

[9] *New Jersey Gazette,* May 24, 1780.

[10] Rochambeau to Montbarey, July 16, 1780, Rochambeau Papers, Vol. VII; Luzerne to Vergennes, July 23, 1780, AAE-cp-(EU), Vol. XIII.

Newport, having recently had experience with an occupation army, was probably not eager to welcome a large French force. Newport officials had no advance knowledge of when the fleet would arrive or whether the French would stay at Newport. After receiving word from Rochambeau, the city fathers tried to make amends for their unintentional error of the previous day. "The Bell rang at New[por]t till after Midnight & the Even[in]g of the 12th Newp[or]t illuminated, the Whigs put 13 Lights in the Windows [,] the Tories or doubtfuls 4 or 6," Ezra Stiles recorded in his diary, continuing, "The Quakers did not chuse their lights sh[oul]d shine before men, & their Windows were broken—a fine subject of Friends Meeting of Sufferings." [11] The General Assembly of Rhode Island honored the French by moving its session from Providence to Newport.[12]

General William Heath greeted Rochambeau at Newport and assured him of American cooperation. Heath quickly called up the militia of the New England states and assigned them to protect the French from overland invasions until the French forces were entrenched. He also requested that local farmers bring their fresh produce to Newport to sell to the French. He asked Rochambeau to pay the farmers in paper currency rather than gold to prevent further depreciation of the Continental currency, to which Rochambeau gladly agreed.[13]

The politeness of the French officers overwhelmed the New Englanders. Heath was more reserved than most when he wrote, "I was always fond of our allies, but I assure you I never was more pleased than with the officers now here." A merchant observed, "The French officers are the most civilized men I ever met. They are temperate, prudent, & extremely attentive to duty. I did not expect they would have so few vices." William Channing seemed surprised that the French looked like normal human beings, "Neither Officers nor men are the effeminate Beings we were heretofore taught to believe them. They are as large & as likely men as can be produced by any nation." [14]

Although favorably impressed by the officer corps, the public accepted the arrival of the French Army with reserve and little comment. Despite the bleak situation of 1780, Americans had become cautious in

[11] Franklin B. Dexter, ed., *The Literary Diary of Ezra Stiles* (New York, 1901), Vol. II, p. 454, July 31, 1780.

[12] *Providence Gazette,* July 15, 1780.

[13] Heath to Washington, July 12, 1780, Heath Papers, Vol. XVI. The request for foodstuffs is in the *Providence Gazette,* July 15, 1780.

[14] Heath to Bowdoin, July 13, 1780, Heath Papers, Vol. XVI; Flint to Wadsworth, July 21, 1780, Wadsworth Papers; Channing to Stiles, Aug. 6, 1780, Dexter, ed., *Diary of Ezra Stiles,* Vol. II, pp. 458–59. The best account of the French at Newport is Mary E. Loughrey, *France and Rhode Island, 1686–1800* (New York, 1944), pp. 24–35, 47–52, 121–37.

what they expected from the French military. Rochambeau and his army were not greeted enthusiastically by the public until the Yorktown campaign. Again, hostility to Great Britain, not trust in France, determined American reactions. A Philadelphian recorded his thoughts in his diary, revealing how distant were his fears of Catholicism and French domination in comparison to the omnipresent danger of Great Britain:

> French Fleet arrived for Certain, may the great and Eternal Jehovah grant that it may be for the best good of these United States for the defeating of the designs of our Cruel Enemies who Thirst for Blood who burn and destroy our defenseless Country Ravish our Virgins and Murder the Innocent. O Lord look down and Judge.[15]

American hopes for an Allied offensive vanished when Admiral Graves joined the British squadron at New York and fifteen British ships appeared off Newport on July 22. Joseph de Valnais prophetically commented that this was "bad news for the operations of this campaign." [16] Fortunately, Clinton did not attack with land forces at once, which enabled Rochambeau to entrench himself around Newport. Washington moved the main army toward New York in a successful feint which drew Clinton and the British Army back into New York. The British, however, had established sea superiority and effectively contained the French in Newport. Offensive operations were hopeless unless the second French division arrived and broke the British stranglehold on Newport. By August the State militia were being dismissed for the year.

The prospect of inactivity disturbed Lafayette. He had matured enough to perceive the political implications of an inactive French Army. Americans, he feared, would suspect the sincerity of the French if they did not fight. He beseeched Rochambeau and De Ternay to launch an assault on New York, but the French commanders declined the advice of their countryman, refusing to move from Newport.[17] Frustrated, Lafayette vented his anger in a letter to Luzerne. Action was politically necessary, he wrote, because Americans worried over the small size of the French force, while the Tories taunted patriots that the French would not send a second division. Lafayette also argued that ac-

---

[15] Diary of George Nelson, July 17, 1780, HSP.

[16] De Valnais to Holker, July 23, 1780, Holker Papers, Vol. XI.

[17] Lafayette to Rochambeau and De Ternay, Aug. 9, 1780; Lafayette to Rochambeau, Aug. 18, 1780, George W. Lafayette, ed., *Mémoires, correspondance et manuscrits du général Lafayette* (Brussels, 1837), Vol. II, pp. 116, 132–33; Rochambeau to Lafayette, Aug. 28, 1780, Arnold Whitridge, *Rochambeau* (New York, 1965), p. 98.

tion was essential to convince Whigs that France was not seeking merely to prolong the war by sending a small defensive force.[18]

Although disappointed, Washington accepted Rochambeau's decision. "The flattering prospect which seemed to be opening to our view in May is vanishing like the Morning Dew." [19] Although many Americans already wondered privately if a second division would ever come, the radical James Warren believed that France had sent the force in an effort to shorten the war.

> The French Fleet and Army are shut in Newport by a Superior British Fleet. A reinforcement has been expected all Summer, it is now time to dismiss all further Expectations of that kind, and satisfy ourselves with Speculation of ill Management of matters somewhere. The Troops and Ships arrived are said to be very fine, and I think if we are disappointed they must be mortifyed. To be reduced to a state of Inaction after crossing the Atlantic with high Expectations must be among the last stages of Mortification to fine officers of high Birth and distinction.[20]

The French officers were disappointed with the strength of the American forces, but did not reveal their opinions to Americans. De Ternay wrote Vergennes that the Revolution was not as far advanced as Europeans believed. In another letter, Ternay complained that American leaders had no plans and without French planning the war would be lost.[21] French officers could not understand why it was difficult to maintain an army if a preponderance of the public supported the Revolution. Luzerne alone pointed out the impossibility of solving the supply problem without foreign loans, even though the public was solidly behind the war.[22]

Rochambeau insisted on a meeting with Washington, who, after much stalling, agreed to a conference at Hartford in the latter part of September. The Americans were wary of the meeting, but Alexander Hamilton, never one to take the defensive in military or political affairs, proposed that Washington suggest that the French were responsible for

---

[18] Lafayette to Luzerne, Aug. 11, 1780, Edmund Burnett and Waldo Leland, eds., "Letters from Lafayette to Luzerne, 1780–1782," *AHR,* Vol. XX (1915), pp. 367–68.

[19] Washington to Samuel Washington, Aug. 31, 1780, Fitzpatrick, ed., *Washington,* Vol. XIX, pp. 482–83.

[20] Warren to John Adams, Oct. 11, 1780, *Warren-Adams Letters,* Vol. I, p. 140.

[21] De Ternay to Vergennes, Sept. 10, 1780, AAE-cp-(EU), Vol. XIII; De Ternay to Vergennes, Oct. 17, 1780, *ibid.,* Vol. XIV.

[22] Luzerne to Vergennes, Aug. 3, 1780, *ibid.,* Vol. XIII.

the inactive campaign. "It is of great importance to us that it would appear we are ready and in condition to act; our allies not," Hamilton argued.[23]

Washington, accepting the substance of Hamilton's strategy, told Rochambeau, "Had the second division of French forces arrived in time, or had the whole come in the 1st instance, the resources of the Country would have poured upon us." [24] Rochambeau was not diverted by such tactics. He quickly established that both sides agreed on the necessity of naval superiority in any operation, and that New York was the primary target. Rochambeau shocked the Americans when he insisted that an attack on New York would require thirty thousand troops. He agreed that France would provide fifteen thousand if the United States furnished the remainder. Washington could give no definite answer on the American quota, thus ending all hopes for definite campaign plans for 1781. On other matters, Washington requested that French troops be sent southward, but Rochambeau explained that he could not separate his land and sea forces. When Washington inquired about a winter offensive against Canada, Rochambeau replied that he could make no commitments until he had talked to Luzerne. Thus the conference concluded without any joint plans for either the winter or summer campaigns of 1781.[25]

Rochambeau and Washington came away from the conference with different feelings. Rochambeau seemed pleased to have met Washington, and indicated satisfaction with the results of the conference. He noted that Americans still believed that the French would be smashed (*écrasés*) because of his small force.[26] He himself remained skeptical that the Americans really had an army, although he believed that they were trying to form one for the upcoming campaign. The basic desire of all Americans, he believed, was to see the men, money, and ships of their "illustrious ally" arrive at Newport.[27]

Washington was disenchanted after the conference. He wrote to Lafayette, "You Must be convinced, from what passed at the interview

[23] "Memo on Proposed conference at Hartford with Rochambeau and Ternay," Syrett, ed., *Hamilton,* Vol. II, p. 392.

[24] "Memo on Conference with Rochambeau," Fitzpatrick, ed., *Washington,* Vol. XX, p. 56.

[25] "Conference at Hartford, Sept. 22, 1780," *ibid.,* Vol. XX, pp. 80–81; another copy is in Rochambeau Papers, Vol. VII, pp. 157–60.

[26] Rochambeau to Montbarey, Nov. 27, 1780, *ibid.,* Vol. VII.

[27] Rochambeau to Montbarey, Dec. 18, 1780, *ibid.,* Vol. VII; the date of this letter is probably in in error, because another copy is in the Archives du Ministère de la Guerre, Correspondance, LC, Vol. MMMDCCXXXVI, dated Oct. 19, 1780, probably the correct date.

at H[artford], that my command of the F[rench] T[roo]ps at R[hode] Is[lan]d stands upon a very limited scale." [28] Washington had reluctantly agreed to try to furnish fifteen thousand troops for the approaching campaign, but he realized that the United States would be fortunate if it could produce a force of ten thousand, so he referred the problem to Congress.[29]

Members of Congress could see no possibility of raising the troops without asking France for another loan. Having called upon Franklin so often, Congress decided to appoint John Laurens special envoy to request the new loan. The selection of an envoy inevitably aroused the remaining radical-moderate antagonisms in Congress. The new appointment implied some dissatisfaction with the moderates' favorite, Franklin, so no radical objected. Thomas McKean, by then drifting loose from his radical moorings and into the moderate bloc, described the prevailing dilemma which most Congressmen foresaw when they appointed Laurens. "The appointment of an Envoy on this occasion seems to imply a want of confidence in our Minister's attention, abilities or something else; however I hope it may not be construed in that light, but rather considered as an evidence of our earnestness in the business." [30] One moderate, Gouverneur Morris, was not so generous, "You desire to know in what quality Lawrence [Laurens] is gone to France. I answer he is gone in Consequence of a Plan to remove Franklin indirectly, a thing which could not for obvious Reasons be accomplished directly." Morris later caught the desperation of Congress at the time of the appointment, "In a word we have sent a young Beggar instead of an old one." [31]

Luzerne wrote Vergennes that, while it would be easier to refuse Laurens than Franklin, the loan was necessary if the American Army was to participate in the approaching campaign. Rochambeau believed that Laurens' mission was too late to be of help in the 1781 campaign.[32] Although Rochambeau was partly correct, Laurens returned with enough gold to enable the United States to pay its most pressing debts during the Yorktown campaign. The supplies, however, did not reach the United States until 1782.

In Paris, Franklin and Vergennes took offense at the Laurens mis-

[28] Washington to Lafayette, Dec. 14, 1780, Fitzpatrick, ed., *Washington*, Vol. XX, pp. 473–74.

[29] Washington to President of Congress, Oct. 11, 1780, *ibid.*, Vol. XX, pp. 161–62.

[30] McKean to John Adams, Dec. 18, 1780, McKean Papers, Vol. I.

[31] Morris to Robert Livingston, Feb. 21, 1781, Livingston Papers, N-YHS, box VI.

[32] Luzerne to Vergennes, Dec. 15, 1780; Dec. 28, 1780, AAE-cp-(EU), Vol. XIV; Rochambeau to Luzerne, Feb. 1, 1781, Rochambeau Papers, Vol. VII.

sion for different reasons. Franklin had already succeeded in negotiating a new loan before Laurens' arrival, so Laurens' primary task became one of choosing supplies and arranging for their dispatch. Franklin was sufficiently offended at the lack of confidence in him shown by Congress that he offered his resignation, which was refused.[33] Vergennes pretended to be offended, but actually he was distressed at a presumed breach in protocol rather than any differences in policy between the Allies. Although he considered Laurens brash, Vergennes thought highly enough of him to recommend that he be appointed Franklin's secretary, a position which Laurens had refused when it was offered to him by Congress in 1779.[34] Luzerne, acting on the instructions of Vergennes, rebuked Laurens for demanding, rather than requesting, supplies from France. Laurens ignored Luzerne's reprimand.[35]

The success of the Laurens mission convinced some moderates that they had been correct in sending him, even if it wounded Vergennes' and Franklin's sensibilities. John Rutledge, whose attitude toward the alliance varied according to the prospects for French aid to regain South Carolina, commented, "I am glad to hear of Colo. John Laurens' Success—it will convince many of what I have often said to you," he wrote the South Carolina delegation in Congress, "that our not having rec[eive]d more powerful Support & effectual Aid, from France, is to be attributed solely, to the want of proper application for it." [36] Rutledge was too engrossed with South Carolina problems to be concerned with the difference between proper application and begging.

Meanwhile, French uneasiness over the reliability of the American Army continued. This uncertainty was aggravated by the mutinies of the New Jersey and Pennsylvania lines in January, 1781. There is no evidence that any of the mutineers were motivated by anti-French feeling, however.[37] Luzerne refused requests from panic-stricken Congressmen that the French Army move to West Point so that Washington could shift his forces southward. He explained to Rochambeau that such a move, made without official permission, would excite jealousies between

[33] Franklin to Cooper, May 25, 1781, Franklin Papers, LC, Vol. IV; Carl Van Doren, *Benjamin Franklin* (3d ed.; New York, 1965), pp. 623–26; Vergennes to Luzerne, March 9, 1781, AAE-cp-(EU), Vol. XV.

[34] Vergennes to Luzerne, Feb. 19, 1781, *ibid.,* Vol. XV. Although Vergennes suggested this before Laurens arrived, he did not withdraw his suggestion after conferring with Laurens.

[35] Luzerne to Vergennes, Sept. 25, 1781, *ibid.,* Vol. XVIII; "The Mission of Col. John Laurens to Europe in 1781," *SCHGM,* Vol. I (1900), pp. 20, 37. John Laurens' papers for his mission are in the Laurens Papers, R. 19.

[36] Rutledge to Delegates in Congress, Oct. 4, 1781, Joseph W. Barnwell, ed., "Letters of John Rutledge," *SCHGM,* Vol. XVIII (1917), p. 160.

[37] Carl Van Doren, *Mutiny in January* (New York, 1943), p. 109.

the two armies.[38] Luzerne wrote Vergennes that Rochambeau was also too short of finances to move his army at this time. The Marquis des Deux-Ponts, in Philadelphia at the request of Luzerne, sent a dispatch with John Laurens to Vergennes reporting that lack of provisions, not disloyalty, caused the mutiny.[39]

The progress of the British forces in the South under Cornwallis, and the detachment under Arnold in Virginia, raised American resentment at the inactivity of the French Army to a fever pitch. The Loyalist press twitted Americans about the role of their ally.

> We hear either General Washington or Green[e], are to go to the Southward to take the Command of an Army to be raised in the Carolinas or Virginia; and that the Rebels in general are much surprized at the Inactivity of their Allies the French, who have done nothing since their Arrival in America, but eat the Provisions designed for the Army under the Command of General Washington.[40]

Thomas Jefferson argued that a campaign against New York was as useless as the repeated and futile assaults on Gibraltar, and he urged Luzerne to use his influence to persuade Rochambeau to send a fleet to the Chesapeake. William Tudor expressed similar dismay at the effort to take Gibraltar when the transfer of a detachment of the combined Spanish and French naval force to America would be "much more conducive to the general Interest of the Alliance." Tudor contended that "France & Spain by acting merely a defensive Part with a View to stifle the Jealousies of their European Neighbors, may protract the War & exhaust the Resources of Great Britain, but America has neither the Patience nor Strength for a Trojan War." [41]

Samuel Huntington, the mild-mannered president of Congress, told Luzerne that French troops should be put in motion to destroy old prejudices against France, and Luzerne believed that Huntington expressed the sentiments of a majority in Congress.[42] Discontent with the French reached the highest pitch in Virginia, which was experiencing large-scale warfare for the first time in the Revolution. Virginians, in-

---

[38] Luzerne to Rochambeau, Jan. 7, 1781, Rochambeau Papers, Vol. XIV.
[39] Luzerne to Vergennes, Jan. 7, 1781; Jan. 11, 1781; Jan. 18, 1781, AAE-cp-(EU), Vol. XV; Deux-Ponts to Vergennes, Jan. 30, 1781, *ibid.,* Vol. XV.
[40] *New York Gazette,* Oct. 23, 1780.
[41] Jefferson to Luzerne, April 12, 1781, Boyd, ed., *Jefferson,* Vol. V, p. 422; Tudor to John Adams, Feb. 5, 1781, Adams Papers, R. 354. John Rutledge also advocated moving the troops of both armies southward, Rutledge to Delegates in Congress, Dec. 8, 1780, Barnwell, ed., "Letters of John Rutledge," p. 48.
[42] Luzerne to Vergennes, Jan. 28, 1781, AAE-cp-(EU), Vol. XV.

stead of blaming themselves for inept planning, vented their hostility against France:

> I live in a Part of the Country remarkable for its Whigism, & Attachment to the Cause of Liberty; and it is with much Concern I find a general Opinion prevailing, that our Allies are spinning out the War, in order to weaken America as well as Great Britain, and thereby leave us, at the End of it, as dependent as possible upon themselves. . . . If our Allies had a superior Fleet here I shou'd have very little Doubt of a favourable Issue to the War; but without it, I fear we are deceiving both them and ourselves, in expecting We shall be able to keep our People much longer firm, in so unequal an Opposition to Great Britain. Wou'd it not be wise & honest to lay this Matter candidly before them; and with decent Firmness, explain how much our mutual Interest requires a Fleet upon the American Coasts, superior to that of our common Enemy? [43]

Rochambeau, undoubtedly at the request of Luzerne, allowed Destouches, who replaced De Ternay after his death in December, 1780, to take fifteen hundred men and two ships of the line to the Chesapeake in the spring of 1781.[44] But Destouches failed to enter the Chesapeake because of a numerically superior British squadron. Virginians were furious at this new example of alleged French inefficiency, which allowed the detested Arnold to sail safely back to New York. "The French do not, as you suppose, bring a single article of military stores for us; nor render us the smallest service by their battle with the English fleet, not having attempted to throw in any succors of land forces," one officer wrote, "but after their action at sea, went safely into the port at Rhode Island, and I suppose there remain, as spectators of very affecting tragedies in these states." [45]

Luzerne noted that Virginians were unhappy over the outcome of the battle, but the incident would probably have been forgotten if the British had not published an intercepted letter from Washington.[46] In the ill-fated letter Washington criticized the French delay in launching

[43] Mason to Virginia Delegates, April 3, 1781, William T. Hutchinson and William Rachal, eds., *The Papers of James Madison* (Chicago, 1962–), Vol. III, pp. 54–55.

[44] Rochambeau to Luzerne, Feb. 24, 1781, Rochambeau Papers, Vol. VII.

[45] Banister to Bland, April, 1781, Charles Campbell, ed., *The Bland Papers* (Petersburg, 1840–1843), Vol. II, p. 65.

[46] Luzerne to Vergennes, March 8, 1781, AAE-cp-(EU), Vol. XV; Washington to Lund Washington, March 28, 1781, Fitzpatrick, ed., *Washington*, Vol. XXI, pp. 385–86. The letter was published in the *Royal Gazette,* April 4, 1781.

the expedition, and suggested that the destruction of Arnold's corps would have been inevitable if the French had acted in time. Washington quickly sought to smooth over the effects of this intemperate and probably inaccurate contention. Rochambeau accepted Washington's clarification of the letter and reported to Ségur that Clinton had caused a "small annoyance" (*tracasserie*) by publishing the letter, but the incident was closed as far as he was concerned.[47]

Washington stretched the truth in making amends to Rochambeau. He was, in fact, embittered by the failure of the expedition. In his letter to Rochambeau, Washington claimed that he had written the published letter to a private person, a relative, and had no copies of what he actually said. Actually Washington wrote four other letters with almost identical wording during the same week. He marked the section "private" in the margin, which was unusual for him.

> How unhappy it is for all our measures, that the adoption of them cannot be in season. Had the French Commrs. at R Island complied (in the first instance) with my request to send the whole Fleet, and a detachm[en]t from their Land force to Virg[ini]a the destruction of Arnold's Corps must have been compleat during the debilitated state of the British Fleet. The undertaking now, is bold and precarious, rendered more so by an unfortunate and to me unaccountable delay of 24 hours in their quitting Newport, after it was said they were ready to Sail; the Wind being as favorable to them and as adverse to the Enemy as Heaven c[oul]d furnish. But it is our true policy to make the most of their assistance without censuring their mistakes therefore it is I communicate this in confidence.[48]

James Lovell wrote his first complimentary words about Washington in years after the publication of the letter, "This does the Genl. great Credit as a private man of Justice." [49]

Rochambeau was beset by many difficulties during his first year in the United States. Although he had specific orders never to break up his forces, his aides criticized this policy because it forced the French to remain inactive while the British under Cornwallis were making spectacu-

[47] Washington to Rochambeau, April 30, 1781, Fitzpatrick, ed., *Washington,* Vol. XXII, pp. 16–17; Rochambeau to Washington, May 5, 1781; Rochambeau to Ségur, May 13, 1781, Rochambeau Papers, Vol. IX.

[48] Washington to Schuyler, March 23, 1781; he wrote the same passage to Joseph Jones, March 24, 1781; to William Fitzhugh, March 24, 1781; to John Armstrong, March 26, 1781, Fitzpatrick, ed., *Washington,* Vol. XXI, pp. 361, 372–73, 376, 379.

[49] Lovell to Gerry, April 10, 1781, Misc. MSS, HU.

lar gains in North and South Carolina and Virginia.[50] Rochambeau defended his policy on two grounds. The French, being financially hardpressed, could not afford offensive action; and the French forces still awaited the second division. Rochambeau unfairly blamed the financial hardships of the army on John Holker, who had written that the army could depend on a stable Continental currency and financing from the profits of French-American commerce. By January the French Army was unable to move until it received specie from France.[51] Although Holker was partly at fault, the error in financing was made in Paris before Rochambeau's departure. Trade with the United States was confined largely to military supplies financed by French loans, so there was no possibility that trade profits could finance the expeditionary force.

The French performance in respect to the second division made the Continental Congress appear a paragon of efficiency. Originally France had intended to send fifteen thousand troops at once. When the troops arrived at Brest to embark, the Navy had ships available for only five thousand. Rochambeau left with the first division, expecting that the second division would follow within a month. The British blockaded Brest, which kept the French from sending the second division. Even so, it is doubtful that the Navy could have provided enough ships for the rest of the troops.

Rochambeau, in his memoirs, accused Luzerne of telling Americans to expect a second division, but in his speech to the Rhode Island General Assembly Rochambeau had said, "At present I only bring over the Vanguard of a much greater Force destined for their [United States] Aid, and the King has ordered me to assure them, that his whole Power shall be exerted for their Support." [52] Americans, their hopes aroused, continually pestered Luzerne for news of the second division.[53] In October, however, Luzerne learned from Vergennes that it was too late to send the second division that season, but it would definitely be sent the

[50] Copy of Memo in Rochambeau Papers, Vol. I; George Barr Carson, Jr., "The Chevalier de Chastellux, Soldier and Philosophe" (unpublished dissertation, University of Chicago, 1942), pp. 137–40; Fersen to Fersen, Oct. 16, 1780, Comte Fersen U. Wrangel, ed., Lèttres D'Axel de Fersen à Son Père pendant la guerre de l'Indépendance d'Amérique (Paris, 1929), p. 80.

[51] Rochambeau to Holker, Oct. 3, 1780; Rochambeau to Necker, Oct. 21, 1780, Rochambeau Papers, Vol. VIII. Rochambeau's resentment against Holker contributed to the dismissal of Holker by Luzerne. See Luzerne to Rochambeau, April 8, 1781, ibid., Vol. XIV; Luzerne to Castries, April 1, 1781; Castries to Luzerne, May 5, 1781, AAE-cp-(EU), Vol. XVI; Castries to Holker, June 21, 1781, ibid., Vol. XVII.

[52] Jean Rochambeau, Mémoires militaires, historiques et politiques de Rochambeau (Paris, 1809), Vol. I, p. 244; Newport Mercury, April 12, 1780.

[53] Luzerne to Vergennes, Dec. 9, 1780, AAE-cp-(EU), Vol. XIV; Luzerne to Vergennes, April 29, 1781, ibid., Vol. XVI.

next spring. Accordingly, Luzerne announced to Congress that the Second division would arrive in time to aid the United States in the 1781 campaign.[54] Vergennes, without consulting Franklin, then informed Luzerne that there would be no second division due to the British blockade.

Actually France did not attempt to send the second division because of finances rather than the blockade. In a memorandum dated a day before Vergennes wrote Luzerne, the cost of financing fifteen thousand troops in the United States was estimated at thirty million livres (or six million dollars) a year. In an undated memorandum, probably written the same month, the author informed Vergennes that it was much cheaper to subsidize the American Army than to send additional French forces.[55] The decision on the second division was made at the same time that France granted John Laurens' requests for aid. Luzerne described breaking the news about the second division to Congress as "difficult and delicate," but at the same time he informed Congress of John Laurens' success. Congress decided to tell the legislatures that it had received "recent proof of His Majesty's friendship," which was a peculiar way to announce that no second division was coming.[56]

American hopes rebounded when Rochambeau and his entire army left Newport in early June to join the American Army on the Hudson in preparation for an attack on New York. After receiving specie from France, Rochambeau had agreed, in a conference with Washington at Wethersfield in late May, to move his troops. When they reached the Hudson, Rochambeau arranged his forces so that they would be separated from American soldiers. The only visits between armies were by officers or men from the Medical and Quartermaster Corps.

To the amazement of everyone concerned, there was little conflict between the two armies. One American staff officer wrote, "The French army and we are in the most perfect harmony, it extends from the Commander in Chief down to the lowest sentinel." After a visit to the two armies, Luzerne also noted the absence of friction.[57] For the first time, the French forces were operating with the main American army, which alone among United States forces had a cohesive officer corps. The

[54] Vergennes to Luzerne, Oct. 22, 1780, *ibid.*, Vol. XIV; Luzerne to Vergennes, April 1, 1781, *ibid.*, Vol. XVI.

[55] Vergennes to Luzerne, March 19, 1781; "Rapport au Roi dur l'augmentation de troupes et munitions demandé par Rochambeau," March 8, 1781, *ibid.*, Vol. XV; "Mémoire sur l'Amérique," undated, *ibid.*, Vol. XIX.

[56] Luzerne to Vergennes, June 1, 1781, *ibid.*, Vol. XVII. Thomas McKean informed Richard Henry Lee in similar words, McKean to Lee, Aug. 13, 1781, McKean Papers, Vol. I.

[57] Knox to William Knox, Aug. 3, 1781, Knox Papers, MHS, Vol. VII; Luzerne to Vergennes, July 21, 1781, AAE-cp-(EU), Vol. XVII.

American officers under Washington's leadership had intimate knowledge of the state of American finances and fully realized their increased reliance on the French. It was imperative that cooperation be maintained. Rochambeau shared this conviction, and the combined staffs subdued potential firebrands in both groups.

Americans expressed pleasure at this auspicious development, recalling the tension caused by past incidents such as Sullivan's outburst at Newport, D'Estaing's call for the British to surrender only to the French at Savannah, and Destouches' failure to enter the Chesapeake the previous March. "The French Troops live with ours on such terms of Cordiality, that every Well-wisher to our Cause is delighted," a Philadelphian wrote, "and I own that I am astonished at the innumerable Instances we hear of unexpected Harmony which reigns in the Two Camps." [58]

Luzerne visited Rochambeau and Washington on the Hudson to discuss a possible shift of French and American forces to Virginia. He carried with him the vital information that De Grasse would arrive from the West Indies for action in American waters around the end of August. Rochambeau and Washington thus agreed that they would determine the most suitable objective after hearing from De Grasse. Neither side had produced the fifteen thousand men agreed upon at Hartford the previous September for an attack on New York. Furthermore, De Grasse would stay on the American coasts only a very short time, so the Allies would have to act quickly to exploit the needed sea power. After learning from Barras, commander of the French Fleet at Newport, of De Grasse's expected arrival in the Chesapeake, Washington ordered both armies southward. But on his way south he made a successful feint at New York which frightened Clinton and consequently allowed Barras time to bring siege guns from Newport to the Chesapeake. [59]

By the time the armies reached Philadelphia, Americans were confident of victory over Cornwallis. Washington and Rochambeau received a gala welcome, as described in a Philadelphia paper:

> On Thursday [August 30] arrived in this city, Their Excellencies General WASHINGTON and COUNT DE ROCHAMBEAU, with their respective suites. They were met and accompanied to town by his Excellency the President of the State [Joseph Reed], the Financier General, and many other Gentlemen of distinction, together with the Philadelphia troop of horse. Every class of citizens seemed to vie with each other in shewing marks

[58] Clajon to Gates, Aug. 7, 1781, Gates Papers, box XVI.
[59] Howard H. Peckham, *The War for Independence* (Chicago, 1958), pp. 170–72.

of respect to the ILLUSTRIOUS PAIR of Defenders of the
Rights of Mankind.[60]

Rochambeau and the French had erased much of the ill feeling toward
them without fighting a battle. Optimism filled the air. For the first time
the papers seemed ecstatic about a French army in America.

> When we reflect upon the generosity of our great and good ally, in
> sending such a body of forces to our assistance, entirely at his
> own expense, to serve the interests of virtue and mankind, we
> cannot but behold with abhorrence and indignation those ungrate-
> ful monsters, the execrable croakers against the French nation,
> who impute those generous proceedings to the blackest motives,
> and such alone as the tyrant of Britain and his abandoned adher-
> ents would be guilty of in similar circumstances.[61]

The marching, colors, and pageantry of the French Army impressed
the Philadelphians. "Had you seen the French troops march through the
Town and exercise, no, you could not have helped feeling a Pain, as a
native of England," one wrote, "and Joy as an American, and an Ally of
France. The British Troops never attained that Degree of Perfection in
marching &c. This is not Enthusiasm, it is the Truth." [62] Unexpectedly,
Rochambeau's army did more to ease American suspicions of French
motives than all the pronouncements of Gérard and Luzerne. Samuel
Fisher, a Quaker who had served over twenty months in prison for refusing to sign a loyalty oath to the state of Pennsylvania, unintentionally
gave Rochambeau the highest compliment on the conduct of the French
Army in the United States.

> A few days after [the arrival of Washington and Rochambeau]
> the French Army passed thro' the City in two or more divisions,
> distant about two days march behind each other. They are said &
> I suppose with Truth to have behaved themselves much better on
> their march than either British or Washington's Soldiers. This I
> conclude cannot be supposed to arise from the general principles
> & morals of the French being better than those of the Inhabitants
> of the British Dominions in Europe & America, but merely from a
> piece of French policy to gain the good opinion of the people of
> America, that they may thereby effect their purposes for the bet-
> ter, for can any man that has the use of his faculties, or is not
> deluded believe that they have meddled as it were in a Quarrell

[60] *Pennsylvania Journal,* Sept. 1, 1781
[61] *Freeman's Journal,* Sept. 5, 1781
[62] Clajon to Gates, Sept. 4, 1781, Gates Papers, box XVI.

between Members of the same Family, Religion, & Language, upon any other motive than to serve their own purposes, which they study to keep covered till a suitable time may arrive to discover the cloven foot? May they never have Strength to establish their Government & religion in any Country where Liberty of Conscience has generally prevailed.[63]

The October victory of the combined forces over Cornwallis at Yorktown assured the eventual success of the alliance. Washington was fêted far more than any other person, but Rochambeau's name appeared frequently in newspapers and private letters. The victory was of such magnitude and significance that papers awarded laurels to all Frenchmen for their assistance. The *Freeman's Journal* printed news of the victory in type which occupied half a page.

BE IT REMEMBERED!

That on the 17th Day of October, 1781,
Lieut. Gen. Charles Earl Cornwallis, with
above 5000 British troops, surrender themselves prisoners of war to his Excellency Gen.
GEORGE WASHINGTON, commander in chief
of the allied forces of France and America.

LAUS DEO! [64]

Church bells in Newport rang all through the night and the next day after the arrival of the news. The *New Jersey Gazette* stressed what became a prominent theme when Americans discussed the alliance, "An Alliance now more firmly cemented by the united effusion of French and American Blood, in a conquest the more agreeable to both nations, for being obtained by their combined efforts as fellow soldiers and fellow victors in the same triumphant cause." [65] Peace and independence apparently assured, with the aid of France, Americans became enraptured with their ally.

The prospect of America is truly glorious. She rises triumphant in one of the most honorable and important contests that ever any people were engaged in: Pressed with uncommon difficulties, she has fortunately found a most faithful and generous, as well as potent Ally. . . . The consequences of our late compleat con-

[63] Anna Wharton Morris, ed., "Journal of Samuel Rowland Fisher of Philadelphia, 1779, 1781," *PMHB*, Vol. XLI (1917), pp. 456–57.

[64] *Freeman's Journal*, Oct. 24, 1781. A good account of Yorktown is Thomas Fleming, *Beat the Last Drum* (New York, 1963), pp. 89–338.

[65] *Newport Mercury*, Oct. 27, 1781; *New Jersey Gazette*, Oct. 31, 1781.

quest at York-Town are vast, and if we know how to improve them, decisive.[66]

After the battle Rochambeau quartered his army at Williamsburg, where he awaited news from Europe in response to the Yorktown victory. In January, 1782, Rochambeau refused Nathanael Greene's request for aid in an attack on Charleston.[67] Rochambeau reported to Luzerne that he refused Greene only because of his orders not to separate his forces. American hopes for another combined offensive were eliminated when the French learned of the defeat of De Grasse by Rodney in the West Indies in May.[68] Rochambeau started moving his troops northward in early July primarily to escape the Virginia summer.

The French Army in Virginia had continued the exemplary conduct which had so impressed Americans to the north.[69] But, although French officers exclaimed about Virginian hospitality, they preferred New England. Luzerne believed that Virginians were indifferent to the Army, because the great fortunes and luxury maintained by slavery led them to perceive French officers as their equals. In contrast, the simple manners and limited fortunes in New England made the public more apt to lionize the French, especially the officers. When the army left Virginia, Luzerne noted a mood of mutual indifference quite unlike the feelings displayed at the departure from New England.[70]

The French had decided to send Rochambeau to the West Indies after the North Cabinet was overthrown and Parliament voted to end offensive warfare in North America. Rochambeau received orders to send his troops to Santo Domingo if it appeared to him that the British were going to evacuate Charleston and New York.[71] He therefore moved his troops to Baltimore, where he expected to embark them for the West Indies.

Rochambeau and Washington held a conference in Philadelphia in mid-July. Luzerne and Rochambeau, who had received their new orders from France, used this occasion to inform Washington that there would be no more offensive operations by the French Army. Before the confer-

[66] *Independent Chronicle,* Nov. 8, 1781.

[67] Rochambeau to Luzerne, Jan. 22, 1782, Rochambeau Papers, Vol. XI; Greene was not deeply offended by his refusal, Greene to Luzerne, Jan. 25, 1782, Greene Papers.

[68] Acomb, ed., *Journal of Von Closen,* pp. 203–204, May 11, 20, 30, 1782.

[69] Madison to Madison, June 15, 1782, Hutchinson & Rachal, eds., *Madison,* Vol. IV, p. 337.

[70] Acomb, ed., *Journal of Von Closen,* pp. 166, 176–77, Nov. 24, 1781, Feb. 16, 1782; Luzerne to Vergennes, Aug. 27, 1782, AAE-cp-(EU), Vol. XXII.

[71] Ségur to Rochambeau, April 30, 1782, Rochambeau Papers, Vol. IV.

ence, Luzerne and Rochambeau had agreed that a campaign against New York would be a waste of men and money. Rochambeau shifted his point of embarkation to Boston, partly because of British sea power in the Chesapeake, and partly in the hope that French troops moving toward New York would prevent the British from sending troops to the West Indies. The conference accomplished nothing, although Washington renewed his perennial request for an invasion of Canada. Rochambeau again declared that he would have to receive orders from France before he could agree.[72]

The French moved northward at a leisurely pace, joining Washington's army at the Hudson in late September. In late October the French forces started for Boston, where they set sail for the West Indies in the last week of December, 1782. Rochambeau was accorded the laurels of a military hero as he made his way north.[73] Each state and almost every city passed resolutions commending him and his army for their aid to the United States. Rochambeau, forever stiff and distant, answered with dignity, but never with warmth. He remained a servant of his King, carrying out his orders in a cautious, conservative fashion, but was never an enthusiast of the American Revolution. Rochambeau could feel justifiable pride that Americans sincerely admired the discipline and honesty of his army and that his troops, placed in a potentially hostile country, never caused a major incident endangering the alliance of his King.

American reactions to French military aid had been varied. Before Rochambeau arrived, many Americans believed that they could win if given sea support. Probably this contention had some validity, because it was the aid of De Grasse rather than Rochambeau which insured victory at Yorktown. The presence of French troops at Newport, however, had made Clinton even more cautious than he had been previously, thus allowing Americans increased freedom of movement in the Middle States during the critical year of 1780.

The reception ultimately given the French Army by Americans of all classes was more favorable than leaders in either country had believed possible. The response was partly due to self-interest, but the French officers contributed more than could have been expected. They were

[72] Luzerne to Washington, July 3, 1782, Archives du Ministère de la Guerre, Correspondance, Vol. MMMDCCXXXVI; Luzerne to Vergennes, July 3, 1782; July 15, 1782, AAE-cp-(EU), Vol. XXI; "Substance of a Conference between Comte de Rochambeau and General Washington," July 19, 1782, Fitzpatrick, ed., *Washington*, Vol. XXIV, pp. 434–35; Rochambeau to Ségur, July 22, 1782, Rochambeau Papers, Vol. XI.

[73] *Ibid.*, Vol. XIII, pp. 84, 100; *ibid.*, Vol. XVII; *Maryland Gazette*, Aug. 15, 1782; *Packet*, Aug. 31, 1782; *Providence Gazette*, Dec. 14, 1782.

well-mannered, bright professionals who cooperated graciously with their American counterparts.

French military aid had proved to be indispensable in the struggle for independence. In the last years of the Revolution, Americans no longer argued that it was solely their war and their fight for freedom. They had to share the laurels. Americans believed that the most important consideration during the last three years of the war was the aid of France. The mere presence of the French Army and Fleet significantly altered British military planning; no longer could British leaders be assured of the sea superiority they needed for land operations. The French, even when inactive, changed the military balance.

If French aid was indispensable, it also meant that Americans had to respond to unilateral French decisions. Because of French refusals, there were no offensive campaigns in the north for three years. The decision to shift to the Chesapeake in 1781 resulted from Luzerne's guarded information about De Grasse. There were no offensive actions in 1782, because the French had become more concerned with their West Indian possessions than with victories in the United States.

Whether Americans wanted to admit it or not, they had no recourse but to agree with Rochambeau and Luzerne in military and diplomatic matters. George Mason, John Rutledge, and like-minded moderates could maintain the fiction that aid from France would be forthcoming if the American plight were properly revealed. Unlike Gouverneur Morris, they failed to realize that aid under the alliance was no longer a question of mutual interest but of the United States beseeching France to continue the American Revolution. The very essence of the radical doctrine of independence and national honor, as expressed by Roger Sherman, was crumbling away. Sherman recorded on the opening page of his account book, "The great principle of alliance, the only Solid effective one, is a right resulting from a firm and dignified national courage to ask the other power to become sharers in our strength, and not partners in our weakness." [74] The new peace instructions of 1781 revealed that the erosion of this concept had advanced even more rapidly in diplomacy than in military affairs.

[74] Roger Sherman account book, undated, Roger Sherman Papers, LC.

XI. The Peace Instructions of 1781

In June, 1781, as Rochambeau's army marched from Newport to join the American forces in the campaign which ended at Yorktown, Congress was again considering diplomatic steps to prepare the United States for possible peace negotiations. In mid-1781 the prospects for gaining independence seemed dim to most Americans. The promising start to the 1780 campaign had faded due to faulty French planning and the collapse of United States credit, and the course of the new campaign was still undetermined. "Our affairs are in a most wretched situation," a Maryland delegate wrote, "Congress is at its wits End—everything at a Stand[still] and unless the French fleet and Army [the second division] arrive very soon we shall in all probability be in the most deplorable situation." [1]

The United States was limited in what it could accomplish by itself, however. Americans had to depend increasingly on French arms and finances to maintain a defensive position; any offensive plans hinged on the timing and type of French military aid. John Laurens had not yet returned from France with news of a new subsidy, and the American position in the South was critical. Powerful British armies seemed on the verge of controlling Georgia, North and South Carolina, and Virginia. Nathanael Greene had demonstrated superb leadership, but had yet to win a major battle in the South or regain an important southern city. The British southern strategy appeared so successful that many American leaders feared British control of all five southern states by the end of the 1781 campaign. "The accounts from the Southward I do not like," wrote one merchant, "Green[e] is much distressed & unless some relief is afforded him I fear the worst." [2]

Pessimism prevailed in Philadelphia, where speculation held that 1781 would be the last campaign no matter which side controlled the South. Southerners particularly feared peace on the basis of *uti possidetis,* control to the power holding possession at the time of the armistice. Consequently, Luzerne could now exert considerable pressure on southern delegates. Maryland joined the confederation due to his influence, and the Virginians, Luzerne noted, were now very humble and less

[1] Jenifer to Hall, May 15, 1781, *LMCC,* Vol. VI, p. 88.
[2] Ridley to Holker, May 22, 1781, Holker Papers, Vol. XV.

pretentious in their claims to the western lands. The Georgia delegates confided in him their fears of peace on the basis of *uti possidetis*.[3]

Joseph Reed believed that after 1781 Great Britain would agree to a treaty on the basis of *uti possidetis* until "a more favorable opportunity offers to recover the whole." [4] Southern delegates detected the difference between their position and that of Reed. A temporary peace would be disagreeable to other sections but not disastrous. For this reason many southerners came to place more faith in Luzerne and the French than in their countrymen from other sections. Nevertheless, "A Whig" resorted to the fighting rhetoric long missing in the South:

> She [Great Britain] will plead the right of conquest, and all the cunning and sophistry of her statesmen will aid the plea. . . . Should the mediatory powers decide in favour of our enemy, we must appeal from their decision to the sword. The moment we cede to Britain one inch of American soil, we fix an eternal stigma on our national character and consent to wear a disgraceful badge of slavery. This is the language of every true whig.[5]

The American cause in Europe had not changed within the past year. John Jay served as bait to keep Cumberland and Great Britain interested in offering Spain an easy way out of the war, but Jay remained unrecognized in Spain, and almost unaided by the Spanish. Although John Adams found Holland more to his liking than Paris, he still had not received Dutch recognition or the needed loans. Francis Dana traveled to St. Petersburg in the chimerical hope that the United States could join the League of Armed Neutrality with Russia. Benajmin Franklin stayed cozy and quiet at Passy, enjoying the unlimited confidence of Vergennes.

Vergennes, exasperated with the protracted war, desperately sought a method to end the conflict on honorable terms for France, if not for the United States. In February, 1781, he secretly proposed a truce on the basis of *uti possidetis*. Believing that peace on these terms would have to come from mediation by other powers, Vergennes was carefully examining the prospects when Austria and Russia surprised him by a joint offer of mediation. Vergennes was not pleased with the European complications of the offer, but accepted it with qualifications. He used the mediation offer to ask the United States to reconsider its ultimata for peace and to rid himself of his personal antagonist from the United States, John Adams.[6]

[3] Luzerne to Vergennes, Jan. 31, 1781, AAE-cp-(EU), Vol. XV.
[4] Reed to Greene, June 16, 1781, Greene Papers.
[5] *Maryland Gazette*, June 21, 1781.
[6] Morris, *The Peacemakers*, pp. 173–90.

Vergennes shuddered to think of Adams as the sole American negotiator for peace. He had disagreed with him over large and small points since the latter's return to France in 1780. Adams insisted on informing the British of his commission to treat for peace, while Vergennes believed that such a step would encourage Great Britain to attempt to seduce the Americans into signing a separate peace treaty. Adams agreed not to inform the British until he had specific authorization from Congress.

In addition to disagreeing with Vergennes about the proper way to approach Great Britain, Adams thrust himself into the role of defender of the United States in areas clearly beyond his jurisdiction. Vergennes shared some responsibility for this, although he never admitted it. He made a mistake when he protested to Adams, instead of Franklin, the congressional act of March 18, 1780, which depreciated the currency at the rate of forty to one. Vergennes claimed that this action caused immense financial damage to French merchants, but Adams retorted that French losses were small and mainly confined to speculators.[7] Vergennes could not tolerate such impertinence from a man he found personally repugnant and had long suspected of being disloyal to the alliance, and retorted:

> To avoid any further discussions of that sort, I think it is my duty to inform you that, Mr. Franklin being the sole person who has letters of credence to the King from the United States, it is with him only that I ought and can treat of matters which concern them, and particularly of that which is the subject of your observation.[8]

Vergennes decided that it was necessary to restrain Adams. He used the forthcoming mediation conference at Vienna as an excuse to ask Congress to limit Adams' powers and, preferably, place them in the hands of the amiable Franklin. Vergennes was less concerned with the Vienna conference, which he did not believe would ever take place, than with making sure that the American negotiator was friendly and under his direct control.

Vergennes had complained about Adams' appointment continually after his return, but he never gave specific instructions for Luzerne to change Adams' commission or seek to replace him. The currency dispute gave Vergennes a pretext to indicate his general dissatisfaction with Adams. At one time he requested that another commissioner with equal powers be appointed. Later, however, Vergennes changed his mind, de-

---

[7] For the running debate between the two on many matters, see Wharton, ed., *Diplomatic Correspondence*, Vol. III, pp. 800–55, *passim*.

[8] Vergennes to Adams, July 29, 1780, *ibid.*, Vol. IV, pp. 17–18.

claring that he would be satisfied if Congress would limit Adams' power or put him under the control of the French Minister at the Vienna negotiations.[9]

Luzerne, with few binding instructions, operated almost independently in Philadelphia; most of the time Vergennes allowed him wide discretionary authority to implement French policy. Luzerne ignored repeated requests to secure Adams' removal or change his instructions, perhaps believing that Vergennes' well-known temper would subside. He also informed Vergennes that it would be impossible to persuade Congress to apologize for depreciating the currency, as Vergennes suggested.[10]

In the last week of May Luzerne received new instructions from Vergennes. Vergennes declared that France would not accept the Austrian-Russian mediation offer until it received word from the United States, and he hoped that Congress would accept the mediation offer and reconsider its ultimata for peace. This time Vergennes gave Luzerne emphatic directions to neglect nothing in persuading Congress to prescribe Adams' powers so that he would have to follow the advice of the King and serve under the ranking French negotiator at Vienna. Vergennes, perhaps remembering the disruptive Arthur Lee controversy, had decided that it would be unwise to seek Adams' recall. This decision made Luzerne's assignment much easier, particularly since Congress was always reluctant to recall a minister from Europe.[11]

Vergennes wanted Luzerne to assure Congress that the mediation would not betray United States interests; the issue of independence would not be negotiable. France would not agree to peace unless the United States was granted independence and the territory of all thirteen states. Vergennes hedged and did not define boundary limits, however. He stated that everything except independence should be subject to modification at the peace negotiations, which made American hopes for gaining territory on their western and northern frontiers precarious.[12]

Except for control of the American negotiator, Vergennes' requests did not differ greatly on territorial questions from the final peace instructions of 1779, and probably appeared generous to many Congressmen. Considering the dismal circumstances of the United States in 1781, most moderates in Congress were undoubtedly relieved to see that

[9] Vergennes to Luzerne, Aug. 7, 1780, AAE-cp-(EU), Vol. XIII; Vergennes to Luzerne, Oct. 22, 1780; Dec. 4, 1780, *ibid.*, Vol. XVI.

[10] Luzerne to Vergennes, March 20, 1781; March 21, 1781; March 28, 1781, *ibid.*, Vol. XVI.

[11] Vergennes to Luzerne, March 9, 1781, *ibid.*, Vol. XV.

[12] *Ibid.*

Vergennes promised full support of independence.[13] "We have the most friendly and unequivocal assurances from our ally," a North Carolina delegate wrote, "that our Interests will be attended to and that he will make good on his part everything that he has undertaken." [14]

John Adams, many agreed, had made himself a nuisance to the only power willing to provide effective aid to the United States. Robert Livingston asked Barbé-Marbois to explain to him "the cause of the coolness, to give it no harsher name, that subsists between Mr. A——— and Count D'Vergennes." He added that Vergennes' disgust "appears to me to be but too well founded." [15] Control of the obstreperous Adams seemed to be a small price to pay for continued French support.

Luzerne now had to test the anti-New England coalition he had nurtured since his arrival in Philadelphia. He emphasized from the outset that John Adams presented the only danger to peace and independence for the United States. Adams' temper and his obstinacy on the fishery issue would unquestionably hinder a speedy peace, Luzerne argued. After cultivating the anti-Adams resentment among Congressmen, Luzerne sought to soften lingering disputes between the two countries. He ignored Vergennes' demands for an apology on the depreciation controversy and instead informed Congress that France had granted a new subsidy through John Laurens.[16]

Luzerne used the critical circumstances of the war and his own control of information to impress Congress with the desperate situation of the United States. He informed a committee of Congress that the British blockade of Brest prevented the dispatch of a second division, while he failed to disclose that De Grasse would visit the American coast in late August. Luzerne hoped to persuade Congress to pass the new instructions before the military campaign started, thus preventing the possibility that the United States would expand its territorial demands with any change in its military fortunes.[17]

At Luzerne's request, Congress appointed John Witherspoon, president of Princeton, to head a committee of five to discuss changes in the instructions, a normal procedure for handling problems of the alliance. Although it had a standing committee on foreign affairs, of which James Lovell was the most prominent member, Congress frequently resorted to

---

[13] For the best discussion of the 1781 instructions, see O'Donnell, *Luzerne,* pp. 117–45; and for the view of a southern delegate, see Irving Brant, *James Madison, The Nationalist* (New York, 1948), pp. 133–45.

[14] Johnston to Burke, June 23, 1781, Burke Papers, NCSA.

[15] Livingston to Barbé-Marbois, Dec. 15, 1780, Livingston Papers, N-YHS, box VI.

[16] Luzerne to Vergennes, June 1, 1781, AAE-cp-(EU), Vol. XVII.

[17] *Ibid.*

ad hoc committees for resolving questions in foreign policy. In such cases the chairman was the most influential member, because he had the greatest responsibility in writing the committee's recommendations. The appointment of Witherspoon, by now universally considered a moderate, was Luzerne's first success, and greatly facilitated the rapidity with which Congress considered the new peace ultimata.

As a gesture of friendship, Luzerne had requested that Witherspoon's son be exchanged on the French prisoners list, which would enable him to be returned much sooner. Luzerne explained that the venerable Witherspoon was too firm in his principles ever to ask such a favor.[18] An unquestioned Patriot favorably inclined to France and opposed to demanding the western lands and the fishery in the peace treaty, Witherspoon was, in Luzerne's opinion, an ideal choice to head this important committee.

Witherspoon and Luzerne worked closely in all matters pertaining to the new instructions. Witherspoon wrote the first draft of the instructions in a private conference with Luzerne, later changing parts which Luzerne regarded as unsatisfactory. The only delay in passing the instructions came through Virginia's demand that the United States be guaranteed the area which is now Kentucky, and that Great Britain not be given exclusive right to what would become the five states in the Northwest Territory. Congress defeated Virginia's attempt to secure her own claims to the West and agreed to let all northern and western boundaries be settled during the peace negotiations. Congress directed Adams to refer to the recommendations on boundaries in his 1779 instructions.[19]

After defeating all attempts to expand territorial claims, Congress took up the problem of controlling John Adams. Luzerne insisted that Adams be completely under the control of the French. He first agreed to instructions which read, "You are . . . to undertake nothing in the negotiations for peace without their knowledge and concurrence." He soon decided, however, that Adams could evade such orders, so he sought and Witherspoon readily agreed to a change reading, "You are . . . to undertake nothing in the negotiations for peace or truce without their knowledge and concurrence; and ultimately to govern yourselves by their advice and opinion." Witherspoon had little difficulty in gaining congressional approval of both drafts of this portion of the instructions. Massachusetts voted against both drafts, but only Connecticut joined her in opposing the vastly more powerful second version.[20]

[18] Luzerne to Castries, May 18, 1781, *ibid.*, Vol. XVI.

[19] Ford, ed., *Journals of CC,* Vol. XX, June 6, 7, 8, 1781, pp. 605–10, 612–13.

[20] The instructions are in Witherspoon's handwriting. See Varnum L. Collins, *President Witherspoon* (Princeton, 1925), Vol. II, pp. 59–62; Ford, ed., *Journals of CC,* Vol. XX, June 8 and June 11, 1781, pp. 614–15, 627.

With French control of Adams secured, Luzerne cared little how many commissioners were named to serve with him. Originally he suggested that Congress consider adding two commissioners, but on June 8 he insinuated that Adams could be put under either Franklin or Vergennes. Three days later Luzerne explicitly demanded that Adams be placed under Vergennes' control, and agreed, for political reasons, to allow the anti-Adams delegates to add two more commissioners. On June 13 he still did not know whether there would be three or five commissioners; the following day he reported that the commission had been expanded to five to insure the inclusion of Franklin.[21]

Congress had floundered hopelessly on the question of adding more commissioners. After the first draft of the instructions was approved on June 8, Congress voted against expanding the commission. After the second and more restrictive instructions were passed on June 11, Congress decided to add two commissioners, and John Jay was unanimously elected to fill one post. On June 14, after three votes, Congress remained deadlocked on whether Thomas Jefferson, Henry Laurens, or Benjamin Franklin should fill the other position. In an effort to insure the inclusion of Franklin, John Sullivan, by this time a French agent, proposed that all three men be added, and this was accepted.[22]

By adding Franklin, Jefferson, and Laurens, Congress was only avoiding controversy, not reaching a sectional compromise. Franklin had the lowest number of votes of the three, so Sullivan wisely devised a stratagem that insured the inclusion of the French favorite on the commission. Since both Laurens and Jefferson were southerners, the conflict between delegates supporting them did not reflect sectionalism; rather, the radical-moderate antagonism had emerged in a new form. Laurens, who had a long-standing reputation of being suspicious of excessive French influence, was passionately anti-Deane and pro-fishery. Jefferson, meanwhile, had remained neutral and enigmatic on the Deane affair, but had changed his position on the western territory and the fishery so that he now agreed with the moderates. The choices for the new commission, although they accidentally represented sectional interests, showed a renewal of the moderate-radical division inflamed by the peace instructions of 1779.

The moderates, now clearly dominant, firmly rejected the radical demand for independence with security, and established that the first priority—and actually the sole concern—was independence in any form. The implications of the peace instructions were significant. They indi-

[21] Luzerne to Vergennes, June 1, 1781; June 8, 1781; June 11, 1781; June 13, 1781; June 14, 1781, AAE-cp-(EU), Vol. XVII.

[22] Ford, ed., *Journals of CC,* Vol. XX, June 9, 11, 14, 1781, pp. 618–19, 627, 648; Luzerne to Vergennes, June 11, 1781; June 14, 1781, AAE-cp-(EU), Vol. XVII.

cated to Americans knowledgeable about Congress that Luzerne was easily the most influential man in Philadelphia. The prestige of Congress sank rapidly, reaching a nadir in 1782 and 1783. The peace instructions demonstrated that Americans were willing to trust their ally more than their own representatives in Europe. Moreover, control of foreign relations moved from Philadelphia to Paris, where the debate on American foreign policy was conducted between the United States commissioners and the French Foreign Office.

Congressmen had displayed surprising unanimity on the new instructions. South Carolina, North Carolina, Georgia, and Pennsylvania agreed with the French position in thirteen different recorded votes on the peace instructions.[23] New Jersey, New Hampshire, and Maryland agreed with the French position 87 per cent of the time, including the vote on the critical question of giving France control over the American commissioners.[24] These seven states assured the seven votes required to pass the new instructions.

The majority, composed of small and Southern States, frustrated Massachusetts and Virginia in their attempts to acquire more territory. Virginia agreed with the French position two-thirds of the time, its opposition coming primarily in the futile effort to guarantee the United States western territory in Kentucky and the Ohio valley. Massachusetts voted in agreement with France only one quarter of the time, but New England solidarity was nonexistent.[25] Only Connecticut agreed with Massachusetts more than half of the time.

The votes on the instructions placing Adams under the control of the French reflected congressional determination to prevent him from seeking the fishery at the expense of other sections of the country. Most delegates did not believe that they were sacrificing national honor, but only controlling Adams' obstinacy on a goal which Congress had repeatedly refused to support. The outspoken Adams had aroused many antagonisms during his long service. The Southern States, in particular, had been consistently anti-Adams since his return from France in 1779. They voted for John Jay in 1779 until a compromise was negotiated, and they resisted all efforts to replace Franklin, partly due to fear that Adams would succeed him as Minister to France.

Congress had often disregarded the pride of its diplomats in 1781. Jay had been instructed to relinquish American claims on the Missis-

---

[23] Ford, ed., *Journals of CC,* Vol. XX, June 6, 7, 8, 9, 11, 15, 1781, July 12, 1781, pp. 605–15, 618–19, 626–27, 650, 746–47.

[24] *Ibid.*

[25] *Ibid.* New York and Rhode Island did not vote, and Delaware voted only once in thirteen roll calls.

sippi in spite of his opposition to this measure.[26] Franklin had been circumvented when John Laurens was appointed to seek a new loan. Adams was the last diplomat to be rudely informed that Congress considered the situation desperate and the need for peace paramount. The votes on the instructions were not wholly an indication of trust in France, although Congress trusted France a great deal more than previously, but also a personal rebuke to Adams with a clear warning not to delay a peace settlement.

Luzerne had achieved a quick and complete victory in the passage of the new instructions. The 1779 instructions had been debated in Congress for eight months with bitter public controversy. The 1781 instructions generated little debate in the press or in Congress, which rapidly agreed to Luzerne's suggestions. The American commissioners were instructed to accept the Russian-Austrian mediation, make no treaty which violated existing treaties or the independence of the Unted States, refer to Adams' earlier instructions on boundaries, and to be ultimately guided by the advice and opinion of the French court in all matters except independence. With little effort Luzerne persuaded Congress to establish, for the first time, United States terms for a truce. These terms, which stipulated that Great Britain must evacuate all parts of the United States and thus avoided *uti possidetis*, were wholly acceptable to Vergennes and Luzerne.[27]

Luzerne, preening with satisfaction, wrote Vergennes about his success.

> I have witnessed the fact, My Lord, that these changes appear suitable to fulfill the desired objective; in fact I view the negotiation as presently being in the hands of His Majesty except for independence and the treaties, and I myself have applauded these two reservations. I wish that you will give your consent to these measures which appear to me to fulfill the instructions which you gave me on the eighth of March last.[28]

Luzerne believed that his success in achieving the passage of the instructions resulted from two considerations. First, Samuel Adams no longer sat in Congress, a fact which Luzerne incorrectly attributed to the influence of Samuel Cooper. Second, the solidarity of the four New England states had disintegrated due, Luzerne believed, to his employment

[26] "Instructions to Mr. Jay as to the Mississippi River," Feb. 15, 1781, Wharton, ed., *Diplomatic Correspondence,* Vol. IV, p. 257.

[27] "Instructions from Samuel Huntington to Adams, Franklin, Jay, Laurens, and Jefferson, June 15, 1781," *ibid.,* Vol. IV, pp. 504–505.

[28] Luzerne to Vergennes, June 11, 1781, AAE-cp-(EU), Vol. XVII.

of John Sullivan.[29] Luzerne was an excellent diplomat, but a poor political analyst. He explained his expense account rather than Congressional action.[30]

For reasons of health, Samuel Adams retired from Congress to take a less strenuous post in Massachusetts. Sullivan, moreover, was joined by a number of other delegates who voted against the wishes of Massachusetts. Samuel Livermore of New Hampshire, for example, agreed with Sullivan on every vote for the peace instructions. Ezekiel Cornell (Rhode Island), Samuel Huntington (Connecticut), and at times James Varnum (Rhode Island) trusted France and opposed Massachusetts on many issues in 1780 and 1781.

In addition to the anti-Adams sentiment, the instructions passed easily because an overwhelming majority in Congress simply depended on France to a much greater degree in 1781 than in 1779. One observer thought that the failure of public credit had particularly affected the attitudes of Congressmen and curtailed their pride. "You formerly thought Congress assumed rather more Dignity and Authority than became them but I assure [you] they are now sufficiently humiliated," wrote Joseph Reed. "The course of Affairs has thrown them into a State of Dependence not very compatible with the dignity of a Sovereign Power." [31]

Furthermore, the composition and outlook of Congress had changed since 1779. New England delegates such as William Whipple, William Ellery, Josiah Bartlett, Henry Marchant, and Elbridge Gerry who strenuously opposed French demands in 1779, were no longer in Congress, primarily for personal reasons. Most of this group later served again in

[29] *Ibid.* Luzerne's interpretation has been accepted by a number of historians who have exaggerated the extent of New England solidarity and Sullivan's role in its disintegration. See O'Donnell, *Luzerne,* pp. 134–35, 139; and Morris, *The Peacemakers,* p. 211; but not Whittemore, *Sullivan,* pp. 177–79.

[30] Luzerne offered a better assessment of radical strength when he wrote a description of over 130 past and present members of Congress in August, 1783. In this list Luzerne designated 25 members as belonging to "the party of the east." In June, 1781, only nine of the 25 still served in Congress, and of these Luzerne stated that at least five had broken with the radicals, notably, Samuel Livermore, James Varnum, John Witherspoon, James Sullivan, and Richard Howly. Three of the four remaining were from Connecticut, Roger Sherman, Samuel Huntington, and Oliver Ellsworth, and the last was James Lovell. Inexplicably, Luzerne did not consider James Lovell's two fellow-delegates from Massachusetts, George Partridge and Artemas Ward, ever to be members of the eastern party. Luzerne described Samuel Huntington as often breaking with the party of the east, but actually Huntington did not do so in the debate over the peace instructions. The original of the "Liste des Membres" is in the Luzerne Papers and is almost identical, except for a few unimportant wording changes and an unfavorable description of Joseph Montgomery of Pennsylvania, to the copy in the Archives du Ministère des Affaires Étrangères, mémoires et documents, États-unis, Vol. I (Paris), pp. 254–287. All references to the list of members are from the original in the Luzerne Papers.

[31] Reed to Greene, Nov. 1, 1781, Reed Papers, Vol. IX.

Congress, but for a time milder, less contentious men like Samuel Huntington replaced them. Barbé-Marbois described Huntington as sincerely attached to the alliance, a "straightforward and unpretentious man, one of the finest citizens of America, whose conduct we have always found worthy of praise." [32]

The disintegration of an always limited New England solidarity had been apparent to a number of observers long before 1781. In 1779 unity prevailed only on the fishery; by 1781 not even a semblance of unity remained. In particular, Ezekiel Cornell and John Sullivan, both former generals with mediocre records, broke radically with their New England colleagues over military measures. Both strongly supported Washington over Gates and held that Washington should be allowed much greater authority in the conduct of the war. Both believed that the Army should be guaranteed a pension for its service. They assumed that the Deane controversy hurt the United States war effort at home and even more in Europe. Unlike other New England delegates, Cornell and Sullivan sought to avoid renewed conflict between the remnants of the Deane and Lee factions still in Congress.[33]

Cornell became an avid convert to French policy. His belated conversion was as much personal as political.

> I hope the people of Rhode Island are as much prejudiced in favor of the French gentlemen at that place, as I am with the Minister here. I must confess, if I ever was prejudiced against the French, it is all at an end, as I think it must be with every American, who has the honor to be acquainted with the Minister, if he can be allowed a true Frenchman.

Cornell went on to praise Luzerne's easy manners, good nature, kindness, and "excessive fondness for Americans as allies." [34]

Sullivan's adherence to French policy is easily explained. He reported the proceedings of Congress to Luzerne, who explicitly named Sullivan in his regular correspondence as his agent.[35] Sullivan's reputa-

[32] Barbé-Marbois to Vergennes, July 11, 1781, AAE-cp-(EU), Vol. XVII.

[33] For Cornell, see Armstrong to Gates, June 15, 1780, Gates Papers, box XIV; Cornell to William Greene, Aug. 1, 1780; Oct. 24, 1780, *LMCC*, Vol. V, pp. 305, 426. On Sullivan, see his two letters to Washington, Sullivan to Washington, Nov. 12, 1780, *ibid.*, pp. 442–43; Sullivan to Washington, March 6, 1781, *ibid.*, Vol. VI, pp. 11–12.

[34] Cornell to William Greene, Aug. 15, 1780, William R. Staples, *Rhode Island in the Continental Congress* (Providence, 1870), p. 306.

[35] Luzerne to Vergennes, Dec. 16, 1780, AAE-cp-(EU), Vol. XIV; Luzerne to Vergennes, May 13, 1781, *ibid.*, Vol. XVI. The initial payment to Sullivan was 4,200 livres or a little over $800. Later Sullivan renegotiated his pay and was given $1,000 a year for his work until at least 1784. Luzerne to Vergennes, June 30, 1781; July 1, 1782; Dec. 21, 1782; July 1, 1783; April 30, 1784, Luzerne Papers.

tion was so great that the British also attempted to bribe him, and around Philadelphia his actions caused suspicion from people opposed to the peace instructions.

> Genl. Sullivan is on his return to New Hampshire. I hope he does not deserve what is generally said of him here, that he is under French influence, surely if it be true, he is most unfit for the Councils of America. I am not surpriz'd that the French should interfere, but am both astonished and grieved that any in our Councils should have adopted the weak policy of being governed by them.[36]

Although weakened by the collapse of New England unity, the meager opposition to the instructions of 1781 was led by the Massachusetts delegation of James Lovell, George Partridge, and Artemas Ward. Lovell, the senior member of the three in length of service and knowledge of foreign affairs, was an enigmatic figure. A former Latin teacher in Boston, he had been selected to deliver the first Boston Massacre oration, and he had been imprisoned by General Gage and held captive in Nova Scotia for almost a year. After his exchange in 1776, Lovell was elected to Congress and served continuously until the fall of 1781.

Lovell thrived as few men did on the everyday workings of Congress. He was one of the first "men of business" in Congress, but not one of its foremost leaders or parliamentary tacticians. He devised the diplomatic codes which the United States used for many years, acted as the decoding expert for intercepted British correspondence, supervised the printing of the Journals, attended almost all debates in Congress, and for close to two years ran the Committee on Foreign Affairs almost singlehandedly. In addition, Lovell coordinated information for many like-minded men through his prodigious private correspondence. He was widely admired within Congress for his activities, although not regarded as a policy leader.

> The Business of Congress in the winter Season is greatly encreased on the necessary Reformation, Plans and Preparation for the succeeding Campaign, and this Time there is half the Number of Members to transact it. Few can stand it as well as our Friend Mr. Lovell; he writes Morning Noon and Night, and sickens once a Fortnight, and devotes a Day to Sleep, after which, like the Sun

---

[36] Mrs. William Shippen to Abigail Adams, Aug., 1781, Adams Papers, R. 355. Mrs. Shippen was a sister of Richard Henry and Arthur Lee. For the British offer, see Holland to Sullivan, June 8, 1781, Clinton Papers. This episode is ably covered in Carl Van Doren, *Secret History of the American Revolution* (New York, 1941), pp. 400–404.

from behind a Cloud, he makes his Appearance with his usual Splendor.[37]

Lovell devoted himself to a monastic existence in Philadelphia, apparently indifferent to the feelings of Mrs. Lovell in Boston. He inquired of the very proper, and still single, Elbridge Gerry, " 'Is it not Time to pay a visit to Mass[achusetts]?' Does my Wife look as if she wanted a toothless grey headed sciatic Husband *near* her? I am more Benefit to her at a Distance than in ♂, as the almanac has it." [38] Lovell also had some practical reasons for his prolonged absence from his wife and five children. "I have neither Farm office nor Store to go where my Industry might as formerly feed & warm me." [39]

Lovell reacted to the demand for the new instructions with resignation, but also with a continuing desire to make independence an honorable concept including territorial security. Although he opposed the instructions adamantly, he feared even to seek a postponement with a majority of Congressmen so overwhelmingly against his position. A week before the passage of the instructions, Lovell predicted that Jay and Franklin would be added to the commission, which, he believed, would give the French complete control even without any changes in the 1779 instructions. His Spartan republicanism offended, Lovell called the majority "the too many soft sycophantic or worse principled diners," a reference to congressional guests at Luzerne's sumptuous dinner table.[40]

Lovell feared that John Adams would consider his new instructions so degrading that he would resign his commission. He made it clear to sympathizer Elbridge Gerry that the instructions were an insult to national honor, but took some consolation in the fact that Adams was still the sole plenipotentiary to negotiate the commercial treaty, which protected the fishery.[41] He surmised that Luzerne did not expect such absolute control to be given France by Congress, but "Suppleness knew not whence to stop especially when under the spur of at least Marbois." [42] Ever since the signing of the alliance, Lovell had contended that the United States should act with gratitude toward France while never sacrificing national dignity. By June, 1781, Lovell was truly one of the few "hardy Watchmen in this political Camp besides the veteran [Roger] Sherman" who considered national honor a concept which required

[37] Gerry to Samuel Adams, Feb. 7, 1778, *LMCC,* Vol. III, p. 76.
[38] Lovell to Gerry, Nov. 20, 1780, Clinton Papers, italics in original. This letter was intercepted by the British.
[39] Lovell to Gerry, July 13, 1781, Gerry-Knight Papers.
[40] Lovell to Gerry, June 5 & 13, 1781, *ibid.*
[41] Lovell to Gerry, June 17, 1781, *ibid.*
[42] Lovell to John Adams, June 21, 1781, Adams Papers, R. 355.

preservation no matter how critical the circumstances of the United States.[43]

In the conflict over the peace instructions of 1779, Massachusetts had a few allies from the Southern States, but radicals such as Richard Henry Lee and Henry Laurens no longer sat in Congress. Thomas McKean, who sided with Massachusetts in 1779, was elected president of Congress in 1781. At the time of his election McKean assured Barbé-Marbois that he approved of putting United States interests in French hands for the peace negotiations.[44] Samuel Adams tried to re-establish their former political alliance in 1781, but McKean ignored Adams, not answering his letters for almost a year.[45] The only southern delegate to agree with Massachusetts in 1781 was Theodorick Bland, a relative of the Lees.

The watchful Lovell did not suspect Luzerne of nefarious actions during the passage of the instructions, but there is limited evidence that Luzerne used every means possible to achieve his objective. In a financial statement written during the discussion of the instructions, Luzerne requested "an unusually large compensation of 30,000 livres [$6,000] in payment for the various losses I have borne."[46] The figure was six times the amount he paid Sullivan or Cooper, and these costs were submitted on an "extraordinary" expense account. John Witherspoon admitted, "At the very Time when this Debate was agitated our most necessary Expenses were supported by them [France] and even the Subsistence and support of many Delegates in Congress was from Bills drawn upon France."[47] The attendance of so many southern delegates at this

[43] Lovell to Gates, June 9, 1779, Gates Papers, box XII.

[44] Barbé-Marbois to Vergennes, July 11, 1781, AAE-cp-(EU), Vol. XVII.

[45] Adams to McKean, Aug. 29, Sept. 19, 1781, McKean Papers, Vol. I; McKean to Adams, Aug. 6, 1782, ibid., Vol. II.

[46] Luzerne to Vergennes, June 13, 1781, AAE-cp-(EU), Vol. XVII. This dispatch is unnumbered and concerned only with finances; there are two written on this date. Luzerne did not generally submit expenses in the middle of the month. Nor was the above figure related to expenses for relief of refugees from the Carolinas and Georgia, since he itemized this in his regular extraordinary expense account. He contributed 10,000 livres, or $2,000, to the relief of refugees in the summer of 1781. Luzerne to Vergennes, Oct. 1, 1781, Luzerne Papers.

[47] This passage was part of a memorandum, the purpose of which has puzzled many. Burnett in LMCC, Vol. VII, p. 111n, suggests that Witherspoon wrote it to Elias Boudinot to acquaint him with the background of the peace instructions. David W. Woods, John Witherspoon (New York, 1906), pp. 257–66, prints all of it except for one paragraph. Neither author knows when or why it was written. Luzerne, however, explained why such a memorandum, fitting the Witherspoon memorandum exactly, would be written. The memorandum he described was written by two members of Congress who worked hard to pass the instructions. They wrote it in August, 1783, as a justification for their conduct in putting the Americans under French control, with the intention of not making it public unless John Adams caused a public controversy over the instructions. James

time appears to be the result of such activities by Luzerne. Georgia had not been able to keep one representative in Congress in the latter part of 1779 and 1780, but during the peace instruction debate three delegates appeared and voted for French policy.

The solid bloc of seven votes for the French position vitiated any opposition efforts to defeat the new instructions. The opposition's best opportunity would have been to work for a postponement until the results of the military campaign were apparent, a tactic Elbridge Gerry had used successfully in 1779. The United States would lose little by waiting to see if the campaign of 1781 proved successful and if Great Britain would agree to the Vienna conference. A Philadelphia paper announced in August that Great Britain had rejected the mediation offer by Austria and Russia, thus making the issue of the new instructions less urgent than many Congressmen believed when voting for them.[48]

But the opposition failed to offer an alternative except for a renewal of demands rejected in 1779. Luzerne was unsure about the question of additional commissioners and even the wording of the instructions; he might have compromised. Yet the failure of the opposition was so complete that Luzerne never had to tip his hand in the discussions. During the debate, no delegate offered an amendment to reduce the power of France. Instead the instructions got progressively stronger as Luzerne realized that an overwhelming majority in Congress would follow his suggestions. Whether Luzerne or the majority would have compromised is problematical, but the opposition, depleted and lacking in confidence, did not pursue the possibility.

During the debate Lovell insisted that the instructions offended national honor, but John Witherspoon retorted that national honor was not in question at the time. He claimed that the essential security of the United States had not been entrusted to France, so there could be no insult to national honor. Furthermore, Witherspoon rarely considered questions of rank and protocol in diplomacy as worthy of Congressional consideration. He did not hesitate to admit that the sole reason he worked to change the instructions was that Vergennes insisted on this after his controversies with Adams.[49] Witherspoon accurately charged

---

Madison was Witherspoon's most likely assistant. Madison was very close politically and personally to Barbé-Marbois, and strongly anti-Adams; there is no evidence in the Madison Papers, LC, to confirm Madison's involvement, yet it appears probable. Everything that Luzerne states about the memorandum makes me certain that the one quoted above is the one to which he referred. See Luzerne to Vergennes, Aug. 8, 1783, AAE-cp-(EU), Vol. XXV.

[48] *Packet,* Aug. 21, 1781.

[49] Witherspoon speech in "Charles Thompson, Notes on Debates," Aug. 9, 1782, *LMCC,* Vol. VI, pp. 436–37; Witherspoon memorandum, [Aug., 1783]; *ibid.,* Vol. VII, pp. 111–17.

that claims of national honor often came from delegates like Lovell and Bland, who wished to expand state boundaries or take possession of areas which the United States had no possibility of gaining by military means. Witherspoon argued that the clause "to ultimately govern yourselves by their advice and consent" became necessary because the combative Adams could not be trusted with discretion in dealing with Vergennes.[50]

Proponents of the instructions also contended that no one American commissioner should be trusted with discretion on boundaries for all sections of the United States. This criticism was aimed at Adams' well-known desire to gain the fishery, but ignored the fact that Adams had been sole plenipotentiary, with power to act as he saw fit, for two years. Edmund Randolph, like most southern delegates, believed it was better to trust France than a New Englander. After Jefferson declined to accept a position on the commission, Randolph wrote him, "There remains no alternative, but either consign southern interest wholly to the management of our present ministers, or to interdict them from the exercise of all discretionary powers." [51]

Randolph's logic was unassailable if French negotiators would or could use discretion about southern interests better than Adams, Jay, or Franklin. But his argument, accepted by a majority of southern delegates, demonstrated a total failure to accept responsibility for continuing a revolution Americans themselves had started long before France had aided the United States. The alliance became a panacea for peace as the Southern States tasted the bitter fruits of military battle. A Delaware delegate observed that "the Great Virginians who alone talked of Conquering Britain, were now reduced to the sad necessity of owning that they were on their knees at the feet and mercy of the French Monarch and had nothing to expect but pra[y] his benevolence." [52]

Most Congressional delegates in 1781 had not held responsible posts during the darkest hours of the Revolution in 1776 and 1777. When affairs again became critical, they lacked faith in the outcome. Neither Great Britain nor France had produced miracles in the long war. There was no reason to trust France to extricate the United States or to foreclose the possibility of another British blunder which would again save the situation. The Revolution and the alliance had been sustained by men like Washington and Samuel Adams who never stopped making the maximum effort. Samuel Adams, much maligned by his enemies in Con-

---

[50] *Ibid.*, pp. 115–17.
[51] Randolph to Jefferson, Oct. 9, 1781, Boyd, ed., *Jefferson*, Vol. VI, p. 128.
[52] Rodney to Caesar Rodney, June 15, 1781, Ryden, ed., *Letters to and from Caesar Rodney*, p. 416.

gress, had a simple, obstinate faith in victory with honor. He once wrote, speaking of 1776, "Our affairs were then at a low Ebb indeed; but *Nil* desperandum was the Motto of the *true* Patriots of America." [53] The words were as true in June, 1781, as they had been in December, 1776.

The primary casualty of the new instructions was Congress, not John Adams. By its vote Congress eliminated itself from any prominent role in foreign affairs for the remainder of the Revolution, and thus provided one of the few instances of a legislative assembly choosing, although undoubtedly with private reservations, to diminish its powers in a critical area. Congress limited its own discretion more than that of its commissioners; any revision of the instructions would now imply a distrust of France. Congress either would have to repeal the instructions in their entirety to change their terms for peace or make supplications to France to gain additional territory for the United States. Elbridge Gerry immediately perceived that, regardless of the question of national honor, Congress had made the repeal of the instructions altogether impractical, or, as another radical put it, "what can be done where so much has been undone I cannot say." [54]

---

[53] Adams to Savage, July 3, 1778, *LMCC,* Vol. III, pp. 319–20, italics in original.

[54] Gerry to Abigail Adams, July 30, 1781, Adams Papers, R. 355; Gilman to Bartlett, Aug. 5, 1782, Bartlett Papers.

XII. Second Thoughts

Victory at Yorktown, shortly after the passage of the new instructions, transformed American hopes from pessimism to optimism. An uneasy interlude of waiting for peace commenced. After Yorktown, both France and the United States believed they should wait until Great Britain decided what steps it would take to end the war. In Philadelphia, dispatches from France became the primary source of reliable news about the expected peace talks, which further enhanced Luzerne's already vast influence over Congress.

Americans now faced the question of what, if any, steps should be taken to modify the peace instructions. The instructions served as a reminder of the total United States dependence on France in critical times, but with the Yorktown victory and Greene's change of fortune in the South, they seemed to be an insult to national honor. Although American pride had rebounded, a change in policy could not be easily accomplished. Repeal of the instructions would indicate a lessening of United States confidence in France, and it would be dangerous, or at least unwise, to risk this at the very time that Great Britain was expected to reveal an interest in opening peace negotiations.

Congressmen were troubled over the new instructions. Thomas Rodney, for one, considered them too large a sacrifice of national dignity. He realized that the instructions made the United States totally dependent on French capabilities of insuring a fair, honorable treaty. But Rodney, like others who shared his reservations, could not conceive of any acceptable alternative to control by France:

> I was against this Clause because I think it must convince the French Court that we are reduced to a weak and abject State and that we have lost all the Spirit and dignity which once appeared in the proceedings of Congress and considering ourselves unable to Carry on the war any longer we are ready to Accept Peace on any Terms; we may be sure they will not hisitate about granting any thing the mediating powers may require respecting us after they Consent to our Independance so that there need be no longer doubt about the Certainty of peace. Yet what is done for ought I know may be best.[1]

[1] Rodney to Caesar Rodney, June 15, 1781, Ryden, ed., *Letters to and from Caesar Rodney*, pp. 415–16.

Daniel Jenifer, a strong supporter of Luzerne, bluntly noted the dilemma of French control, but did not want to change the instructions. "I fear that our Interests will not be so immediately attended as we might wish:" he wrote, "however, I think France must procure us tolerable terms, or She cannot expect to keep us long in her interest, therefore, I trust more to her policy than to her Justice." [2]

Gouverneur Morris, now an assistant to Robert Morris, heatedly denounced the new instructions in a letter to Jay. Gouverneur Morris had been a favorite of Gérard for his strong opposition to New England in 1779, but he was never as intimate with Luzerne. Morris, despite his many inconsistencies, was a strong nationalist and regarded the instructions as a negation of responsibility and sovereignty. "But when you come by your instruction that you must ultimately obey the dictates of the French minister," he wrote Jay, "I am sure there is something in your bosom which will revolt at the servility of the situation." Later Morris castigated Congress for its lack of courage, "No other Congress will surrender all, as this has, to an ally. I am more moved on this occasion that I ever have been, and therefore it is possible I may be mistaken, but I think so strong, so deep an impression cannot be false." [3]

Luzerne quickly sensed that, on second thought, many supporters of the instructions questioned the wisdom of their action. Massachusetts delegates, in particular, chided others for agreeing to change masters instead of standing firm for independence. Luzerne scolded delegates from two unidentified states for even harboring such thoughts. He argued with considerable force that the King had been scrupulously fair in maintaining his obligations under the alliance and certainly should merit trust in negotiations. Luzerne reported to Vergennes that the well-intentioned delegates accepted the French position after his reprimand.[4]

Luzerne had become an oracle of all knowledge about foreign affairs. The naive delegates believed that they could ask Luzerne about the reliability of the King of France and receive an objective answer. Many never questioned the ability of France to insure the essential interests of the United States. Proponents of the instructions failed to assess France's military prowess against Great Britain or its failure to induce Spain, an ally, to give effective aid to the United States. An answer to these questions would have revealed the limited capacity of France to find solutions to these problems. The dismal circumstances of the Allied cause in mid-1781 were not all the fault of the United States.

No public debate on the instructions ensued, however. For the most

[2] Jenifer to Weedon, June 5, 1781, *LMCC*, Vol. VI, p. 112.
[3] Morris to Jay, June 17, 1781, Johnson, ed., *John Jay*, Vol. II, pp. 38–39.
[4] Luzerne to Vergennes, June 23, 1781, AAE-cp-(EU), Vol. XVII.

part, Congressmen honored their pledge not to discuss the proceedings of Congress for a year. Leaders throughout the country had been informed of the proposed Austrian-Russian mediation, and many knew that France had asked Congress to determine the United States peace terms. Some learned by private channels that France fully backed independence and the boundary claims of the 1779 instructions. From the information available to most leaders, there was little cause for apprehension. Few knew that France had ultimate control over the commissioners and the final word on western boundaries.

William Clajon wrote the only article in the press attacking the instructions, but his criticism was not anti-French; rather, he believed Congress had renounced any claims to western lands. Clajon, a former secretary to General Gates, wrote in a letter at the time of the instructions, "It seems that France requires the Ultimatum of Congress respecting Peace. But, Sir, I trust they will obtain better Terms for us than will be proposed by Congress." [5] In his article Clajon made the first challenge to the power of Congress to ratify treaties.

> O ye, sages, who direct OUR SUPREME council, never forget that every FINAL POWER must remain inviolate in the hands of the people—in those hands which lifted you to your present high stations! You are fully authorised to combine proposals; but, in every sense, a treaty is a LAW; and, to ratify these, is a sacred right, which cannot be wrested from your constituents at large.
>
> They [Congress] should declare that we will not sheathe our swords before Britain has evacuated and ceded to us the thirteen states in our confederation; before she has evacuated all her other possessions on this continent, and left it to the free option of the inhabitants there, to continue under her government or accede to our union. Congress ought to declare, that these are the outlines of our
>
> SINE QUIBUS NON [6]

Clajon's attack evoked no response in the Philadelphia papers, perhaps because no one in Congress wanted to discuss the issue publicly. Most Americans believed that public controversy over the peace ultimata in 1779 gave the British undue advantage, and caused incalculable harm to the American cause in Europe by revealing a lack of unanimity about the objectives of the war. American diplomacy, now removed

[5] Clajon to Gates, June 13, 1781, Gates Papers, box XVI. Clajon admitted that he was the author of the article in Clajon to Gates, Aug. 7, 1781, *ibid.*, box XVI. Barbé-Marbois incorrectly identified the author of the protest as a member of Congress; Barbé-Marbois to Vergennes, July 11, 1781, AAE-cp-(EU), Vol. XVII.
[6] *Freeman's Journal,* July 11, 1781.

from the public arena, proceeded by the more traditional European methods of secrecy. Details about peace negotiations were so well guarded that a Providence paper reported in 1782, "It is said that passports are sent over to Amsterdam for Mr. Adams, the only person in Europe invested with the power to negotiate from the American Congress, and that he is expected in London next week for the purpose of opening a treaty." [7]

Many delegates did not inform their state governments about the new instructions. Daniel Jenifer described conflicts over the instructions in private correspondence, but in letters written to the Governor of Maryland he made no mention of the instructions. Theodorick Bland and Joseph Jones failed to inform Washington, although both were his frequent correspondents.[8]

As a result of congressional secrecy, a number of prominent leaders did not know the basic details about the changes in the instructions. As late as November, Nathanael Greene did not know that additional commissioners had been selected. James McHenry, formerly an aide to Washington and currently in Virginia with Lafayette, knew only of the mediation offer.[9] Washington probably did not know the contents of the instructions until 1783. Washington, however, admitted knowledge only of information which Congress had officially given him in dispatches. Elias Boudinot, president of Congress, wrote Washington in March, 1783, describing conflicts caused by the instructions and French anger over the American commissioners' signing of a separate peace treaty. "I read it [Boudinot's letter] with great pleasure and gratitude," Washington answered, "and beg you to accept my sincere thanks for the trouble you have taken to communicate the several matters therein contained many parts of which 'till now were altogether New to me." [10]

The Massachusetts delegates, the backbone of opposition to the in-

---

[7] *Providence Gazette,* May 11, 1782.

[8] Jenifer and Carroll to Thomas Sims Lee, June 12, 1781 (two letters); June 26, 1781, J. Hall Peasants, ed., *Archives of Maryland,* Vol. XLVII, pp. 284–85, 316; Bland to Washington, June 19, 1781; Jones to Washington, June 20, 1781, Washington Papers, Vol. CLXXVII; Bland to Washington, July 2, 1781, *ibid.,* Vol. CLXXVIII.

[9] Greene to Lovell, Nov. 21, 1781, Greene Papers; McHenry to Smith, July 30, 1781, McHenry Papers, LC, Vol. I. Ebenezer Smith, the head of the Post Office, did not know in September. See Hazard to Belknap, Sept. 5, 1781, *Belknap Papers,* Vol. II, pp. 107–108. It is not clear when Alexander Hamilton learned of the instructions, but Madison records him as saying that "he had disapproved it [the instructions] uniformly since it had come to his knowledge." "Remarks made by Hamilton on provisional peace treaty on March 19, 1783," Syrett, ed., *Hamilton,* Vol. III, pp. 294–95.

[10] Washington to the President of Congress, March 30, 1783, Fitzpatrick, ed., *Washington,* Vol. XXVI, pp. 272–73, marked private by Washington.

structions, refrained from public criticism as long as John Adams retained his commission to negotiate a commercial treaty with Great Britain. They believed that Adams could delay any final peace treaty by refusing to sign a commercial agreement, thus protecting the demand for access to the fishery. Luzerne overlooked this possible loophole, but Barbé-Marbois perceived that Adams might be able to evade French control after a Massachusetts delegate boasted that his state had again outmaneuvered the French.[11]

Barbé-Marbois persuaded his frequent companion, James Madison, to introduce a motion revoking Adams' commission for a commercial treaty. The motion passed the same day it was introduced by a seven to two margin; only Massachusetts and Connecticut were in opposition.[12] Congress took no further action on a commercial treaty with Great Britain for over a year. Every southern delegate voted to revoke Adams' commission, which eliminated New England's best hope for gaining the fishery without French support. James Lovell sounded the alarm to Elbridge Gerry, who then started to organize a sustained campaign to repeal the instructions.

> Mr. John Adams has no distinct powers. You recollect where we placed our Security for the haddock. But now it is judged that Great Britain will continue to settle all Points respecting trade in the treaty of peace. And our Side to be ultimately decided by France according to the instructions given; which, producing the most happy Effects possible, cannot fail to do us *infinite* [*disgrace*] with all wise & spirited Men of the present and future generations.[13]

Whatever the second thoughts about the instructions, the most pressing task for individual delegates was to make sure their particular nominee accepted a new commission. Private channels were used to convince the new appointees to assume the positions. Henry Laurens presented no immediate problem, because he was in the Tower of London, where he had been imprisoned since October, 1780, after being captured on his voyage to Holland. After Laurens was formally exchanged in September, 1782, Robert Livingston sent him his commission.[14] Laurens even-

[11] Barbé-Marbois to Vergennes, July 11, 1781, AAE-cp-(EU), Vol. XVII.

[12] Ford, ed., *Journals of CC,* Vol. XX, July 12, 1781, pp. 746–47.

[13] Lovell to Gerry, July 13, 1781, Gerry-Knight Papers. Because of the cipher and to confuse the British if they intercepted the letter, Lovell stated the last phrase this way, "cannot fail to do us *infinite Honor* with all wise & spirited Men of the present and future generations. Say Disgrace!" Lovell commonly resorted to such tactics, putting the real meaning in cipher while writing the opposite meaning in normal style. Italics in original.

[14] Livingston to Laurens, Sept. 17, 1782, Livingston Papers, N-YHS, box IX.

tually signed the preliminary treaty, but did not take part in the negotiations preceding the signing.

Thus southern hopes for a participating member of the commission depended on Thomas Jefferson. Meriwether Smith, who nominated Jefferson, told him that he should accept the post so that southern interests would be represented. For the first time Smith indicated some second thoughts about the wording of the instructions, although he did not change his mind or advocate repeal. "I am not at Liberty to communicate to you explicitly by *a Letter* their *Objects* that will require your attention or the *Nature* of the *Restrictions* by which you will be bound:" he wrote Jefferson, "You will therefore not be able to determine whether the Embassy will be agreeable and honourable." Jefferson first refused to accept the new assignment because of the illness of his wife, but he accepted when the position was offered again in the fall of 1782, after her death, making no objection to the wording of the instructions.[15]

Benjamin Franklin, the favorite of Vergennes, had thrown his supporters into a quandary when he offered to resign due to John Laurens' appointment to negotiate a loan. Congress did not act on Franklin's proposal, and Daniel Jenifer soothed his wounded pride, "I can assure you that Congress have the greatest reliance on your abilities, integrity, and address, in so much, that it is with pleasure that I can inform you in the late choice of Ministers to negotiate a peace you were unanimously elected." [16] Franklin, mollified by what he considered a vote of confidence, warmly accepted the new commission.

> It gave me great Satisfaction to find, by the unanimous Choice you mention, that my services had not been unacceptable to Congress. . . . It was my Desire to quit public Business fearing it might suffer in my Hands thro' the Infirmities evident in my Time of Life. But as they are pleased to think I still may be useful, I submit to their Judgment, and shall do my best.[17]

John Jay, a unanimous choice for the commission, had received support from all sections of the country. Southerners respected Jay for leading congressional opposition to the fisheries in 1779 and for his work as Minister to Spain, where he fought valiantly for effective aid without renouncing United States claims to the West. New England delegates considered Jay the lesser of two evils. They did not believe he opposed New England as strongly as they suspected Franklin did, and they hoped that

[15] Smith to Jefferson, June 21, 1781; Jefferson to McKean, Aug. 4, 1781; Livingston to Jefferson, Nov. 13, 1782; Jefferson to Livingston, Nov. 26, 1782, Boyd, ed., *Jefferson*, Vol. VI, pp. 99–100, 113, 202, 206, italics in original.

[16] Jenifer to Franklin, July 6, 1781, *LMCC*, Vol. VI, p. 138.

[17] Franklin to Jenifer, Sept. 13, 1781, Franklin Papers, LC, Vol. III.

Jay's appointment would facilitate Franklin's exclusion from the commission.

John Jay's irascible disposition had not improved during his service in Spain. The Spanish government under Floridablanca procrastinated, making no concrete commitments to assist the United States while insisting that the United States relinquish its claims in the West. Jay also had troubles with his staff. He argued about personal matters with Henry Livingston, his nephew and private secretary, and about political issues with William Carmichael, his official secretary.

Jay accepted the new assignment, but with a blistering attack on the instructions startling to their adherents in Congress. "But, Sir, as an American I felt an interest in the dignity of my country, which renders it difficult for me to reconcile myself to the idea of sovereign independent States of America submitting," he wrote, "in the persons of their ministers, to be absolutely governed by the advice and opinions of the servants of another sovereign, especially in a case of national importance." [18] A Massachusetts delegate sensed a kindred spirit after Jay's letter was read in Congress, "Mr. J[ay] gives us his Sentiments on the Subject which appear to me rational and independent." [19]

Jay's strong feeling about the instructions was significant because of his overwhelming support in Congress. Luzerne believed that Jay's opinions had more influence in Congress than those of either Franklin or Adams, because Jay "appears to be the least passionate, either for or against us." [20] Congress had added commissioners partly to heal the divisive split between Franklin and Adams. After Jay's letter it appeared that difficulties about authority and honor might again break out among American diplomats in Europe.

James Lovell provided information and persuasion to secure John Adams' acceptance of his emasculated commission. After the revocation of Adams' powers to negotiate a commerical treaty, Lovell informed him matter-of-factly, "I persuade myself no dishonor for you [was] intended. The business greatly, in every view chagrins me." [21] Lovell hoped that Adams would accept the new commission, but he believed

---

[18] Jay to President of Congress, Sept. 20, 1781, Wharton, ed., *Diplomatic Correspondence*, Vol. IV, pp. 716–18. John Adams had a copy of this letter, but probably did not receive it until Sept., 1782, after Jay sent Adams a copy of the intercepted Barbé-Marbois letter. Adams' notation reads, "Mr. Jay to President of Congress about a *certain* instruction, Septr. 1781," Adams Papers, R. 355. Barbé-Marbois in his letter attacked Samuel Adams and Massachusetts for wanting the fishery. He stated that if France excluded the United States from the fishery then the United States would be more dependent on France after the war.

[19] Partridge to Gerry, Dec. 22, 1781, *LMCC*, Vol. VI, p. 283.

[20] Luzerne to Vergennes, Sept. 25, 1781, AAE-cp-(EU), Vol. XVIII.

[21] Lovell to Adams, July 21, 1781, Adams Papers, R. 355.

there was little he could do other than indicate his disapproval of congressional actions and rely on Adams' political wisdom.

Lovell had not considered the reaction of the better half of the Adams family. Abigail reacted to the instructions as any proud, spirited wife would to a slight on her husband's honor. Her fury rose when she heard that Congress had chosen the detested Franklin to serve with her husband. She wrote Lovell, "I see nothing but dishonor and disgrace in the union." [22] After a month's brooding, Abigail unleashed her moral indignation on the helpless Elbridge Gerry.

> One [John Adams] will speak a bold & firm language becoming a free sovereign & Independent nation, the other [Franklin] will be indecisive gelding fauning flattering. . . . If after all the efforts of the Friends of Liberty C[ongre]ss should join them you may be assured my Friend will resign his commission. I shall intreat him to, but he will not want persuasion yet.[23]

Gerry realized that New England hopes for the fishery depended on John Adams' acceptance of his reduced powers. While agreeing that the actions of Congress were disgraceful, he asked Abigail to await further word from Lovell.[24] Gerry sent Abigail's personal ultimatum to Lovell, who set out to smooth her ruffled feathers. Reversing everything he had previously written about the instructions, Lovell gave Abigail a highly dubious interpretation of the entire affair. "I do really think that no pique or ill will against Mr. A[dams] exists here. . . . I am not induced to suppose La Luzerne otherways than Friendly & respectful," he wrote, later adding, "I wish you not to suffer any Vexation of Mind beyond that I do myself. There is no such Idea here as any Criminality in Mr. A[dams]. He is much esteemed." [25] A month later Lovell took Abigail to task for her hostility to Franklin, but described Franklin's unsympathetic judgment of the Adams-Vergennes conflict as "a most unkind and stabbing one." [26]

Time and Lovell's letters calmed Abigail. When she wrote John she appealed to his vanity, including poignant reminders about the political effects of an overly tenacious defense of personal honor. "I really am in suspense whether you will hold you garbled commission— . . . but if you resign—I am not the only person by hundreds who dread the consequences," she wrote. "You will do what you esteem to be your duty, I doubt not, fearless of consequences and eternity [?] will discriminate the

---

22 Abigail Adams to Lovell, June 30 [1781?], *ibid.,* R. 359.
23 Abigail Adams to Gerry, July [20?], 1781, *ibid.,* R. 355.
24 Gerry to Abigail Adams, July 30, 1781, *ibid.,* R. 355.
25 Lovell to Abigail Adams, Aug. 10, 1781, *ibid.,* R. 355.
26 Lovell to Abigail Adams, Sept. 15, 1781, *LMCC,* Vol. VI, p. 219.

Honest Man from the Knave tho the present generation seems little disposed to." [27]

John Adams did not lack a sound sense of political reality. He accepted the commission without protest to anyone in the United States, although he denounced the instructions to Francis Dana.[28] Adams used Abigail's opinions as needed moral support, but dismissed her fears about insults to his honor, "Dont distress yourself neither about any malicious attempt to injure me in the Estimation of my Countrymen." He ended his letter on a rare hypocritical note, "I laugh, and will laugh before all posterity at their [his enemies'] impotence. Rage and Envy they could not help blushing themselves if they were to review their conduct." [29]

Vergennes, now that he had the desired control of the impudent Adams, congratulated Luzerne on his success and reported his pleasure with the new instructions.[30] Although Vergennes never clarified his intentions on the clause giving him ultimate control over the Americans, he wanted it more for protection than for a direct exercise of authority. Vergennes wished to have close personal friendship and confidence between himself and any American negotiator. He hoped that a diplomat whom he could respect, such as Franklin, would be named leader of the American delegation.

After Franklin showed Vergennes his new commission, Vergennes notified Luzerne that the King would consider it a rebuke if Congress changed the instructions.[31] Since Congress had passed the instructions by a top-heavy majority, Vergennes reasoned that threats of French displeasure would obstruct any attempts at repeal. Later, however, he raised the cost of repealing the instructions. Luzerne was instructed to inform Congress that France would take no part in any congressional consideration of repeal, but if Congress did alter the instructions, the United States would have to fend for itself in making peace with Great Britain. Such a position, Vergennes predicted, would reveal the weakness of the "anti-Gallicans" in Congress, consequently reducing them to silence.[32] Vergennes gave Congress a clear-cut choice of following the instructions as they were or, for all practical purposes, giving up the advantages of the alliance.

Vergennes knew that French strength in Congress was at an all-time peak even before Yorktown. Only two states had opposed putting the

[27] Abigail Adams to John Adams, Sept. 29, 1781, Adams Papers, R. 355.
[28] Adams to Dana, Dec. 11, 1781, Dana Papers, MHS.
[29] John Adams to Abigail Adams, Dec. 2, 1781, Adams Papers, R. 355.
[30] Vergennes to Luzerne, Sept. 7, 1781, AAE-cp-(EU), Vol. XVIII.
[31] Ibid.
[32] Vergennes to Luzerne, Oct. 7, 1781, ibid., Vol. XIX.

commissioners under his control. Opponents of the instructions would have to change the votes of five states. Even if a solid New England and Virginia coalition developed in favor of repeal, it would still need the votes of two additional states. Repeal of the instructions was therefore a virtual impossibility, and Luzerne and congressional opponents of the instructions knew it.

Nevertheless, the minority was not reduced to silence, as Vergennes had predicted. Motions to alter the instructions were proposed four times in 1781 and 1782, usually by radicals such as William Ellery, James Lovell, or Arthur Lee. The Massachusetts delegates worked unremittingly to repeal the instructions, although their efforts were foredoomed. No more than three states ever voted for repeal in any attempt.

William Ellery, who returned to Congress in the fall of 1781, introduced the first motion to expand the ultimata for peace. Ellery did not specify where he wished to expand them, but he undoubtedly wished to gain the fisheries in exchange for support for southern territorial ambitions in the West. Ellery's motion, made before the outcome of Yorktown, was defeated, five to two. Massachusetts and—inexplicably— Georgia, voted for it. Ellery's own vote was canceled out by Ezekiel Cornell.[33]

James Lovell, refreshed by his first visit home in five years, led the next effort to repeal the instructions in January, 1782. Lovell's attempt came too soon after Yorktown. Congressmen, in spite of their reservations, could see no advantage in changing their position until they learned how Parliament would react to the latest British defeat. Lovell then resurrected an argument he had used in the debates on the peace ultimata of 1779; he contended that France would be obliged to give the United States a portion of her own fishery if unsuccessful in gaining part of the fishery for the United States in peace negotiations with Great Britain. Lovell's argument was sophistry, but he wanted to reveal alleged French determination to exclude the United States altogether from the Grand Banks. Although Luzerne noted, "The fisheries are always defended with an extreme vigor by Mr. Lovell," the January vote was five to two, the same as in October.[34] John Sullivan's absence in no way changed the New England vote on the instructions. Three of the five New England delegates outside of Massachusetts voted against repealing or changing the instructions. Again, only Georgia sided with Massachusetts.

The most serious effort to repeal the instructions came in August,

[33] Secret Journal, Oct. 18, 1781, Papers of Continental Congress, NA, pp. 44–45.
[34] *Ibid.*, Jan. 18, 1872, pp. 39–40; Luzerne to Vergennes, Jan. 5, 1782, AAE-cp-(EU), Vol. XX.

1782. By this time attention focused on western lands, and how little France had aided the United States in gaining Spanish support. The Southern States were by now more confident of their position and less fearful of peace talks being held in Europe. Great Britain, evincing an unmistakable interest in peace, had opened informal negotiations with Franklin in Paris. Furthermore, the redeployment of British forces indicated that the United States would not be heavily involved if war broke out again in the Western Hemisphere. Sir Guy Carleton was sending troops to the West Indies, arranging for the settlement of refugees in Nova Scotia, and preparing the final evacuation of Charleston. The South Carolina delegates' appetite for western land increased as total British evacuation of the South appeared imminent.

John Jay set off the spark which ignited the debate in Congress again. Jay announced that he was leaving Madrid because of the apparent impossibility of reaching an agreement with Spain. He informed Congress that the primary reason for failure was French indifference to American needs. James Madison, whose predilection for French policy was so pronounced that a close friend warned, "I hope you are not under his [Luzerne's] influence," believed the opposition to be stronger than ever.

> This circumstance with some other passages of Jay's letter which cannot be here recited, were fresh leaven to the anti gallic ferment and revived the motion lately mentioned to you. It was again suspended by an adjournment but will be renewed and pressed to a decision. From the present temper of congress I infer that the decision if not reversive of the power given to France in the negotiation of peace will denote such a degree of discontent and distrust as will greatly impair the confidence on the side of our ally and may if discovered inspire the enemy with new hopes for a protraction of the war. It is very probable that this affair will eventually be adjusted on some middle ground. The venom against France will not be assuaged without some such expedient.[35]

Madison was far too pessimistic about French strength in Congress. Most members of Congress saw no reason why relations with Spain should cause a break in the alliance with France. The promising outlook for peace made Congress reluctant to make any significant changes when a sweeping victory was within grasp. Any vote showing a lack of confidence in France would do the United States needless damage. The situation had been reversed in the last year. There was little harm in showing continued trust in France, because the United States held the advantage.

[35] Rev. James Madison to Madison, Jan. 13, 1783, Madison Papers, R. 1; Madison to Randolph, Aug. 5, 1782, LMCC, Vol. VI, p. 420.

If war broke out again, it would be on the seas and in the West Indies.

Reconsideration of the instructions was successfully parried by Madison, who proposed a committee to reconsider revisions. Madison's motion carried by a vote of eight to three, with Massachusetts, Connecticut, and Virginia in opposition. Virginia changed its vote on this issue when Arthur Lee and Theodorick Bland combined to override Madison. Madison, appointed chairman of the new committee, effectively pigeonholed any proposal which would substantially change the intent of the instructions.[36]

The final attempt to alter the instructions came in December, 1782, after Congress received a copy of the Barbé-Marbois dispatch on the fisheries, which the British had intercepted and given to John Jay in Paris. A motion was introduced to reconsider the instructions, but it was postponed indefinitely on another motion by Alexander Hamilton providing that Congress should wait until it had more information with which to check the authenticity of the Barbé-Marbois letter. Massachusetts delegates held their tongues, for a change, because Jay's letter and information from John Adams indicated that Jay had been converted to a position of insisting on the fishery in the peace treaty.[37]

Until Jay's letter denouncing French policy arrived in December, opponents of the instructions had been in a hopeless position. Now John Jay's position guaranteed Massachusetts its objective, even without repeal of the instructions. The failure of repeal efforts indicated fear of insulting France rather than trust. The alliance itself was at stake at the very time when victory seemed closest. Nevertheless, Samuel Osgood correctly noted a Herculean effort by a few members of Congress to repeal the instructions despite the damage such a step would do the alliance.[38] But the ultimatum from Vergennes on the price of repeal and the favorable circumstances of 1782 outweighed pleas to make the United States master of its own negotiations for peace and independence.

James Lovell, now serving as a receiver of Continental taxes in Boston, still waged a private campaign against the instructions. He did not hesitate to admit the obvious fact that any modification of the instructions would indicate American distrust of France, but consistently argued that self-interest required a fine discrimination to keep trust from becoming control.

> . . . we are committed, (as we cannot [commit] ourselves into the Hands of the Supreme Being) into the hands of our Great,

36 Secret Journal, Aug. 8, 1782, *Papers of Continental Congress,* pp. 53–54.

37 Ford, ed., *Journals of CC,* Vol. XXIII, Dec. 30, 1782, from Madison's notes on debates, p. 874.

38 Osgood to John Adams, Dec. 7, 1783, *LMCC,* Vol. VII, pp. 382–83.

generous, powerful, & alas wise [ally]. Our Country are left two objects; one is our Independence, the other is to avoid any concessions inconsistent with our Treaties with Fr[ance] & as they are constituted our Guardians, I think this latter might have been omitted, as they will doubtless take care of themselves, but our Fishery, the Extent of our Union, East, W[est] N[orth] S[outh], the Return of Progress, the Return of their [Tories'] Estates, the Extent of our Trade, the limitation of our Navy & everything you can conceive to be the object of Liberty is committed to those who care most for us, but as I have taken up a queer Idea that every Man & nation Love themselves best & will consult their own Interests, & that it is dangerous to trust any affair entirely to the Disposition of another.[39]

[39] Lovell to Langdon, Aug. 30, 1782, Langdon Papers, HSP.

French Ministers To The United States

CONRAD ALEXANDRE GÉRARD, first French Minister to the United States, became embroiled in political controversy. (*Independence National Historical Park Collection*)

CHEVALIER DE LA LUZERNE, second French Minister to the United States, understood the revolutionary implications of the American struggle. (*Independence National Historical Park Collection*)

Radicals

Upper Left: RICHARD HENRY LEE, an early supporter of an alliance with France. (*Independence National Historical Park Collection*) Upper Right: JOSEPH REED, a quiet but consistent radical. (*Independence National Historical Park Collection*)   Lower Left: HENRY LAURENS, a critic of excessive French influence. (*Independence National Historical Park Collection*)   Lower Right: ROGER SHERMAN, a "hardy Watchman" in the defense of national honor. (*Cirker and Cirker, Dictionary of American Portraits*)

Moderates

Upper Left: Thomas McKean, originally a radical, shifted to the moderate bloc in 1781. (*Dictionary of American Portraits*) Upper Right: Benjamin Rush, objected to radical territorial demands, but refused to give uncritical support to the French. (*Independence National Historical Park Collection*) Lower Left: James Iredell, supported the alliance yet lamented the "miserable but necessary disunion" from Great Britain. (*Library of Congress*) Lower Right: Daniel of St. Thomas Jenifer, fed Gérard's distrust of the radicals. (*Enoch Pratt Free Library, Baltimore*)

The Deane–Lee Dispute

Upper Left: SILAS DEANE, commissioner to France, whose private commercial activities precipitated a bitter foreign policy dispute. (*Dictionary of American Portraits*)   Upper Right: GOUVERNEUR MORRIS, who with other moderates sympathetic to Deane received Gérard's favor. (*Dictionary of American Portraits*)   Lower Left: ARTHUR LEE, accused Deane of speculating with public funds. (*Independence National Historical Park Collection*)   Lower Right: SAMUEL ADAMS, led support for Arthur Lee and American aspirations for the fishery. (*Dictionary of American Portraits*)

Agents For The French

Upper Left: REV. SAMUEL COOPER, served both Gérard and Luzerne. (*Williams College Museum of Art, Williamstown, Massachusetts*) Upper Right: HUGH HENRY BRACKENRIDGE, prolific but uninspired in his articles for the French. (*Dictionary of American Portraits*) Lower Left: THOMAS PAINE, who was subsidized by both the American and French governments. (*Dictionary of American Portraits*) Lower Right: JOHN SULLIVAN, reported the proceedings of Congress to Luzerne. (*Dictionary of American Portraits*)

Moderate Congressional Leaders
After 1779

ROBERT R LIVINGSTON, Luzerne's personal choice as secretary of foreign affairs. (*Dictionary of American Portraits*)

JOHN WITHERSPOON, composed the peace instructions of 1781 in a private conference with Luzerne. (*Independence National Historical Park Collection*)

Radical Congressional Leaders
After 1779

ELBRIDGE GERRY, who with James Lovell led the powerful Massachusetts political organization in Congress. (*Independence National Historical Park Collection*)

WILLIAM ELLERY, unsuccessfully urged repeal of the peace ultimata of 1781. (*Independence National Historical Park Collection*)

The Clergy
And The Press

Upper Left: REV. WILLIAM GORDON, ardent radical from Boston. (*Massachusetts Historical Society*) Upper Right: REV. EZRA STILES, president of Yale, expressed the new American nationalism. (*Dictionary of American Portraits*) Lower Left: JAMES RIVINGTON, publisher of the *Royal Gazette*. (*Dictionary of American Portraits*) Lower Right: JOHN DUNLAP, publisher of the *Pennsylvania Packet*. (*Dictionary of American Portraits*)

XIII. From Yorktown to Peace

The resounding victory at Yorktown had renewed American enthusiasm for the French. After years of impatient waiting, Yorktown demonstrated the advantages of the alliance. Initial elation over the treaties of 1778 had dimmed with the frustration of the 1779 and 1780 campaigns, and some Americans had come to doubt the value of French support. The Yorktown victory seemed to assure peace and independence at last. Americans, believing peace to be near, abandoned the war effort and took refuge in the security provided by their French ally.

The period between Yorktown and the arrival of the peace treaty saw public affirmations of the benefits of the alliance and the indestructible bond between the United States and France, yet the public belief in the imminence of peace meant that the commitment to France was increasingly superficial. The mutual interests of the two allies would end with independence. Americans realized, however, that the United States could gain better terms from Great Britain by preserving Allied unity until independence was secure, whatever their private reservations about France.

Americans had overwhelmingly supported the alliance because they considered it the best means of achieving these goals. With the attainment of both objectives at hand, there was little reason to exacerbate friction with France. The Continental Congress, reduced in prestige and power, concerned itself with domestic controversies rather than war planning in 1782. Ebullient Americans did not heed the lonely public officials exhorting them to continue the war. Peace was secure, Americans believed. Everything revolved around this feeling in the year and a half following Yorktown.

No discouraging news in 1782 could dispel American confidence in peace. Rodney's victory in April over De Grasse in the West Indies was seen as causing difficulties for France, not the United States, although the alliance guaranteed France its West Indian possessions as of the war's end. After De Grasse's defeat, a widespread rumor held that Great Britain would offer the United States independence while continuing to fight France and Spain in the West Indies. A Maryland observer optimistically predicted, however, "that G[reat] B[ritain] is Sincere, and wishes a general peace and [I] hope by this time the Preliminaries are Signed." [1]

Americans had great difficulty actually determining how close they were to peace, due to the lack of reliable information from France. Congress did not hear any official information about the opening of peace negotiations for a six-month period in 1782.[2] The press abounded in unsubstantiated but hopeful rumors. A Connecticut paper reported, "The disaffected [Tories] now believe that Peace and a full Recognition of American Independency by the Court of Great Britain are not far distant." A Rhode Island paper rounded out details on negotiations, "Since Yesterday a report is spread that the negotiation for peace is broken off; but some people of credit, who pretend to know what passes assure us of the Contrary." An Annapolis paper misinformed its readers that the Ministers from Holland and the United States "have already publicly declared, that they no longer doubt that peace is about to take place." [3]

Most news about peace came from following the debates in Parliament. In 1782 Americans could read more about the actions of Great Britain in their papers than they could of those of Congress or France. Furthermore, they assumed that Parliamentary debates provided the best indications of peace prospects. Political changes within Great Britain, rather than military events, were seen as the key to peace. By 1782 Americans had resigned themselves to the impossibility of recapturing Charleston and New York, but they believed Great Britain would cease fighting and therefore awaited news of any changes in the North Cabinet.

American hopes rose with the resignation of Lord Germain and, shortly thereafter, the fall of the entire North Cabinet with the resultant accession to power by those persistent critics of the war, the Rockingham Whigs. Although Americans believed they understood the operation of Parliament, Shelburne's accession as Prime Minister in July, 1782, disturbed them because of the unknown quality of his policies. "At the first of the Season, the Expectations of America were much raised, in Consequence of the Change of the Ministry and Measures of Parliament; but Events have shewn that their hopes have risen too high," Washington wrote. "The Death of the Marquis of Rockingham, the Advancement of the Earl of Shelburne, and the Delays of Negotiations, have given us very different Impressions from those we at first re-

[1] Carroll to Tilghman, Aug. 25, 1782, Emmet Collection, NYPL.

[2] Madison to Randolph, Aug. 5, 1782; Aug. 20, 1782, *LMCC,* Vol. VI, pp. 420, 453; Luzerne to Vergennes, Sept. 5, 1782, AAE-cp-(EU), Vol. XXII.

[3] *Connecticut Courant,* Sept. 3, 1782; *Providence Gazette,* Sept. 21, 1782; *Maryland Gazette,* Nov. 28, 1782.

ceived." [4] Washington acknowledged, however, that the ouster of Lord North was still the most important indication that peace might come in 1782.

A Maryland paper had prematurely announced the overthrow of the North Cabinet, but confirmation of his ouster did not arrive until May.[5] The news, accompanied by the Parliamentary resolution ending offensive warfare in America, electrified Americans. A correspondent of James Madison summarized the changes which he believed assured the best prospects for peace since 1775, "The British Empire is shaken to its foundation," but Great Britain, he predicted, will try to "separate us from our great Ally, to whom under Providence, we are principally indebted for the present humiliating situation of our Enemy." [6]

Congressional delegates close to the French tried to dampen the enthusiasm of Americans who expected an easy peace. A slightly dense Georgia delegate reported that the ministerial changes gave no reason to hope that Great Britain would grant the United States independence. Those expressing such views constituted a decided minority in Congress, however. Elias Boudinot noted that "not withstanding all the News lately made, I doubt not but we shall have Peace in the Spring." According to another observer, many people in Massachusetts believed "that peace is near & that our inde[pendence] is acknowledged by the British King." [7]

British actions in Europe and the United States strengthened public confidence that peace was near. The appointments of Oswald, Grenville, and Fitzherbert to negotiate peace were considered the best indication that the British wanted to terminate the war. A Connecticut editor speculated on the ways in which Great Britain might seek to compensate for the loss of the United States.[8] Other Americans were equally sanguine. Little news after May, 1782, convinced them that Great Britain intended to continue the war.

Since Great Britain planned no offensive warfare, Americans had to decide what policy would exact the maximum benefits. All groups agreed on a policy of public affirmation of the binding link between France and the United States. "A Citizen" expounded on the wisdom of the United States living up to its treaty commitments with France:

[4] Washington to Franklin, Oct. 18, 1782, Fitzpatrick, ed., *Washington,* Vol. XXV, pp. 272–73.

[5] *Maryland Gazette,* March 21, 1782; *Packet,* May 2, 1782.

[6] Amber to Madison, May 18, 1782, Hutchinson and Rachal, eds., *Madison,* Vol. IV, p. 252.

[7] Few to Jackson, June 2, 1782, *LMCC,* Vol. VI, p. 362; Boudinot to Hannah Boudinot, Sept. 17, 1782, Stimson-Boudinot Collection, PU; Holten to Osgood, Aug. 15, 1782, Samuel Holten Papers, LC.

[8] *Connecticut Courant,* Dec. 24, 1782.

Peace is now the general cry, the general topic of conversation: Peace intended: and peace offered by Great Britain! Not to the allies and associates in the war; but to revolted colonies. There is nothing in the power of human expression more shocking to virtue, national faith, and honor. An attempt to debauch the United States, and cause a violation of their virgin promise. . . . Could we be guilty of so much ingratitude, as to separate from our best friend and only Ally, we should forever forfeit all pretentions to a name among the nations of the earth, and justly feel the horrors of British vengence. Perhaps the people of England are tired of the war; what then? The minority in Parliament has gained its point, by changing the men of Administration: And, to command with some facility the feelings and purses of the nation, the mode, but not the nature of the war has changed.[9]

Even those who had been "anti-Gallicans" favored fidelity to the alliance. Horatio Gates argued, "True to Allies, they [France] cannot fail being true to us." He continued, noting his long standing apprehension about France upsetting the balance of power, "I will not indulge a thought that they will ever imitate the Bad Policy of G[eorge] the 3rd and his advisors." [10]

James Madison made a transparent effort to determine the feelings of Arthur Lee, but the cagey Lee would not be trapped into denouncing the alliance. Lee questioned that "we can dishonorably abandon Allies who have assisted us, for Enemies who have endeavored to destroy us, merely because these endeavors have been frustrated." He continued by reciting the litany of self-interest and honor which radicals considered their distinctive contribution to foreign policy. To negotiate separately would mean that "we would of choice adopt a character of the extremest folly & perfidy when we can with more security adhere to honorable engagements & enjoy a reputable name." [11]

Despite pro-alliance declarations, the approaching peace lessened Luzerne's influence on congressional decisions. His influence decreased because he could not counteract the widespread belief that Great Britain, and not France, was the key to peace. In February, 1782, Luzerne reported that Congress impatiently awaited news from Great Britain. Later he noted that peace dominated the conversation of Americans of all classes after they reviewed the debates in Parliament.[12]

[9] *Providence Gazette,* May 18, 1782.

[10] Gates to Henry, May 10, 1782, Gates Papers, box 19D.

[11] Lee to Madison, May 16, 1782, Hutchinson and Rachal, eds., *Madison,* Vol. IV, p. 244.

[12] Luzerne to Vergennes, Feb. 9, 1782; April 6, 1782, AAE-cp-(EU), Vol. XX.

Luzerne concluded that the public mood made it unwise to demand settlement of potentially divisive issues between the two allies. He complained about the complacency of Congress, which failed to prepare for the upcoming campaign. Luzerne refrained, however, from taking action on John Temple's presence in Boston, although he believed Temple to be an agent of the British government. Any public step to banish Temple, he wrote, would "be rather dangerous." [13] Luzerne knew that the bonds of the alliance depended on the reservoir of good will created by the victory at Yorktown, and he planned his moves cautiously to conserve that good will for a dire emergency.

Luzerne foresaw no serious difficulties, however. He reported that the news of the ministerial changes caused a sensation in Philadelphia, but no one advocated listening to expected British proposals for a separate peace. Luzerne confidently assured Vergennes that Americans were levelheaded about peace and intended to fulfill their obligation under the alliance. If Luzerne was overconfident about the fidelity of Americans, Vergennes was even more deluded. He informed Luzerne that he feared no American, because the United States had nothing to gain by defecting.[14] Throughout 1782, Vergennes and Luzerne arrogantly assumed that Great Britain would not offer sufficient inducements, such as the fishery or western lands, to make Americans risk breaking the alliance.

Luzerne's predictions of American fidelity seemed to be confirmed by the response to offers to negotiate by General Carleton and Admiral Digby. Congress absolutely refused to enter into any discussions with Carleton's emissaries. Great Britain, through Carleton, did not propose enough more than was contained in the scorned North proposals of 1778. As long as Carleton and Digby could give no assurance that they had the authority to grant independence without qualification, there was no possibility that they could succeed in opening negotiations.

Luzerne believed that Carleton would try to implement his offer by a system of bribery on the state level. If the states seemed to desire negotiation, the Carleton offer would create a pressure opposed to the refusal of Congress to discuss terms.[15] Congress, adamant in its refusal, passed a resolution stipulating that all discussions for peace must take place in Europe. Carleton, if he did bribe any state legislators, had little success, because by July Congress and all thirteen states had passed formal resolutions rejecting the negotiation bid by Carleton and Digby.[16] Any devi-

[13] Luzerne to Vergennes, Feb. 9, 1782, *ibid.*, Vol. XX.
[14] Luzerne to Vergennes, May 6, 1782, *ibid.*, Vol. XXI; Vergennes to Luzerne, June 28, 1782, *ibid.*, Vol. XXI.
[15] Luzerne to Rochambeau, May 6, 1782, Rochambeau Papers, Vol. IV.
[16] Luzerne to Vergennes, June 3, 1782; July 22, 1782, AAE-cp-(EU), Vol. XXI.

ation from the terms of the alliance would have to come from the American commissioners in Paris.

At this point Luzerne decided to remind Americans of their obligations to France through official announcement of the birth of the Dauphin. He had a pavilion built to accommodate the six hundred guests invited to celebrate the birth. An additional twelve thousand people watched the fireworks display or enjoyed hand-outs in front of the Minister's residence, according to one paper's estimate.[17] The cost of the celebration ran to almost thirty thousand livres, or six thousand dollars. The Philadelphia press carried elaborate descriptions of the gala evening, the biggest social event in Philadelphia since parties given during the British occupation.

> The engaging manner of the minister, the judiciousness of the decorations, the satisfaction and joy that diffused itself on every countenance, manifesting the unfeigned zeal of every guest in support of our alliance on this pleasing occasion, and the affability and decorum of all, rendered it most agreeable, and delightful ever seen or exhibited on this continent.[18]

James Madison summarized the underlying reasons for public celebration at the birth of the Dauphin, "It was deemed politic at this crisis to display every proper evidence of affectionate attachment to our Ally." [19] During the sentimental outpouring for the Dauphin in the following months, nearly every state and sizable city formally passed resolutions expressing their joy at the event. So extensive was the American reaction that a Loyalist writer commented, "And what a fuss and bother had there been made on the news of the birth of a Dauphin of France, if a promised King of America had been born, there could not have been greater rejoicings." [20]

The demonstrations of affection were as superficial as they were political. Politicians could safely take a stand without fear of retribution. A Boston paper described the elaborate Massachusetts celebration, concluding with a homily on monarchy:

---

[17] Luzerne to Vergennes, May 14, 1782, *ibid.,* Vol. XXI; the cost is given in Luzerne to Vergennes, July 25, 1782, *ibid.,* Vol. XXI; *Packet,* July 18, 1782.

[18] *Freeman's Journal,* July 17, 1782; a description of the party is in Rush to [Ferguson?], July 16, 1782, Butterfield, ed., *Rush,* Vol. I, pp. 278–82.

[19] Madison to Randolph, May 14, 1782, Hutchinson and Rachal, eds., *Madison,* Vol. IV, p. 242.

[20] Quote from *Royal Gazette,* Dec. 11, 1782. For a few of the many examples, see *Maryland Gazette,* July 11, 1782; *Packet,* May 21 and 25, 1782; *Providence Gazette,* Aug. 17, 1782; *Connecticut Courant,* June 4, 1782; *New Jersey Gazette,* June 19, 1782.

Indeed every order of men in its own way, shouted benediction of the Dauphin, which is a compliment not only upon the patriotism, but the good sense of the people, who did well to consider of what importance (in an hereditary kingdom) is the Dauphin; who not only from his infancy may be educated for the throne, but (life preserved) may save immense bloodshed, which so often happens where the right of a crown is disputed. This alone is a reason why republicans, as far as they are friends of mankind, may rejoice when the heir to a great empire is born.[21]

The Dauphin's birth, however, could not erase all suspicion of French motives. Robert R Livingston's brother-in-law asked him "if ever you had discovered in the Conduct of the *French* a wish to change our Government, arising from natural causes, their prejudices in favour of Monarchy, & the difficulty of transacting business with many Heads?" [22] Lingering skepticism about France increased as peace approached. General Charles Lee, disgraced and befriended only by his pet dogs, denounced the action of Congress in not declaring a separate peace. This meant in "plain English," Lee argued, that France would take all of the British possessions in the East and West Indies, "which added to her immense resources will enable her to give law to the whole world." [23]

Although Charles Lee was widely considered to be anti-French, other Americans also started wondering about the role of France in the peace negotiations and the international politics of future years. Radical leaders who had first complained of excessive French influence in 1779 again took up the cudgels to attack France for delaying peace. Richard Henry Lee commented, "It must be very hard, tho, if they [France] will not let us say, that a War ought to have at least one years duration less than that which was waged for the *fairest woman* [Helen of Troy] in the World." [24] Lee expressed a growing dissatisfaction with the binding nature of the alliance, a subject even moderates began to re-examine in 1782. The Reverend James Madison, president of the College of William and Mary, revealed the extent to which anti-French suspicions had increased since Yorktown.

[21] *Continental Journal,* June 20, 1782; this may be Cooper's handiwork, see Cooper to Luzerne, June 13, 1782, Cooper Papers.

[22] Tillotson to Livingston, Jan. 6, 1782, Livingston Papers, N-YHS, box VII, italics in original.

[23] Lee to Robert Morris, July 20, 1782, Stan V. Heckels (Catalogue), *The Confidential Correspondence of Robert Morris* (Philadelphia, 1917), pp. 145–46.

[24] Lee to Shippen, Jan. 7, 1783, Ballagh, ed., *Lee,* Vol. I, pp. 277–78, italics in original.

But if the Independence be bona fide admitted, What can be the obstacles to Peace? France as well as this Country will then have obtained the Object of their Contest, at least the avowed object, and will it not have a considerable Influence upon the Councils of the Other European Powers, if it appears, that she does not rest satisfied with that Acquisition. [?] As to the part which America ought to act, whether she be obliged to attend Her Friend beyond the Mark first aimed at, or whether it be not as damnable in Politics as in Religion to desert the Source of our Salvation, I will not presume to determine.[25]

Damnable or not, a number of Americans incorrectly believed that France had obstructed peace in August, 1782, and this increased their doubts about the future of the alliance. The misconception about France came from a confused understanding of the debate between Vergennes and John Jay over Jay's insistence that Oswald's commission be worded to recognize the American commissioners.[26] By the end of 1782 more and more Americans, impatient for news of a peace treaty, grasped at any rumor to blame France and Spain as much as Great Britain.

The most persistent suspicion of French motives came from Massachusetts, where leaders murmured threats of disunion unless the United States received a share of the fishery. William Gordon, a late convert to Francophobia, suggested to John Adams "that if C[ongress] in their instructions betray their constituents, you will prove instrumental in saving the liberties of your Country. You will be safe though you break orders that would break your owners [France]." [27]

Massachusetts had exhausted all procedures within Congress to guarantee United States participation in the fishery. Its leaders were now forced to consider more drastic action than merely suggesting to John Adams that he break his instructions. Massachusetts, at this time, had only one major bargaining point left—a threat to break up the alliance and reach an agreement with Great Britain. It is doubtful that Massachusetts would ever have attempted such a radical move, but Elbridge Gerry was willing to consider it in 1782.

Whatever may be our Prospects in every other Respect, they are not favorable as they relate to the Fishery. Should the want of a thorough Knowledge in Congress of the Importance of this Right, to the United States, or an Inattention in this Point of their

[25] Rev. James Madison to James Madison, Sept. 18, 1782, Hutchinson and Rachal, eds., *Madison*, Vol. V, p. 138.
[26] Gordon to Gates, Feb. 26, 1782, Gates Papers, box XVI; a newspaper account of the affair is in *Freeman's Journal*, March 12, 1783.
[27] Gordon to Adams, Nov. 30, 1782, Adams Papers, R. 359.

Interest, (on the Part of our allies) deprive Us of the Fishery, the *Union & Alliance* so far as they respect this State will no Longer be natural, because, repugnant to its true Interest; & G[reat] Britain will be furnished with powerful Means by offering a participation in her Fisheries, to detach this State from the Confederacy & Alliance with France & make it an Ally of her own. I have however too much Reliance on the Wisdom of Congress & the Councils of France, to suppose that they will admit so dangerous a Measure, as they cannot be insensible, that States as well as Individuals are governed by the Ideas they have of their own Interest.[28]

Luzerne believed that Massachusetts' threats to gain the fishery by fair means or foul warranted action to protect French interests and prevent United States participation in the fishery. He suggested that France invade and control Cape Breton to guarantee French rights, and at the same time recommended that France and Great Britain sign a no-conquest treaty for that area.[29] Later Luzerne renewed his proposal that France prevent United States participation in the fishery by secretly taking over Isle Royale. He further suggested that the final peace treaty say nothing about the fishery, thus leaving control completely in the hands of France and Great Britain.[30]

Gérard had enunciated French policy when he insisted that France would not support the United States claim for the fishery. France's official position on this had not changed, but Luzerne's attitude had hardened appreciably. Vergennes had contended from the beginning of the alliance that the fishery question should not delay the peace treaty. Luzerne, however, held that France should work to insure the exclusion of the United States, even if Great Britain were willing to grant United States participation. Few Americans perceived that the trusted French Minister had become the strongest advocate of excluding them from the Grand Banks.

Luzerne sometimes worked at cross-purposes with his own recommendations, however. He encouraged Benjamin Rush to write a series of articles advocating the expansion of the American Navy,[31] but quickly realizing the implications of this action, shifted his course. He predicted that an American Navy would not protect commerce as he had origi-

---

[28] Gerry to Dana, June 13, 1782, Adams Papers, copy, R. 358. James Warren threatened the same measures, Warren to Arthur Lee, March 14, 1783, Richard Henry Lee, *Life of Arthur Lee* (Boston, 1829), Vol. II, p. 279. Italics in original.
[29] Luzerne to Vergennes, Jan. 16, 1782, AAE-cp-(EU), Vol. XX.
[30] Luzerne to Vergennes, May 19, 1782, *ibid.,* Vol. XXI.
[31] Luzerne to Vergennes, Aug. 9, 1782, *ibid.,* Vol. XXII.

nally hoped; instead, to strengthen United States claims for a share of the fishery, it would launch attacks on the very islands Luzerne had marked for French acquisition.[32]

Congress and particularly Robert R Livingston, the Secretary of Foreign Affairs, continued to have a deep personal trust in Luzerne. Livingston, Luzerne's personal choice for the position, accepted the office at the urging of Barbé-Marbois.[33] Livingston did not advocate claiming the western lands or making a special effort to obtain the fishery. An easygoing man, he was an ineffective policy-maker. The choleric Arthur Lee described Livingston's performance harshly but accurately, writing, "Whatever you see or receive from him you may consider as dictated by the French Minister. He made him what he is, and policy, or gratitude, keeps him from disobeying or renouncing his maker." Luzerne acknowledged a degree of validity in Lee's description when he commented that Livingston "has shown very great attachment and confidence in us." [34]

Livingston's trust in France became irrelevant in late December when American papers carried news of the new commission which authorized Richard Oswald to treat with the American commissioners. The Oswald commission seemed to confirm the optimistic hopes of Americans. Elias Boudinot aptly phrased it: "the Rubicon is passed." One paper commented on this tacit acknowledgment of United States independence, "All that can be said at present is, that what has hitherto appeared to be the greatest obstacle to a general accommodation, seems now to be got over." [35] Since the news of Oswald's commission was more than three months old before it reached Congress, Americans expected to hear of the final peace treaty with each incoming ship. With independence apparently secure, only waiting and lip service to the alliance were required.

While Oswald's commission caused elation in Congress, other dispatches from John Jay accused France of undermining the American negotiating position.[36] Jay sent Congress the intercepted Barbé-Marbois dispatch of March 13, 1782, in which the author strongly reiterated the French position on the fishery. The dispatch, although it reflected no

---

[32] Luzerne to Vergennes, Dec. 27, 1782, *ibid.,* Vol. XXII.

[33] Barbé-Marbois to Livingston, Jan. 2, 1781, Livingston Papers, N-YHS, box VI.

[34] Lee to Dana, July 6, 1782, *LMCC,* Vol. VI, p. 379; Luzerne, "List of Members," Luzerne Papers. A good account of Livingston and the French is George Dangerfield, *Chancellor Robert R. Livingston of New York* (New York, 1960), pp. 134–80.

[35] Boudinot to Pintard, Dec. 24, 1782, Boudinot Papers, HSP; *Packet,* Dec. 24, 1782. Quote from *Independent Ledger* (Boston), Jan. 13, 1783.

[36] Jay to Livingston, Sept. 18, 1782; Oct. 13, 1782, Wharton, ed., *Diplomatic Correspondence,* Vol. V, pp. 740, 809.

change in French policy, was significant because of its effect on Jay and the timing of its arrival in the United States. The Oswald commission and British peace preparations in the United States allowed underlying distrust of French motives to burgeon into heated denunciations of French insincerity.[37] The dispatch confirmed the past suspicions of the Massachusetts delegates and the opponents of the 1781 peace instructions.

James Madison, a strong advocate of French policy, admitted, "Candor will suggest however that the situation of France is and has been extremely perplexing. . . . This policy [to make the United States realize her weakness] if discovered tended on the other hand to spoil the whole." [38] Madison was one of many French supporters in Congress forced to re-evaluate their position and confess, at least privately, that they had put too much confidence in Luzerne's assurances that France would never work against the best interests of the United States.

Robert Livingston, however, remained unconvinced by the Barbé-Marbois dispatch. Livingston, who had earlier described himself as "sometimes a little hurt by his [Jay's] *dogmatick* manner & incommunicableness," castigated Jay for believing the document.[39] He wrote, "what is said of the great Bank [fishery] is nonsense or if it conveys any sentiment I think it is not such as a man of common sense would speake." [40] Livingston went even further in a private memorandum, apparently for himself, which he probably wrote in early 1783.

> An Idea has also gone forth & it is fomented by the disaffected [from France] that France wishes from interested views to monopolize the fishery at least to exclude all other competitors but G[reat] B[ritain]. Those who have attended to the disinterested conduct of France during the war oppose to this sentiment the honor & good faith of their ally. The little interest that he [the King of France] can have in excluding a people from a right which w[oul]d not interfere with his, since France does little more than supply itself & the New England fishery for the most parrt only supplys the continent and Islands of America. They see the care with which France has endeavoured to cultivate a good understanding between that Kingdom & these States & they are persuaded that so inconsiderable an object will not be put in competi-

[37] See Madison notes on debates in Ford, ed., *Journals of CC*, Vol. XXIII, pp. 870–75; *ibid.*, Vol. XXV, p. 845; also Osgood to Adams, Dec. 7, 1783, *LMCC*, Vol. VII, pp. 378–88.

[38] Ford, ed., *Journals of CC*, Vol. XXIII, p. 871.

[39] Livingston to Morris, June 13, 1778, Livingston Papers, N-YHS, box IV, italics in original.

[40] Livingston to Jay, Dec. 30, 1782, *ibid.*, box X.

tion with the harmony which ought to subsist between them or administers food to these unwordly jealousies.[41]

Livingston demonstrated the unstinted trust with which a number of American leaders viewed French policy. He cannot be blamed for being mistaken about the true intentions of France on the basis of the Barbé-Marbois dispatch, but his observations directly contradict the public position taken by Gérard and Luzerne since the beginning of the alliance. Livingston's self-deception was partly due to his firm belief "that as we owe our success in war to his [Louis XVI's] magnanimity & generosity we may be equally indebted to his justice & firmness for an honourable peace." [42] There is little doubt as to why Luzerne wanted Livingston as Secretary for Foreign Relations.

Luzerne received no word of the intercepted dispatch from Livingston or pro-French members of Congress. He speculated that letters arriving from Paris had caused suspicion of France among some Congressmen. But he believed that they were angry primarily because Rayneval, first secretary to Vergennes, had made a trip to see Shelburne without American participation.[43] The French information system failed on this occasion, because there were no agents such as Sullivan in Congress.[44]

There was little to do in early 1783 except await additional news from Paris. The first news of the signing of the preliminary treaty came from the Loyalist press in New York, which reprinted excerpts from the King's speech to Parliament of December 5, 1782. A Philadelphia paper, quoting the *Royal Gazette* of February 9, reported that the King had declared the United States independent with the signing of the preliminary treaty. Having been taken in too many times by James Rivington, the same paper commented three days later, "but this is too absurd

[41] "Consideration on the U.S. and the Peace Treaty," [Jan., 1783?], *ibid.*, box XI.

[42] *Ibid.*

[43] Luzerne to Vergennes, Dec. 30, 1782, AAE-cp-(EU), Vol. XXII. Luzerne later argued that the letter had indeed made a deep impression on Congress and eroded the trust in France by many members of Congress. He also stated that he still had not seen a copy of the Barbé-Marbois letter presented to Congress, Luzerne to Vergennes, March 20, 1784, Luzerne Papers.

[44] When Luzerne learned of the dispatch he first suspected that it was one of his that had been intercepted. Vergennes informed him that the Americans were given the Barbé-Marbois dispatch of March 13, 1782, by the British. Luzerne to Vergennes, April 19, 1783, AAE-cp-(EU), Vol. XXIV; Vergennes to Luzerne, Sept. 7, 1783, *ibid.*, Vol. XXV. Madison noted that the French learned about the dispatch via Boston. Madison to Jefferson, May 13, 1783, *LMCC*, Vol. VII, pp. 162–63. Probably Cooper read one of the copies of the dispatch sent back by John Adams and relayed the information to Philadelphia.

and inconsistent to be credited; because all powers at war must have signed at the same time." [45]

In spite of Luzerne's vain efforts to discount the rumors, most Americans believed reports of the peace treaty. One almost illiterate Congressman wrote: "The day is now Come when the sun will Rasie on amirrica never to set." [46] A patriotic poet contributed "On American Independency."

> When pregnant Nature strove relief to gain,
> Her nurse was Washington, her midwife Paine.
> The infant Independence scarce began,
> To be, e'er he had ripen'd into man;
> France his god father, Britain was his rod,
> Congress his guardians, and his father GOD.[47]

"I believe the next arrival from Europe will bring us the good News," Elias Boudinot wrote.[48] Captain Joshua Barney, who carried news of the preliminary treaty, stopped in the West Indies, revealing to one and all that he sailed with a British passport and carried some very important documents for Congress.[49] Barney docked on March 11, and arrived in Philadelphia the next day with a copy of the preliminary articles of peace signed November 30, 1782.

The preliminary treaty which Captain Barney delivered to Congress had been signed in Paris by the four American commissioners, who had violated both the defensive treaty and the 1781 peace instructions. Once negotiations commenced between Great Britain and the United States in Paris in the summer of 1782, each American commissioner—starting with Benjamin Franklin, whom Vergennes believed the most trustworthy, followed by John Jay and John Adams, and finally the much-maligned Henry Laurens—broke his instructions to confide in the French Minister and ultimately follow his advice. Franklin started secret negotiations with Richard Oswald, and John Jay broke openly with Vergennes over the wording of Oswald's commission, which, after Jay's objections, recognized the United States. John Adams, who still called

[45] *Royal Gazette,* Feb. 9, 1783; *Packet,* Feb. 15, Feb. 18, 1783. Other papers carried the news but had no way of confirming the information. The *Independent Chronicle,* Feb. 27, 1783, stated that it had informally heard from Captain Barry acknowledging the existence of a peace treaty; the *Newport Mercury,* Feb. 22, 1783, carried a dispatch from Antigua; other papers carrying the news were *Connecticut Courant,* Feb. 25, 1783; *Providence Gazette,* March 1, 1783; *Maryland Gazette,* Feb. 20, 1783.

[46] Luzerne to Vergennes, Feb. 9, 1783, AAE-cp-(EU), Vol. XXIII; Montgomery to Magaw, Feb. 13, 1783, *LMCC,* Vol. VII, p. 43.

[47] *Independent Gazetteer* (Philadelphia), Feb. 18, 1783.

[48] Boudinot to Greene, Feb. 13, 1783, *LMCC,* Vol. VII, p. 42.

[49] *Packet,* Feb. 27, March 6, 1783.

Franklin "the old conjurer" and suspected Jay of being hostile to New England interests, was surprised to learn after his arrival in late October that Franklin and Jay agreed with him that the progress of the negotiations should be kept secret from the French. Only Henry Laurens, whom Vergennes and Luzerne most suspected, protested violating the defensive treaty with France by signing a separate peace with Great Britain, although he added his signature to the final document.[50]

Vergennes was furious at the Americans for violating their instructions, but realistically acknowledged that the benefits for the United States were too extensive to be resisted by any diplomat. In addition to independence, Great Britain granted the United States access to the Newfoundland fisheries and agreed to avoid settlement of the explosive Loyalist question in the peace treaty. Furthermore, Great Britain and the United States agreed that each would share navigation rights on the Mississippi. The United States gained the valuable western lands beyond the Appalachian mountains to the Mississippi and from the thirty-first parallel in the south to the supposed source of the Mississippi in the north. The boundary between Canada and the United States was based on the desire of Americans to have a defensive frontier running through the Great Lakes, up the Saint Lawrence, and down the Saint Croix River to the Atlantic. The Americans thus acquired an enormous expanse of undeveloped territory with natural and defensible borders. "You will notice that the English buy peace more than they make it," a stunned Vergennes wrote his secretary. "Their concessions, in fact as much as to the boundaries as to the fisheries and loyalists, exceed all that I should have thought possible." [51]

Luzerne, in his final report, wrote that never in the eighteenth century had one belligerent displayed such generosity to another; the Americans had won everything they had asked on boundaries, fisheries, and Loyalists. Great Britain's desertion of the Tories he believed to be an action unworthy of a great nation.[52] Vergennes and Luzerne must have secretly admired the American commissioners, although temporarily resenting the facility with which their American allies abandoned both their treaty commitments and the instructions in which the French placed such confidence.

Congress welcomed the news of the preliminary treaty and immediately ordered that the states be informed. This procedure allowed the Pennsylvania state legislature to receive the news the same day; a mem-

[50] Morris, *The Peacemakers,* pp. 264, 273–74, 310, 336, 356–57, 377; Van Doren, *Franklin,* pp. 665–99.
[51] Vergennes to Rayneval, Dec. 4, 1782, Wharton, ed., *Diplomatic Correspondence,* Vol. VI, p. 107.
[52] Luzerne, "Final Report," Luzerne Papers.

ber of the legislature leaked the contents of the treaty, except for the secret article on Florida, to the press. One paper reprinting the treaty sold out several hundred extra copies within hours.[53] The papers seemed indifferent to the fact that the articles were only preliminary, one of them stating the obvious fact apparent to all Americans, "America, however, is no longer the object of the war; the British having acknowledged our independence." [54]

The surprisingly good terms of the preliminary treaty pleased almost everyone. Only the recommendation of reparations payments to the Loyalists caused scattered protest.[55] Although Luzerne warned Washington that the treaty was only provisional, he observed that Great Britain had granted the United States "everything they could desire," adding that French "satisfaction had been complete." [56] Luzerne did not mention to Washington, or any of his other correspondents, French displeasure over the violation of the terms of the defensive treaty.

American satisfaction with the terms of the preliminary treaty put the French in a difficult position. Luzerne could not protest the violation of the alliance too harshly, because the United States had gained all its goals and would be a useless ally if the war continued. "It appears to me the British for once played the Game of Negotiating with tolerable address," Joseph Reed commented, "if they make Peace they attain their End—if Peace fails thro[ugh] our Allies, we shall be very cold in the Prosecution of the War, no longer necessary for the Establishment of our Claims." [57] Reed, a quiet but constant critic of excessive French influence, softened his hostility to France. The United States, he realized, had more than redeemed itself from past insults to national honor. Although the generous terms of the treaty diminished hostility toward France, the alleged indignities of the past had already hardened some attitudes toward the alliance. Nevertheless, the success of Jay, Adams, and Franklin in circumventing the opposition's fears and the arrival of the provisional treaty marked the end of anti-French expressions.

Congress now faced a delicate problem with the provisional treaty. It could not disavow such a generous treaty, yet it had to find a method to placate France. The easiest procedure seemed to be to censure the commissioners for violating their instructions, while not rejecting the re-

[53] *Independent Gazetteer,* March 18, 1783; the paper reprinted the treaty on this date because the March 15, 1783, edition had sold out so quickly.

[54] *Freeman's Journal,* March 19, 1783.

[55] Gilman to Weare, March 12, 1783, *LMCC,* Vol. VII, p. 72; Floyd to Clinton, March 12, 1783, *ibid.,* p. 73; Lee to Warren, March 12, 1783, *ibid.,* p. 77; Collins to Greene, March 13, 1783, *ibid.,* p. 78.

[56] Luzerne to Washington, March 15, 1783, Washington Papers, Vol. CCXVII.

[57] Reed to Greene, March 14, 1783, Reed Papers, Vol. X.

sults of their actions.[58] "The dilemma to which Congress are reduced is infinitely perplexing. If they abet the proceedings of their ministers all confidence with France is at an end which in the event of a renewal of the war must be dreadful as in that of peace it may be dishonorable," a needlessly worried James Madison wrote. "If they avow the conduct of their ministers by their usual frankness of communication the most serious inconveniences present themselves." [59] Actually, very few feared that the war would continue, and the commissioners had far too much support to allow Congress to pass a motion of censure. The dilemma was resolved by the well-worn method of procrastination resulting in no formal decision at all.

Meanwhile, Luzerne directed his efforts to insuring that American officials fully grasped the provisional nature of the treaty. He accepted the American withdrawal from the war, even though the final treaty was not signed immediately. Luzerne may well have known about the secret article concerning Florida, because he noted that it was impossible to stem American antagonism for Spain.[60] Luzerne achieved limited success in his insistence that the papers describe the treaty as provisional, but this qualification was weak and stipulated no military obligations which Americans would have to fulfill. A Philadelphia paper pointed out that peace was by no means assured and that "We have to this moment rejected with distain [sic] every proposal of a defection." [61]

Despite Luzerne's efforts, the news spreading rapidly from Philadelphia was received as the final conclusion of the Revolution. Ceremonial toasts were offered and salutes fired to the United States and France. Perhaps the saddest case of news reporting occurred in Newport, where the paper inserted the following message about the preliminary treaty:

> We are favoured last Evening by a Gentleman with a Philadelphia Paper of the 17th inst. containing the REAL AUTHENTICATED ARTICLES, for a treaty of Peace, subscribed at Paris the 30th of November last, by the British and American Commissioners; but the Paper, by some Accident, being so mutilated and torn, we are unable to gratify our Readers with them, in this Day's Publication.[62]

The festering tension between France and the United States over the signing of the preliminary articles disappeared when news of the treaties

[58] Gaillard Hunt, ed., *The Writings of James Madison* (New York, 1900), Vol. I, pp. 402–23, carries Madison's notes of the Congressional debates.

[59] Madison to Randolph, March 18, 1783, *LMCC*, Vol. VII, p. 90.

[60] Luzerne to Vergennes, March 15, 1783; March 19, 1783; March 22, 1783, AAE-cp-(EU), Vol. XXIII.

[61] *Packet,* March 22, 1783.

[62] *Newport Mercury,* March 29, 1783.

between the remaining powers arrived on March twenty-fifth. Since there were no changes from the preliminary treaty of November 30, 1782, the news was anticlimactic.[63] Congress, now left to await the definitive treaty, concerned itself with financial problems which were exacerbated by a threatened army mutiny, and a public eager to return to peacetime conditions demanded the evacuation of New York.

French errors were forgotten as conversation about the alliance shifted to the past tense. "I hope on this occasion America will hold in Eternal remembrance the good offices and benefits she has received from our great and good Ally, by conferring on her a beneficial preference to all nations," Theodorick Bland wrote. "Eternal remembrance" needed to be seen in perspective, however. "She [France] surely merits every thing we can do, which is consistent with the Dignity and interest of our own Country," concluded Bland.[64]

The interest of the United States became the foremost consideration; past benefits from France were to be weighed only by future prospects. A minister at Ipswich, Massachusetts, enunciated the more nationalistic sentiment prevalent after the arrival of the peace treaty. Briefly mentioning France, he thanked her for helping the United States defeat Cornwallis and then concerned himself with the future of the new country. The fishery, in contrast to the alliance, warranted considerable attention, "The *fishery* so important to our commerical interests, granted to us with such ample privileges, must afford us a living and an inexhaustible fund of wealth and traffic: a fund of superior worth to all the glittering mines of Peru." [65]

The alliance had originally been signed because of the mutual interests of France and the United States. When independence was granted, the bond of mutual interest dissolved. The alliance died in practice, if not legally. The foreign policy of the United States now focused on the country's new relations with Great Britain and her West Indian possessions. France became one of many European powers, one which unfortunately did not offer the prospect of lucrative trade. France was fêted for her aid, but memories are short in diplomacy. Independence solved the major problem of the United States, freeing Americans to concentrate on domestic issues. The alliance between the Catholic monarchy and the Protestant republic had achieved its goal, and both countries proceeded to pursue their separate national interests.

[63] *Packet,* March 25, 1783.
[64] Bland to Washington, March 25, 1783, *LMCC,* Vol. VII, p. 109.
[65] Levi Frisbie, *An Oration Delivered at Ipswich at the Request of a Number of Inhabitants, on the twenty-ninth of April, 1783; on the Account of the Happy Restoration of Peace Between Great Britain and the United States of America* (Boston, 1783), p. 14, italics in original.

XIV. End of the Alliance

The French-American defensive alliance ended in fact when news arrived of the termination of hostilities between France and Great Britain in March, 1783. Americans assumed that the alliance would officially end with the arrival of the definitive treaty of peace which formally acknowledged United States independence. Radicals and moderates from all sections agreed that the adhesive bond of mutual interest disintegrated with achievement of the goal. They immediately began to evaluate the new status of the United States, with the first casualties being the wartime connections with Europe. Non-commercial pacts were now shunned like a contagion. Congress ordered Francis Dana to desist from seeking admission to the League of Armed Neutrality; interest in Spanish credits evaporated with peace. Americans contemplated retaining only the commercial treaty with France.

During the war the United States sought the friendship of the powerful. In peace the United States desired the amity of commercially-minded nations, and foremost among the latter group was Great Britain. Americans expected the definitive treaty to include a commercial treaty allowing American merchants access to the British West Indian trade. Merchants flocked to the wharves to welcome each incoming British ship and quickly glutted the American market with the goods of their former adversary. The war, judging by the tastes of American consumers and the preferences of merchants, seemed to be but an unfortunate interruption of normal trade relations.

The alliance, because of its success, rapidly receded from public awareness. Future relations with France now had to stand the test of increased trade and credit with other powers. Hastening the dissolution of the alliance was the failure of France to cement lasting ties with influential groups in the United States. The alliance had greatly affected the military and congressional machinery during the last years of the Revolution, but now the Army disbanded and Congress, deprived of continued French subsidies and lacking revenue power, declined in authority. The alliance had only superficially affected state and local government, and most parts of American society remained untouched.

Commerce might have been a source of continuing French influence, but trade with France was confined to a handful of merchants associated with John Holker in supplying military goods. Luzerne described the French merchants in the United States as "a Parcell of little Rascals, *petits Coquins,* and Adventurers who have sold the worst Merchandises, for great Prices." [1] This unfortunate wartime experience did little to encourage Americans to expand their trade with France. The alliance, if anything, seemed to be a hindrance to new American aspirations. France, with her own European interests, was likely to pursue long-standing policies which would inhibit Americans from establishing trade connections with all of Europe.

The decline of the alliance to inanition did not preclude the hope of better trade relations with France, however. John Jay suggested that if France wanted to encourage trade, it must extend longer credits to American merchants. Jay also proposed a relaxation of French trade restrictions so that American products in addition to tobacco could be imported.[2] The best prospect for expanded trade would be to allow the United States to export food supplies to the French West Indies.

France, however, clung to her mercantile policies and refused to open West Indian ports to American trade. Individual governors could and did grant permission to trade on a yearly basis, but this policy was too haphazard for stable commerce. Between 1782 and 1789, French trade with the United States fell sharply from the peak established in 1781. Even the limited trade with the West Indian islands drained specie from France, which the United States could in turn use in its mushrooming British trade. Because French officials believed the triangular trade benefited Great Britain, it was discouraged.[3]

The post-war financial crisis in France contributed to the decline of French-American commerce. Jeremiah Wadsworth, the leading American supplier to the French, had to travel to France to collect legitimate bills for supplying the French Army. John Holker, the deposed French consul general, suffered large losses when prices dropped with the news of peace.[4] Holker, too, left for France to rearrange his financial affairs. As British ships were arriving weekly, two of the biggest merchants in Franco-American trade could not continue their wartime commercial activities. Many American merchants quickly returned to their pre-war agreements with British merchant houses, from which they imported

---

[1] Butterfield, ed., *Diary of John Adams,* Vol. II, p. 388, June 21, 1779.

[2] "Memoir regarding Commerce between France and the United States," May 26, 1783, AAE-cp-(EU), Vol. XXIV.

[3] Jacques Godechot, "Les Relations Économiques entre la France et les États-Unis de 1778 à 1789," *French Historical Studies,* Vol. I (1958), pp. 34, 38.

[4] Wadsworth and Carter to Castries, May 15, 1783, Correspondance commerciale générale, B111, Vol. CDXLVIII, AN; Pringle to Holker, March 29, 1783, Holker Papers, Vol. XX.

primarily textiles and other necessities. The trade with France, by contrast, was composed of luxury items and included almost no industrial products; brandy alone accounted for 30 per cent of the United States imports from France.[5]

If the prospects for profitable commercial relations were dim, Americans still hoped France would remain a friendly, but not dominating, influence in political affairs after independence. John Langdon, a Portsmouth merchant who saw signs of excessive French influence in Congress, nevertheless wished that the French would "use their power so as to secure our affections when we shall no longer need Protection." [6] Affection, however, would not determine future relations or solve the problem of domination, and the degree of independence and security would. Oliver Ellsworth summarized the basic American position, "If Great Britain induced thereto by the former administration, must make us independent of herself, it is wise to do so with grace and *in a manner* that shall also keep us independent of France." [7]

The definitive treaty granted the United States independence on such liberal terms that Americans, whether moderate or radical, believed they had enough security to commence evaluating all European powers on the basis of the future advantages they could bring to the United States. France deserved consideration, but not to the detriment of harmonious relations with Great Britain. Only gratitude could lead Americans to regard France in a more favorable light than other powers. Self-interest, unfortunately for France, motivated United States foreign policy more than gratitude in 1783.

James McHenry reflected the dispassionate American attitude toward foreign relations in a memorandum written in 1783. McHenry, with insight rare for him, systematically outlined the current status of the alliance. In 1778 France "took up the American cause as instrumental to her political views in Europe. America likewise, accepted the allian[ce] with France for her separate view, viz., for the establishment of independence." This being the case, "the alliance is therefore completed and terminated without leaving behind it any political principle or true permanent connection between them." Similar circumstances might force both countries to sign another temporary alliance, but since France's primary interest was in Europe the United States could gain no advantages from a permanent alliance. For the present, McHenry con-

[5] Merrill Jensen, *The New Nation* (New York, 1950), pp. 185–88, 201–204; James B. Hedges, *The Browns of Providence Plantations* (Cambridge, 1952), pp. 258, 259.

[6] Langdon to Gilman, Aug. 31, 1782, Langdon Papers.

[7] William G. Brown, *The Life of Oliver Ellsworth* (New York, 1905), p. 100, italics in original. Brown states that the date of this statement was May 6, 1783.

cluded, permanent ties and increased trade could not be expected of France. Hence, "It would be vain to expect in the French any such ally, as newly established states ought to look out for to give maturity and firmness to their constitutions." [8]

McHenry also analyzed future relations between the United States and Great Britain. He believed that the great areas of territory granted the United States "contain an inexhaustible source of riches industry and future power." American society would be fundamentally altered by the acquisition of the new territory, the development of which depended upon "intercourse between Great Britain and America." The United States and Great Britain were linked "inseparably either as friends or foes." This was an "awful and important truth, these are considerations not to be thought of lightly, not to be prejudged in passion, nor the arrangements of them to be hastily foreclosed." [9]

Luzerne, with regret but not surprise, reached virtually the same conclusions as McHenry. He agreed that few French-American connections would remain after peace, although the fishery might possibly become a source of conflict.[10] Later, Luzerne set forth his ideas about the role of France and the United States in the future. He predicted an increase in the "natural interests" drawing Great Britain and the United States together, with a consequent weakening of the ties between France and the United States. United States commerce with Great Britain, he speculated correctly, would increase rapidly, while French-American commerce would remain static. France could do little to stop this realignment, nor was it in France's best interest to resist it. Luzerne believed that United States independence in itself would benefit French interests in the Western Hemisphere, but attempts to influence American policy could needlessly antagonize the United States.[11] Vergennes congratulated Luzerne on his astute analysis, noting his own agreement with the conclusions. He wrote that France would "allow things to follow their natural movement." [12]

Luzerne reflected on Great Britain's policy after the peace settlement in his final report. The generous terms of the treaty meant that the United States would not retain a deep animosity toward Great Britain. Furthermore, the borders agreed upon were natural and easily defended. Thus Great Britain would pursue a defensive strategy toward the United

[8] "Memorial on the British negociation," June 1, 1783, James McHenry Papers, Vol. II.
[9] Ibid.
[10] Luzerne to Vergennes, April 12, 1783, AAE-cp-(EU), Vol. XXIV.
[11] "Observation Sur les principes de conduite à tenir vis à vis les Américains," April 30, 1783, ibid., Vol. XXIV.
[12] Vergennes to Luzerne, July 21, 1783, ibid., Vol. XXV.

States, and the need for American dependence on France would disappear, Luzerne reasoned.[13] Implicitly, French and American leaders agreed there was little rationale for even pretending that the alliance would or should be instrumental in future United States foreign policy.

This mutual, though informal, understanding about the end of the alliance must have relieved the burdened Vergennes, who seemed more than willing to allow it a peaceful death. The French-American venture had caused a severe financial crisis for his country, which for five years had fought the leading power in Europe without any significant reward except independence for a weak and divided country three thousand miles away.

The very weakness of the United States prevented France from pursuing any goals other than the general reduction of British power. By the end of the war, France was providing supplies and subsidies for the American Army; loans to support its currency; and fleets and an army in an effort to keep the infant ally in the war. Long-term dominance of this sort would be too expensive, and future support from the United States too unpredictable, to justify continued inclusion in a policy centered in Europe. Furthermore, Vergennes found the Americans to be impetuous, cynical, and generally unreliable as allies.

Despite repeated proclamations of cooperation and gratitude, Americans had indeed proved to be demanding. The United States, while quick to request territory, credits, and supplies, was indifferent to legitimate French concerns in the West Indies. Ultimately, Americans showed no qualms about violating the provision of the defensive treaty prohibiting either country from signing a separate peace. By the end of the war the alliance had become a French prop for the United States instead of a partnership, yet the Americans, with unabashed self-righteousness, freely ignored its terms.

But even with independence American leaders did not want to sever all ties with France, since they realized that in a future emergency the United States would need France more than France would need the United States. If ties were permanently broken, the United States would again be at the mercy of Great Britain's overwhelming power.

In 1783, Americans had to determine the degree to which the United States would enter into European affairs. Responsible leaders recognized that isolation was impossible and, more important, undesirable. They wanted to avoid permanent dependence on France, while establishing a policy which would give the United States enough flexibility to sign another alliance in case of a temporary crisis. The United States, according to this policy, could be independent, yet protected

[13] Luzerne, "Final Report," Luzerne Papers.

from aggression by a European power. War had taught American leaders how insignificant the United States was in European diplomacy. The United States lacked sufficient power to be influential in European affairs, even when protecting only its own interests. It had to adjust its policy to work within the prevailing European rivalries.[14]

Acknowledgment of the lowly position of the United States in European politics strengthened a long-standing American sentiment against permanent alliances. Noting that the alliance had changed in conception between 1778 and 1782, Henry Laurens regretfully conceded that France's superior power gave her effective control of peace negotiations.[15] Laurens was merely later than many Americans in admitting the French superiority which Gérard had considered the basis of diplomacy between the two nations. American recognition of the miniscule role of the United States accentuated the underlying disposition against alliances except in times of emergency. The lack of external threats during the rest of the 1780's reinforced this attitude, and a combination of interest and inclination meshed neatly until the French Revolutionary wars.

Samuel Adams, for example, believed that the United States must strengthen itself or its fate would rest on the whims of Great Britain and France. To avoid European dominance or permanent connections, the United States must begin by punctually paying its debts. Adams distinguished between foreign influence and dominance. It was natural, he wrote, for a weak country to have foreign influences in its domestic politics; the primary problem would be "to guard against the evil Effects of them." The purpose of post-war foreign policy, according to Adams, should be to reduce the opportunities for British or French domination, which would at the same time obviate any need for alliances.[16] Roger Sherman offered a similar appraisal of the lessons to be drawn from the alliance. "The more attention we pay to our resources and the less we rely upon others, the more surely shall we provide for our own honor and success," he wrote, "and retrieve that balance between the contending European powers." [17]

Benjamin Franklin reached like conclusions about the future needs of the United States. Great Britain, Franklin warned, might one day try to reconquer the United States, but he did not recommend another alliance with France to forestall this. "In these Circumstances we cannot be too careful to preserve the Friendships we have acquired abroad, and

---

[14] Gilbert, *The Beginnings*, pp. 76–89.
[15] Laurens to John Adams, Aug. 27, 1782, Adams Papers, R. 357.
[16] Samuel Adams to John Adams, Nov. 4, 1783, *ibid.*, R. 361.
[17] Roger Sherman Account Book, no date, Roger Sherman Papers, p. 1.

the Union we have established at home," he advised Congress, "to secure our Credit by a punctual Discharge of our Obligations of every kind, and our Reputation by the Wisdom of our Councils." Franklin then expressed the basic policy of a majority of American leaders after the demise of the alliance. A policy of friendship was essential, he argued, "since we know not how soon we may have a fresh Occasion for Friends, for Credit, and for Reputation." [18]

A possible exception to the prevailing judgment, greatly overemphasized by later historians, was the viewpoint of John Jay and John Adams when attempting to negotiate a commercial treaty with Great Britain in 1783. They denounced all connections with Europe, but they were in a decided minority and their arguments were ignored in the United States.

Jay's and Adams' position can be traced, in part, to their efforts to find justification for breaking their instructions from Congress. Being sound lawyers, neither was content, as Franklin was, to remain silent about their action; instead they changed the basis of argument from the issue of violating the instructions to xenophobic lectures on the inherent evil of any political connection with Europe. Later, Jay as Secretary of Foreign Affairs and Adams as Minister to Great Britain acted on the contrary assumption that the United States would need alliances in times of emergency.

The foreign policy views of men such as Franklin, Samuel Adams, and Washington, who saw the necessity of limited involvement with Europe for survival, were in fact challenged by a small minority which advocated breaking all connections with Europe. This view, dating to the initial wilderness settlements, saw the primary mission of America as creating a separate society distinct from European antecedents. The development of the West became the main theme of George Mason, Hugh Henry Brackenridge, William Gordon, and a variety of others who conceived of foreign policy only as an adjunct to speed autonomous American development. They held many of the same views as the wartime radicals, but the radicals, by contrast, wanted territory for security within the European power system. The Seven Years' War had greatly encouraged a belief in the unlimited exploitation of the West, and the Revolution contributed even more to this vision.

In a very real sense, those who wished to terminate European connections saw the Revolution and independence as assuring the removal of any obstacle to the development of the hinterland. Part of their vehemence against the British during the Revolution derived from the conviction that Great Britain had repeatedly restricted the opportunities for

[18] Franklin to Mifflin, Dec. 25, 1783, Franklin Papers, LC, Vol. V.

western expansion promised by the victory in the Seven Years' War. Disparate groups—at first mostly concentrated in the rural inland regions, and often in violent conflict with one another—held a common confidence in the United States as an unsoiled, self-contained society drawing on its own vast physical resources. Disciples of evangelical religion, simple republicanism, and western land speculation found themselves in agreement on a foreign policy rejecting American involvement with Europe.

George Mason emerged from seclusion to make a rare pronouncement that caught the substance of this nascent philosophy, "I wish America would put her trust in God and herself, and have as little to do with the politics of Europe as possible." [19] A persistent exponent of the new vision of America was William Gordon, a prominent Massachusetts clergyman. "I wish to have no jarrings & janglings, either between States, or the United States & any foreign power," he wrote. "May we have peace with the world & among ourselves, & may our affairs be conducted with such wisdom & uprightness, that we may not be embroiled in any European quarrel!" Gordon then castigated any attempts to centralize United States government, a position which was to become a cardinal virtue to Jeffersonians. If the United States centralized its government, "we shall in a century or two be so formidable, that European kingdoms will be jealous for their own security & join in wars against us." [20]

Gordon, who shortly thereafter returned to Great Britain to live, declared to John Adams, "Peace being once settled upon equitable principles, America has nothing to do with wars." Like most advocates of this embryonic manifest destiny, Gordon thought that the development of the West offered the United States a unique opportunity to separate itself profitably from Europe. This conviction emanated from the Revolution itself, with its drastic break from the past as well as the old Puritan belief in a new society unfettered by the corruptions of Europe. The idealized West would allow the United States alone to rid itself of the cause of wars, since there would be no balance of power, no alliances, no aggression, no covetous neighbors. "Let Europeans who have not an extensive country fight & destroy. America should be separated from their quarrels; & by multiplying people fill the back country for ages to come." [21]

The alliance itself had created the situation in which this early ver-

---

[19] Mason to Henry, May 6, 1783, Kate Mason Rowland, *The Life of George Mason* (2d ed.; New York, 1964), Vol. II, p. 47.
[20] Gordon to Washington, Feb. 26, 1783, Washington Papers, Vol. CCXIV.
[21] Gordon to Adams, Sept. 19, [1782?], Adams Papers, R. 361.

sion of manifest destiny became a possible alternative to a policy which recognized the interdependence of the United States and Europe. Yet with independence and an unexpected degree of security, proponents of the two views shared more than they disputed. Both considered the preservation of peace mandatory, with dissension coming over the necessity and purpose of connections with Europe. For more than a decade after the Revolution proponents of either concept could support United States foreign policy, although from slightly differing points of view.

The group headed by Washington held the reins of government for many years after the Revolution. Motivated by their understanding of American interests, they carefully avoided foreign alliances. Much of United States foreign policy in the 1790's reflected their experiences under the French alliance. Unsure of their union but more certain of the limits of American power, early leaders sought to steer a course of non-involvement and remain at peace during the French Revolutionary wars. Although delighted by the French Revolution, widely and incorrectly regarded as a replica of their own struggle, they saw little purpose in risking the existence of the United States for the sake of French policy. Nor did the course of neutrality reflect a contradiction or change of attitude, as many Frenchmen charged. American leaders who had been the foremost advocates of the alliance always assumed that self-interest would take precedence over ideology in foreign relations. They had seen no contradiction when the French monarchy aided a republic for reasons of self-interest; likewise, they saw no disgrace in declining to aid another republic when this would not serve the interests of the United States.

It was altogether consistent, if not gracious, that those who most enthusiastically welcomed the French Revolution, including Jefferson and the party forming around him, would with clear conscience advocate neutrality. The American Revolution might well serve as an example to Europe, but Jeffersonians agreed that the United States position should not be endangered by intervening in European wars. Only when the Jay Treaty appeared to reverse the direction of neutrality to favor Great Britain did a bitter split over foreign policy occur. Americans continued an unequivocal identification of Great Britain as their greatest threat until 1795—an attitude that had earlier facilitated the alliance. When disagreements arose about the primary source of external danger, foreign policy became more controversial.

Close observers of the American scene did not expect either self-interest or sentiment to plunge the United States into the cause of the French Revolution. After peace was secured, the role of France in establishing American independence rapidly faded from memory. It was as if

Americans suffered from collective amnesia. Perceptibly, but probably unintentionally, the Americanization of the American Revolution occurred. If the French role were remembered at all, it pertained only to Lafayette's part and Rochambeau's assistance to the "illustrious Washington" at Yorktown. John Warren, one of the few to refer to the alliance, stated in a Fourth of July oration, "Nor shall the powerful Aids of a magnanimous Ally be suffered here to pass unnoticed: the generous terms in which assistance and support were granted, shall leave impressions of esteem and friendship which time and age shall not be able to efface." [22]

The impressions proved more fleeting than Warren had suggested. When a local artillery company celebrated peace in Providence, not one of the thirteen traditional toasts commemorated the role of France. Even Washington, in his resignation speech to Congress in 1783, failed to mention the alliance.[23] Of course, other celebrations did pay homage to France, but in 1782 no public address on the Revolution had failed to mention her significant role. Americans seemed determined not to share the laurels of victory after independence.

Post-War nationalism contributed to the slighting of France because it was difficult to exult in the glory of America while at the same time stressing the recent dependence on France. Nationalism in the United States has generally been more intense and openly chauvinistic after a war than before it, and this was the case at the nation's origin. Americans felt a heightened awareness of their country's bountiful future and unprecedented liberties after the Revolution. The very newness and promise of the American experiment made it difficult for them to acknowledge the proper role of the French.

Americans could rationalize their new attitude toward the alliance by insisting that Great Britain had been more generous than France in the peace negotiations. France apparently fought United States participation in the fishery, while Great Britain granted Americans liberty to tap this vital source of wealth. Pre-war stereotypes of French subtlety and duplicity, revised and embellished, again circulated. Furthermore, memories of the degrading peace instructions of 1781 continued to linger, despite the redeeming actions of the American commissioners and French acceptance of them. But the most important reason for the change in attitudes was that the ties of mutual interest had dissolved; Americans no longer needed to stress French help.

[22] John Warren, *An Oration, Delivered July 4th, 1783, At the Request of the Inhabitants of the Town of Boston, in Celebration of the Anniversary of American Independence* (Boston, 1783), p. 24.

[23] *Providence Gazette*, May 3, 1783. Luzerne was quick to note Washington's omission. Luzerne to Vergennes, Jan. 2, 1784, Luzerne Papers.

The alliance had nevertheless changed a number of American attitudes. In international affairs it gave Americans a much-needed lesson in power politics. After the war, Americans could make choices in foreign policy with more confidence in their ability and yet with an increased understanding of the limitations of American strength. The alliance had its most profound effect at the personal level, causing a considerable number of Americans to alter their parochial prejudices against France. When John Jay admitted that he was attached to France "in a degree that I could not have thought myself capable ten years ago," he expressed a new tolerance felt by many leaders.[24] The alliance, although it did not end American intellectual bondage to Great Britain, broke the former British monopoly and allowed Americans to draw on a broader source of European political and philosophical thought. American colleges, for example, started acquiring the latest scientific and philosophical works from France, in addition to appointing French teachers to their faculties.

The alliance also revealed a dangerous administrative problem to American leaders: the inability of a government to function effectively in foreign relations without revenue. Many had defended the instructions of 1781 because of the desperate situation of the United States, but the problems then included more than adverse military developments. Edmund Randolph wrote after Yorktown that his state "every month publishes to the world, that Virginia has paid nothing to the treasury of the U.S.," and Patriot newspapers carried reports that four states contributed no taxes to Congress in 1782.[25] The final humiliation had not yet fallen upon Congress, however. When it ratified the treaty of peace, Congress lacked the money to send a messenger back to Europe, and Luzerne had to pay for his passage.[26] National honor could receive slight protection under such circumstances. By 1783 American leaders recognized that sovereignty, national credit, and revenues were inextricable, and, moreover, indispensable in foreign relations.

Both moderates and radicals considered the financial question the most serious problem facing the United States after independence, though the radicals did not become Nationalists or lessen their belief in republicanism.[27] James Lovell, who accepted an appointment as a receiver of Continental taxes in Boston and who knew Congress as well as

---

[24] Jay to Franklin, April 27, 1780, Wharton, ed., *Diplomatic Correspondence,* Vol. III, p. 633.

[25] Randolph to Madison, Nov. 16, 1782, Hutchinson and Rachal, eds., *Madison,* Vol. V, p. 282; *Salem Gazette,* Jan. 2, 1783.

[26] Luzerne to Vergennes, March 30, 1784, Luzerne Papers.

[27] Cf., Jensen, *The New Nation,* pp. 28–84; Jackson Main, *The Anti-Federalists* (Chicago, 1964), pp. 72–102.

anyone, regarded the refusal to pay taxes as a breakdown of republican government. He maintained that republicanism could not survive unless the people voluntarily accepted the responsibility to finance it.[28] Radicals felt that government had to have revenue power in order to fulfill its responsibilities.

Richard Henry Lee personified what became the anti-Federalist or states' rights position, but he was in a decided minority among the wartime radicals.[29] States' rights had not been part of the radical program during the Revolution. To the contrary, radicals, more than others, had defended congressional prerogatives, and they realized that without taxing power Congress would be ineffective in foreign affairs.

It is more than coincidental that both radicals and moderates closely connected with the alliance in 1781 and 1782 supported the new Constitution in 1787 and 1788. Certainly those who supported the Constitution had other motives for backing it, but throughout 1783 when they speculated about foreign policy, they invariably returned to the problem of finances and the international credit of the United States. Even Elbridge Gerry, who opposed the Constitution, wanted to give Congress revenue power. Although Richard Henry Lee, Theodorick Bland, and others who opposed the Constitution in 1787 and 1788 had been critics of excessive French influence during the war, they were not an organized political group, nor did their views derive from conflicts over the alliance. More Massachusetts Congressmen supported the Constitution than opposed it, but all had opposed French policy on the fishery after 1779. Samuel Adams, for one, admitted that the powers of Congress needed to be strengthened, and eventually supported the Constitution. Although the alliance drew very limited mention in the Constitutional Convention or the public debates over ratification, the question of finances loomed large, and this was intimately connected with foreign policy.

Whatever effect the alliance may have had on domestic controversies over the power of government, for most Americans it did not serve as an admonition against signing future alliances. American leaders agreed that the United States had received tremendous advantages from the alliance; most could foresee future circumstances when they might be willing to enter into another alliance with France. Washington in his Farewell Address distinguished between permanent and temporary political alliances. It was the prohibition against permanent alliances that be-

[28] Lovell to Langdon, Aug. 30, 1782, Langdon Papers.

[29] See the exchange of letters between William Whipple and Richard Henry Lee, Lee to Whipple, July 1 and 7, 1783; Whipple to Lee, Sept. 15, 1783, Lee Family Papers, R. 7. It is difficult to find any other prominent radicals, whether in or out of Congress, who agreed with Lee in opposing the 5 per cent impost.

came a central tenet of early United States foreign policy. Later, as circumstances changed, Americans increasingly imposed a different interpretation on the alliance, using its problems to warn against any foreign connection. No responsible leader in the eighteenth century took this position, however.

A final assessment of the alliance must consider the advantages that accrued to the United States as a result. Without the alliance, the United States probably would not have achieved independence. Most certainly, it would not have gained the western lands and the fishery which made independence secure. The alliance served as a warning to European powers that in an emergency the United States would seek aid wherever offered, which perhaps increased Great Britain's reluctance to contemplate reconquering the United States. By these standards the alliance was an unparalleled success in American foreign policy.

With the exception of independence, the alliance with France was the sharpest break with the previous experience of Americans. Yet they had supported their new political connection with surprising enthusiasm. Many assented only passively to the alliance, but a great number of persons, from all sections of the country, worked diligently to make it function smoothly. After Newport, Savannah, the failure to capture Arnold in Virginia, and many other incidents, Americans made a concerted effort to stifle criticism of the alliance. Although strongly encouraged by American leaders, public declarations of renewed loyalty to the alliance were voluntary and not attributable to governmental or French control of vital channels of public opinion such as the press or pulpit.

The primary reason for the absence of dissent about the alliance was that it offered no tangible threat to the United States. Loyalists ceaselessly pointed out the differences in French and American manners, morals, and religion, but to no avail. Americans accurately believed that the alliance was a limited pact between governments for clearly defined objectives. Conflict between factions during the alliance, particularly in the Deane-Lee affair, was limited to debate over American goals and the degree of support France should give the United States; neither moderates nor radicals ever suggested that the alliance be abandoned.

Dissent was rare because self-interest and prevailing moral standards seemed highly compatible under the alliance. When Americans discussed it, they stressed self-interest as much as morality, but they did not believe them to be in conflict. The alliance did not require the United States government to undertake actions unacceptable to the people. Critics often objected not to United States obligations under the alliance, but to what they regarded as France's failure to fulfill its commitments, as at Newport.

Revolutionary leaders accepted the alliance for what it was, a pact dictated by temporary mutual interests. The motives of France did not need to be altruistic, nor were they diabolical. Samuel Adams could write in late 1783, "I will say it for my Countrymen, they are, or seem to be, very grateful. All are ready to freely acknowledge our obligation to France for the part she took in our late Contest." Adams did not conclude with this specious sentiment, however. Generosity, he noted, did not motivate France, which "doubtless foresaw & probably never lost Sight of" the advantages of a total separation of Great Britain and the United States. The strength of the alliance was that both countries could simultaneously pursue their own interests. The results of such a policy were clear to Adams, "America with the assistance of her faithful Ally has secured and established her Liberty & Independence. God be Praised!" [30]

[30] Samuel Adams to John Adams, Nov. 4, 1783, Adams Papers, R. 361.

Bibliography

ESSAY ON SOURCES

The research for this study concentrated on private letters in manuscript collections, Revolutionary War newspaper files, and diplomatic correspondence. A great many of the letters contained little information relating to the alliance, except for notations of elementary details such as celebrations or letters of introduction to or from prominent Frenchmen. Correspondents wrote with restraint, due to the precarious postal system and the pernicious effects of having a letter intercepted by the British; this undoubtedly reduced the number of comments critical of the French. Newspapers were an important source, but they must be used with caution, because publishers—with the exception of the Loyalist press, of course—consistently excluded unfavorable references to the alliance. In addition, most of the essays in the press dealt with state problems of taxation and currency and rarely with foreign relations.

Microfilming of manuscript collections is invaluable for research in the Revolutionary era. Foremost among all collections used in this study are the Adams Papers on deposit in the Massachusetts Historical Society. After John Adams returned to Europe in 1780, his correspondence dropped noticeably, but Abigail Adams maintained a regular correspondence with Massachusetts political leaders which is indispensable for information about radical attitudes toward the alliance. The incoming correspondence for this period is in reels 349–361, and John Adams' letters are in reels 92–97, 102, 106–107, and 110. The Henry Laurens Papers on deposit at the South Carolina Historical Society, reels 7–19, and the Lee Family Papers issued on microfilm by the University of Virginia, reels 4–7, supplement the Adams Papers for information on the radicals and debates in Congress until 1780.

The Benjamin Franklin Papers and those of his secretary, William Temple Franklin, are of incalculable value for the views of moderates, particularly those from the Middle States. Unfortunately, Franklin rarely offered his opinions about either the alliance or other Americans in his letters. Of the Franklin correspondence on deposit at the American Philosophical Society, I used reels 5–24, and reels 51–52 of the William Temple Franklin material included in the same collection.

The Library of Congress has copies or photostats of almost all the relevant French Foreign Office or Ministry of War archives. However, the copies of the Archives du Ministère des Affaires Étrangères, États-Unis, Mémoires et Documents are incomplete and lack some necessary material which is available at the Archives du Ministère des Affairs Étrangères in Paris. The

Archives du Ministère des Affaires Étrangères, correspondance politique (États-Unis), containing all of the dispatches of Gérard and Luzerne, constitute the best organized and most extensive commentary on Congressional and Pennsylvania politics during the Revolution. John J. Meng, editor, *Despatches and Instructions of Conrad Alexandre Gérard* (Baltimore, 1939), reprints all of the Vergennes-Gérard correspondence concerning the United States. Nevertheless, care should be taken in considering Gérard's views on American politics and domestic controversies because of his deep involvement with the moderates after the beginning of 1779.

Luzerne was much more politically astute and more sensitive to the effects of the Revolution, but it should be remembered that modesty was not one of Luzerne's stronger traits and the total effect of reading over three hundred of his dispatches may lead the reader to consider him more influential than he actually was. The Luzerne Papers at the Archives du Ministère des Affaires Étrangères are quite helpful, and they contain the only copies of his secret expense accounts, in addition to the original of his Liste des Membres, which is different in some respects from the copy available in the Mémoires et Documents collection at the same location. Although Henry Doniol's massive compilation from the French archives, *Histoire de la Participation de la France à l'Établissement des États-Unis d'Amérique* (Paris, 1886–1892), is suggestive for French policy, his editing is too unreliable for use as a primary source.

The consular correspondence between the French Minister in Philadelphia and the French consuls in various American cities was destroyed by fire, but the John Holker Papers include some copies of consular dispatches from Boston in 1778 and 1779, and the Rochambeau Papers contain scattered references to the work of the consuls. These collections, both of which are in the Library of Congress, are also helpful for other facets of the French role in the alliance. The Sir Henry Clinton Papers at the William L. Clements Library include a few intercepted consular letters, but the overwhelming bulk of this vital correspondence is lost. Clinton's intelligence reports from inside American lines contain only fleeting references to the alliance.

A number of American generals left a vast quantity of papers, but this correspondence pertains mostly to military matters and includes very few personal letters. The Washington Papers at the Library of Congress are an important exception because of Washington's increasing influence within the United States. Washington, moreover, was the only general who had prolonged correspondence with the French, and he received an immense number of letters from persons in every section of the country that are extremely useful. Another exception is the Horatio Gates Papers in the New-York Historical Society, since Gates was the most politically active of the American generals and his correspondents offered many opinions on the alliance. Unfortunately, Gates did not preserve much of his own private correspondence. Other generals whose papers were of more limited use for this topic are the Benjamin Lincoln, Henry Knox, and William Heath Papers in the Massachusetts Historical Society, the Philip Schuyler Papers in the New York Public Library, and the Nathanael Greene Papers in the William L. Clements Library.

The other collections of the greatest value were the Samuel Adams Papers at the New York Public Library, and the Gerry-Knight Papers for James Lovell's correspondence in 1781, the William Livingston Papers, and Mathew Ridley Papers, all at the Massachusetts Historical Society. Any study of the Revolution cannot ignore either the Robert R Livingston Papers or the Joseph Reed Papers at the New-York Historical Society. For this study, the small collection of the Samuel Cooper Papers at the Huntington Library, read on microfilm, was helpful. The huge but cumbersome Dreer and Gratz autograph collections at the Historical Society of Pennsylvania contain a great many letters of value. At the same location are the Thomas McKean and John Langdon Papers, which include letters with many comments on the alliance and foreign affairs. The Josiah Bartlett Papers at Dartmouth College and the Benjamin Franklin and William Whipple Papers at the Library of Congress also contain many interesting items on the alliance.

For the views of southern leaders, in addition to the Laurens and Lee Papers, I found the James Iredell Papers at Duke University and the Charles E. Johnson Papers, which include the bulk of Iredell's Revolutionary correspondence, at the North Carolina State Archives to be the most enlightening. The Thomas Burke Papers at the North Carolina State Archives and the Southern Historical Collection at the University of North Carolina are meager but of value in understanding this complex man. The Josiah Smith Letterbook in the Southern Historical Collection provides important details on religion in the South during this period, and contains some helpful information on John Zubly, which can be supplemented by the Zubly Diary and Papers at the Georgia Historical Society.

The most useful newspapers were the *Independent Chronicle, Maryland Gazette, Pennsylvania Packet,* and Rivington's *Royal Gazette.* Some of the newspapers were read on microfilm, but fortunately a majority were available in the excellent collection at the William L. Clements Library. The *Freeman's Journal,* which started in April, 1781, is by far the most entertaining and in many ways the most informative of the papers. Francis Bailey, its publisher, and Philip Freneau, its editor, seemed to thrive on controversy, and each held a broad conception about the amount of dissent permissible and needed in wartime. Many of the essays that indirectly attacked excessive French influence in state or national politics were printed in this paper, which often drew the ire of Luzerne and the moderates.

The printed sermons, which served as source material for the sections on religion, are all available on microcard in the Early American Imprint Series, and the William L. Clements Library has copies of a great many of the sermons cited. Unfortunately, not many sermons were printed in the Middle and Southern States and fewer still have been preserved. None of the few comments on the clergy in the South indicates appreciable disloyalty to the

Revolution, however, so the clerical response to the alliance in that area was probably similar to that in New England. Although simplifying the division in American religion and not giving theological liberals enough consideration for their role in supporting the alliance, Alan Heimert's *Religion and the American Mind* (Cambridge, 1966) makes a notable contribution to this field, and surpasses all other works on this topic for the Revolutionary period.

The amount of printed primary material is prodigious, and the letterpress editions of many figures will increasingly facilitate research in this period. The most important collection for this study is Edmund Burnett, editor, *Letters of Members of Continental Congress* (Washington, 1921–1936). Burnett's ability as an accurate editor and thorough researcher makes this work an indispensable source. If space limitations had not restricted Burnett, the collection would be even more valuable. There is no discernible bias in his deletions, but in a number of isolated instances he did omit material on the alliance, which prevented total dependence on the series. To compensate for this, I read the originals of as many letters as possible or referred to a printed copy of the full text when available.

John Fitzpatrick, editor, *The Writings of George Washington* (Washington, 1931–1944), suffers in comparison to the later letterpress editions, because it fails to print any of Washington's incoming letters. *The Papers of Thomas Jefferson* (Princeton, 1950–   ), edited by Julian Boyd, are useful as are *The Papers of James Madison* (Chicago, 1962–   ), edited by William Rachal and William Hutchinson. The Madison Papers will give the most detailed account of a congressman in the later stages of the war published since Burnett's work mentioned above. Harold Syrett, editor, *The Papers of Alexander Hamilton* (New York, 1961–   ), provide supplementary material for many of Washington's dealings with the French. Francis Wharton did a very complete job in editing *The Revolutionary Diplomatic Correspondence of the United States* (Washington, 1889). The forthcoming editions of the John Jay and Benjamin Franklin Papers for this period, when combined with the Adams and Laurens Papers on microfilm, will contain most of the material Wharton missed.

Various state historical journals contain letters of importance. The *South Carolina Historical and Genealogical Magazine* includes many letters of prominent South Carolinians, due to the efforts of Joseph Barnwell. The "Original Letters and Documents" section of the first decades of the *Pennsylvania Magazine of History and Biography* is quite useful. In the same journal are a number of diaries from the immense collections of the Historical Society of Pennsylvania. Two journals of recent origin and short duration, the *French-American Review* and the *Franco-American Review,* contain numerous articles on the French in the United States during the Revolution.

Many Frenchmen left memoirs of their experience in the United States, and a number of staff officers kept journals which have been printed. Overall, the memoirs left by the French are mediocre, and some are unreliable in the most basic facts. Among the best are Evelyn Acomb, editor, *The*

Revolutionary Journal of Baron Ludwig Von Closen, 1780–1783 (Chapel Hill, 1958), and Thomas Balch, editor, *Journal of Claude Blanchard* (Albany, 1876), which is more detailed than the French edition, *Journal de Campagne de Claude Blanchard* (Paris, 1869). Howard C. Rice, Jr., editor, *Travels in North America in the Years 1780, 1781, and 1782* (Chapel Hill, 1963) by the Marquis de Chastellux cannot be ignored, although Chastellux was far more enamored of Americans than any other officer, with the possible exception of Lafayette. Although somewhat dated, Frank Monaghan's *French Travelers in the United States, 1765–1932* (New York, 1933) is a great aid for the Revolutionary period.

Among secondary works, Herbert James Henderson, Jr., "Political Factions in the Continental Congress, 1774–1783," a doctoral dissertation done at Columbia University in 1962, deserves special mention. Henderson argues that there were discernible political blocs in the Continental Congress, identifiable by roll call analysis, and that the delegates from New England can be called a political party with shared goals. He sees the binding link among members as religion. His contentions on the solidarity exhibited by New England delegates and the binding link of religion are at variance with the conclusions reached in this study. The differences are matters of degree and somewhat, but not wholly, attributable to the different criteria used for determining the level of agreement to call a group a party. Henderson uses the individual voting records of each member for comparison, while I consider the votes of the entire state delegation as a unit. In my judgment, however, even a breakdown by roll call analysis of different categories of issues such as military, economic, and foreign affairs—which has yet to be done—would yield no new substantive findings about the political composition of Congress. What is actually needed is a study that analyzes the reduced prestige of Congress in the last years of the Revolution and the period preceding the adoption of the Constitution.

Another study useful for politics during the Revolution is Merrill Jensen's *The New Nation* (New York, 1950), which is much sounder than his *The Articles of Confederation* (Madison, 1948). The western land problem in Congress has been more than adequately covered in Thomas P. Abernethy, *Western Lands and the American Revolution* (New York, 1959), and Philip C. Phillips, *The West in the Diplomacy of the American Revolution* (Urbana, 1913). E. James Ferguson's *The Power of the Purse* (Chapel Hill, 1961) and Jackson T. Main's *The Anti-Federalists* (Chicago, 1964) are valuable. Also helpful are Edmund Burnett, *The Continental Congress* (New York, 1941); Margaret B. MacMillian's underrated effort, *War Governors in the American Revolution* (New York, 1943); Richard P. McCormick, *Experiment in Independence: New Jersey in the Critical Period, 1781–1789* (New Brunswick, 1950); Robert L. Brunhouse, *The Counter-Revolution in Pennsylvania* (Harrisburg, 1942); and Paul Goodman, *The Democratic-Republicans of Massachusetts* (Cambridge, 1964).

The most important secondary work used for this study is William E.

O'Donnell's fine study, *The Chevalier de la Luzerne* (Louvain, 1938). Edward Corwin's *French Policy and the American Alliance of 1778* (Princeton, 1916) is still sound, despite his reliance on Doniol and the passage of more than fifty years. Many of the ideas on commerce and eighteenth century diplomacy in this study are from Felix Gilbert's scintillating book, *The Beginnings of American Foreign Policy* (New York, 1965). Another debt is owed to Louis Gottschalk for his work on the important, but boring, Lafayette, particularly *Lafayette Joins the American Army* (Chicago, 1935) and *Lafayette and the Close of the American Revolution* (Chicago, 1942). J. J. Jusserand's *With Americans of Past and Present Days* (New York, 1916) is a series of lectures given when the author was the French Ambassador to the United States. The book, based on the French manuscript collections in the Library of Congress, has considerable merit, although it is actually a gracefully written piece of propaganda urging the United States to intervene in World War I on the side of Great Britain and France. The best study of France and the United States in the Revolutionary period is Durand Echeverria, *Mirage in the West* (Princeton, 1957), to which this study owes more than is apparent in the footnotes. Also useful are Robert R. Palmer, *The Age of the Democratic Revolution: The Challenge* (Princeton, 1959), and Gerald Stourzh, *Benjamin Franklin and American Foreign Policy* (Chicago, 1954).

A number of specialized studies aided greatly in filling out certain areas. Foremost among these works is Alexander Lawrence's *Storm Over Savannah* (Athens, 1951) on the siege of Savannah in 1779. Also of merit are Mary E. Loughrey, *France and Rhode Island, 1686–1800* (New York, 1944); Kathryn Sullivan, *Maryland and France, 1774–1789* (Philadelphia, 1936); and Allen Forbes and Paul Cadman, *France and New England* (Boston, 1925). Two studies of Catholicism which reveal how little the religious issue affected the alliance are Charles Metzger, *Catholics and the American Revolution* (Chicago, 1962), and Mary Augustina Ray, *American Opinion of Roman Catholicism in the Eighteenth Century* (New York, 1936). Richard Morris' *The Peacemakers* (New York, 1965) fills a needed gap on the activities of the diplomats in Europe concerning peace negotiations, although I still prefer Samuel Bemis' *The Diplomacy of the American Revolution* (Bloomington, 1961).

Two studies of moderates in the later stages of the Revolution are quite valuable for understanding the actions of Congress in 1781 and 1782, namely, George Dangerfield's *Chancellor Robert R. Livingston* (New York, 1960) and Volume II of Irving Brant's *James Madison* (New York, 1948). Brant and Dangerfield both detect an ill-defined nationalism in their subjects, which is difficult to reconcile with the credulity they displayed to Luzerne and their hostility to John Adams' and John Jay's reports from Europe. Douglas S. Freeman's *George Washington*, Volumes IV and V (New York, 1951 & 1952) are helpful as are David D. Wallace's *The Life of Henry Laurens* (New York, 1914) and Carl Van Doren's *Benjamin Franklin* (New York, 1965).

A number of biographies published in the early nineteenth century, often by grandsons or other relatives, still have not been surpassed. Included in this group are James Austin, *The Life of Elbridge Gerry* (Boston, 1828); Theodore Sedgwick, *A Memoir of the Life of William Livingston* (New York, 1833); William B. Reed, *Life and Correspondence of Joseph Reed* (Philadelphia, 1847); and Richard Henry Lee, *Life of Arthur Lee* (Boston, 1829). Of all the prominent Revolutionary figures, Richard Henry Lee and Arthur Lee are the most in need of biographies which will put their substantial contributions in better perspective. A study of James Lovell would go far in increasing understanding of the radicals in the Continental Congress after 1778.

William Gordon, *History of the Rise, Progress, and Establishment of the United States of America* (London, 1788), is still a valuable source and has been unfairly underrated because of plagiarism from the *Annual Register*. Gordon did interview a great many American leaders after the war, had some access to the private papers of the Continental Congress, and saw many private letters of prominent individuals. Gordon would have had a more accurate history if he had kept a copy of his own lively correspondence during the Revolution, because he was well informed about political affairs. William Trescot's *The Diplomacy of the Revolution* (New York, 1852) is an intriguing study, and many of the conclusions about the foundations of American foreign policy have a surprisingly modern tone.

The following list is not exhaustive but includes the primary or secondary sources which were useful for background material and relevant for this study.

PRIMARY SOURCES

Manuscript Collections

American Philosophical Society
  Benjamin Franklin Papers
  Nathanael Greene Papers
Archives du Ministère des Affaires Étrangères
  Chevalier de La Luzerne Papers
  Finances du Ministère
  Mémoires et Documents (États-Unis)
Archives Nationales
  Correspondance commerciale générale, sub-series B[111]

Boston Public Library
    Chamberlain Collection
    Miscellaneous MSS Letters
Columbia University
    John Jay Papers
    Gouverneur Morris Papers
Connecticut Historical Society
    Jeremiah Wadsworth Papers
    Oliver Wolcott Papers
Dartmouth College
    Josiah Bartlett Papers
Duke University
    James Iredell Papers
    Ephriam Kelly Papers
Georgia Historical Society
    John Zubly Diary
    John Zubly Papers
Harvard University
    Arthur Lee Papers
    Miscellaneous MSS Letters
    Jared Sparks MSS
Historical Society of Pennsylvania
    Balch Papers, Shippen Correspondence
    Elias Boudinot Papers
    Cadwalader Papers
    D'Estaing Manuscript Journal, 1778–1779
    Dreer Autograph Collection
    Henry Drinker Papers
    Etting Collection
    Benjamin Franklin Papers
    Gratz Autograph Collection
    John Langdon Papers
    Henry Laurens Papers
    John Laurens Commonplace Book
    Logan Papers
    Thomas McKean Papers
    Christopher Marshall Diary and Letterbook
    Robert Morris Papers
    Diary of George Nelson
    Shippen Family Papers
    Society Collection
    Papers of James Wilson
    Jasper Yeates Papers
Huntington Library
    Samuel Cooper Papers

Library of Congress
  Archives du Ministère des Affaires Étrangères, correspondance politique (États-Unis).
  Archives du Ministère des Affaires Étrangères, correspondance politique (États-Unis, Supplément).
  Archives du Ministère des Affaires Étrangères, États-Unis, Mémoires et Documents.
  Archives du Ministère des Affaires Étrangères, B[1], Consular Correspondance.
  Archives du Ministère de la Guerre, Correspondance.
  Archives du Ministère de la Guerre, Correspondance Supplément, A[4].
  Papers of Elias Boudinot
  Silas Deane Papers
  Benjamin Franklin Papers
  Nathanael Greene Papers
  John Holker Papers
  Samuel Holten Papers
  James McHenry Papers
  James Madison Papers
  Minutes of the French Legation in the United States
  Gouverneur Morris Papers
  Robert Morris Papers
  Rochambeau Papers
  Roger Sherman Papers
  George Washington Papers
  William Whipple Papers
  John Witherspoon Papers
Massachusetts Historical Society
  Adams Family Papers
  Bowdoin-Temple Papers
  Thomas Cushing Papers
  William Cushing Papers
  Dana Family Papers
  Elbridge Gerry Papers
  Gerry-Knight Papers
  John Hancock Papers
  William Heath Papers
  Henry Knox Papers
  Benjamin Lincoln Papers
  William Livingston Papers
  Mathew Ridley Papers
  Robert Treat Paine Papers
  Artemas Ward Papers
  Meshech Weare Papers

National Archives
    Papers of Continental Congress
New-York Historical Society
    Horatio Gates Papers
    Robert R Livingston Family Papers
    Samuel Osgood Papers
    Joseph Reed Papers
    Jeremiah Wadsworth Papers
New York Public Library
    Samuel Adams Papers
    Emmet Collection
    Robert R Livingston Papers
    William Livingston Papers
    Phillip Schuyler Papers
North Carolina State Archives
    Thomas Burke Papers
    Charles E. Johnson Papers
Princeton University
    Elias Boudinot Papers
    De Coppet Autograph Collection
    William Churchill Houston Papers
    Stimson-Boudinot Collection
    Stockton Additional Papers
    John Witherspoon Papers
South Carolina Historical Society
    Henry Laurens Papers
    Arthur Middleton Papers
    Miscellaneous MSS
University of North Carolina
    Thomas Burke Papers
    Richard Caswell Papers
    Edmund Pendleton Papers
    Josiah Smith Letterbook
University of Pennsylvania
    Benjamin Franklin Papers
University of Virginia
    Lee Family Papers
William L. Clements Library
    Sir Henry Clinton Papers
    Nathanael Greene Papers
    John Holker Papers
    Miscellaneous MSS
    Earl of Shelburne Papers
    Abraham Whipple Papers

Primary Printed Sources

OFFICIAL RECORDS

Bartlett, John Russell (ed.). *Records of the State of Rhode Island and Providence Plantations.* VIII, IX. Providence, 1863–1864.

Ford, Worthington C. *et al.* (eds.). *The Journals of Continental Congress.* 34 vols. Washington, 1904–1937.

Hastings, Hugh (ed.). *Public Papers of George Clinton.* 10 vols. Albany, 1899–1914.

Meng, John J. (ed.). *Despatches and Instructions of Conrad Alexandre Gérard.* Baltimore, 1939.

Peasants, James H. (ed.). *Archives of Maryland.* XLVII. Baltimore, 1930.

PUBLISHED JOURNALS AND LETTERS

Acomb, Evelyn (ed.). *The Revolutionary Journal of Baron Ludwig Von Closen, 1780–1783.* Chapel Hill, 1958.

Adair, Douglass, and Schutz, John A. (eds.). *Peter Oliver's Origin & Progress of the American Rebellion.* San Marino, 1961.

Adams, Charles Francis (ed.). *Familiar Letters of John Adams and His Wife Abigail Adams during the Revolution.* Boston, 1875.

Ballagh, James Curtis (ed.). *The Letters of Richard Henry Lee.* 2 vols. New York, 1911 & 1914.

Balch, E. W. (ed.). "Narrative of the Prince de Broglie of a Visit to America, 1782," *Magazine of American History,* I (1877), 180–86, 231–35, 306–309, 374–80.

Balch, Thomas (ed.). *Journal of Claude Blanchard, 1780–1783.* Translated by William Duane. Albany, 1876.

Barnwell, Joseph W. (ed.). "Correspondence of Hon. Arthur Middleton, Signer of the Declaration of Independence," *South Carolina Historical and Genealogical Magazine,* XXVI (1925), 183–214, XXVII (1926), 1–29, 51–80, 107–55.

———. "Letters of John Rutledge," *South Carolina Historical and Genealogical Magazine,* XVII (1916), 131–46, XVIII (1917), 42–49, 131–42, 155–67.

———. "Letters to General Greene and Others," *South Carolina Historical and Genealogical Magazine,* XVII (1916), 3–13, 53–57.

Bates, Albert (ed.). *The Deane Papers, 1771–1795.* (Connecticut Historical Society, *Collections,* XXIII.) Hartford, 1930.

Belknap Papers. 3 vols. (Massachusetts Historical Society, *Collections,* fifth series, II–IV.) Boston, 1877 & 1891.

Bowdoin and Temple Papers. (Massachusetts Historical Society, *Collections,* sixth series, IX.) Boston, 1897.

Boyd, Julian, *et al.* (eds.). *The Papers of Thomas Jefferson.* Princeton, 1950–.

Burnett, Edmund C. (ed.). *Letters of Members of Continental Congress.* 8 vols. Washington, 1921–1936.

Burnett, Edmund and Leland, Waldo (eds.). "Letters from Lafayette to Luzerne, 1780–1782," *American Historical Review,* XX (1915), 341–76, 577–612.

Butterfield, Lyman H. *et al.* (eds.). *Adams Family Correspondence.* (Series II), 2 vols. Cambridge, 1963.

———. *Diary & Autobiography of John Adams.* (Series I), 4 vols. New York, 1964.

Butterfield, Lyman H. (ed.). *Letters of Benjamin Rush.* 2 vols. Princeton, 1951.

Campbell, Charles (ed.). *The Bland Papers,* 2 vols. Petersburg, 1840–1843.

Chase, Eugene P. (ed.). *Our Revolutionary Forefathers: Letters of François Marquis de Barbé-Marbois.* New York, 1939.

Chinard, Gilbert (ed.). "Journal de guerre Mai 1780–Octobre 1781 of Brisout de Barnevillèle," *French-American Review,* III (1950), 217–78.

———. *The Treaties of 1778.* Baltimore, 1928.

Coleman, Mary Haldane (ed.). "Randolph and Tucker Letters," *Virginia Magazine of History and Biography,* XLIII (1935), 41–46.

"Correspondence between Hon. Henry Laurens and his Son, John, 1777–1780," *South Carolina Historical and Genealogical Magazine,* VI (1905), 3–14, 47–52, 103–10, 138–60.

Cruickshanks, Eveline (ed.). *Memoirs of Louis Philippe Comte de Ségur.* London, 1960.

Cushing, Harry Alonzo (ed.). *The Writings of Samuel Adams.* 4 vols. New York, 1904–1908.

Dawson, Warrington (ed.). "Au Garde Suisse de Louis XVI au Service de L'Amérique: Le Baron Gaspard de Gallatin," *Le Correspondant,* no. 1653 (Aug. 10, 1931), 321–38, no. 1655 (Sept. 10, 1931), 672–92.

———. "With Rochambeau at Newport: The Narrative of Baron Gaspard de Gallatin," *Franco-American Review,* I (1936), 330–40.

Dexter, Franklin B. (ed.). *The Literary Diary of Ezra Stiles.* 3 vols. New York, 1901.

"Diary of a French Officer: Presumed to be Cromot du Bourg," *Magazine of American History,* V (1880), 205–14, 293–308, 441–52, VII (1881), 283–94.

Diary of Frederick MacKenzie. 2 vols. Cambridge, 1930.

"Diary of James Allen, Esq. of Philadelphia, Counsellor-at-Law, 1770–1778," *Pennsylvania Magazine of History and Biography,* IX (1885), 175–96, 278–96, 424–41.

Doniol, Henri (ed.). *Histoire de la Participation de la France à l'Établissement des États-Unis d'Amérique.* 5 vols. Paris, 1886–1892.

Douglass, R. B. (ed.). *Charles Albert, Comte de More, Chevalier de Pontigibaud, A French Volunteer of the War of Independence.* New York, 1898.

Duane, William (ed.). *Extracts from the Diary of Christopher Marshall.* Albany, 1877.

Dumas, Mathieu Count. *Memoirs of His Own Time.* London, 1939.

Ellery, Henrietta C. (ed.). "Journal of Route and Occurrences in a Journey to Philadelphia from Dighton, begun October 24, 1778," *Pennsylvania Magazine of History and Biography,* XII (1888), 190–99.

Ezell, John S. (ed.). *The New Democracy in America, Travels of Francisco de Miranda in the United States, 1783–1784.* Translated by Judson P. Wood. Norman, 1963.

Fitzpatrick, John C. (ed.). *The Writings of George Washington.* 39 vols. Washington, 1931–1944.

Foner, Philip (ed.). *The Complete Writings of Thomas Paine.* 2 vols. New York, 1945.

Ford, Paul L. (ed.). *The Journals of Hugh Gaine.* 3 vols. New York, 1902.

Ford, Worthington C. (ed.). *Correspondence and Journals of Samuel Blachley Webb.* 3 vols. New York, 1893.

———. *Letters of Joseph Jones 1777–1787.* Washington, 1889.

———. *Letters of William Gordon.* (Massachusetts Historical Society, *Proceedings,* LXIII.) Boston, 1931.

———. *Letters of William Lee.* 3 vols. New York, 1891.

Gottschalk, Louis (ed.). *Letters of Washington and Lafayette.* New York, 1944.

Green, Samuel A. (ed.). *Journal of Count William des Deux-Ponts.* Boston, 1868.

Hammond, Otis G. (ed.). *Letters and Papers of Major-General John Sullivan of the Continental Army.* (*Collections of the New Hampshire Historical Society,* XIII–XV.) Concord, 1930–1939.

Heartman, Charles Fred (ed.). *Letters written by Ebenezer Huntington During the American Revolution.* New York, 1915.

Henkels, Stan V. (catalogue) *The Confidential Correspondence of Robert Morris.* Philadelphia, 1917.

Hunt, Gaillard (ed.). *The Writings of James Madison.* 9 vols. New York, 1900–1910.

Hutchinson, William T. and Rachal, William, *et al.* (eds.). *The Papers of James Madison.* Chicago, 1962–.

Isham, Charles (ed.). *The Deane Papers, 1774–1790.* 5 vols. (New York Historical Society, *Collections,* XIX–XXIII.) New York, 1887–1890.

"Izard-Laurens Correspondence," *South Carolina Historical and Genealogical Magazine,* XXII (1921), 1–11, 39–52, 73–88.

James Thatcher's Military Journal, revised edition. Boston, 1827.

Johnson, Amandus (ed.). *Naval Campaigns of Count de Grasse.* Philadelphia, 1942.

Johnson, Henry P. (ed.). *Correspondence and Public Papers of John Jay.* 4 vols. New York, 1890–1893.

Jones, Charles C. (ed.). *The Siege of Savannah in 1779.* Albany, 1874.

Journal de Campagne de Claude Blanchard. Paris, 1869.

Kennett, Lee (ed.). "Charlestown in 1778: A French Intelligence Report," *South Carolina Historical Magazine,* LXVI (1965), 109–11.

Kite, Elizabeth (ed.). *Correspondence of Washington and de Grasse.* Washington, 1931.

Lafayette, George W. (ed.). *Mémoires, correspondance et manuscrits du général Lafayette.* 12 vols. Brussels, 1837–1839.

"Letters from Commodore Alexander Gillon in 1778 and 1779," *South Carolina Historical and Genealogical Magazine,* X (1909), 3–9, 75–82, 131–35.

"Letters from Marquis de Lafayette to Hon. Henry Laurens, 1777–1780," *South Carolina Historical and Genealogical Magazine,* VII (1906), 3–11, 63–68, 115–29, 179–93, VIII (1907), 3–18, 57–68, 123–31, 181–88, IX (1908), 3–8, 59–66, 109–14, 173–80.

"Letters of General Nathanael Greene to Colonel Jeremiah Wadsworth," *Pennsylvania Magazine of History and Biography,* XXII (1898), 211–16.

Letters of Joseph Clay, Merchant of Savannah, 1776–1793. (Georgia Historical Society, *Collections,* VIII.) Savannah, 1913.

Lévis-Mirepoix, Emmanuel de (ed.). "Quelques Lettres du Baron Montesquieu sur la Guerre d'Indépendance Américaine," *Franco-American Review,* II (1938), 192–204.

Marsh, Philip M. (ed.). *The Prose of Philip Freneau.* New Brunswick, 1955.

Massey, Edouard R. (ed.). "Rhode Island in 1780 by Lieutenant J. B. S. Roberneir." (Rhode Island Historical Society, *Collections,* XVI.) Newport, 1923, 65–78.

Meras, E. Jules (ed.). *Memoirs of Duc de Lauzun.* New York, 1912.

"Mission of John Laurens to Europe in 1781," *South Carolina Historical and Genealogical Magazine,* I (1900), 13–41, 136–51, 213–22, 311–24, II (1901), 27–43, 108–25.

Moore, Frank (ed.). *Correspondence of Henry Laurens.* New York, 1861.
———. *Diary of the Revolution.* Hartford, 1876.

Morgan, Marshall (ed.). "Alexandre Berthier's Journal of the American Campaign," *Rhode Island History,* XXIV (1965), 77–88.

Morris, Anna W. (ed.). "Journal of Samuel Rowland Fisher of Philadelphia, 1779–1781," *Pennsylvania Magazine of History and Biography,* XLI (1917), 145–97, 274–333, 399–457.

"Original Letters and Documents," *Pennsylvania Magazine of History and Biography,* V (1881), 107–108.

"Original Letters and Documents," *Pennsylvania Magazine of History and Biography,* V (1881), 476–77.

Paine, Thomas. *Letter to Abbé Raynal.* Albany, 1792.

Papers of Charles Thomson. (New-York Historical Society, *Collections,* I.) New York, 1879.

Parsons, Jacob Cox (ed.). *Extracts from the Diary of Jacob Hiltzeimer of Philadelphia, 1765–1798.* Philadelphia, 1893.

Pattee, Fred L. (ed.). *The Poems of Philip Freneau.* 3 vols. 2d. ed. New York, 1963.

Paullin, Charles O. (ed.). *Out Letters of the Continental Marine Committee and Board of Admiralty, 1776–1780.* 2 vols. New York, 1914–1915.

Peckham, Howard (ed.). "Dr. Berkenhout's Journal, 1778," *Pennsylvania Magazine of History and Biography,* LXV (1941), 79–92.

Peden, William (ed.). *Thomas Jefferson, Notes on the State of Virginia.* Chapel Hill, 1955.

Rice, Howard C., Jr. (ed.). *Travels in North America in the Years 1780, 1781, and 1782 by Marquis de Chastellux.* 2 vols. Chapel Hill, 1963.

Robin, Abbé. *New Travels Through North America.* Translated by Philip Freneau. Philadelphia, 1783.

Rochambeau, Jean Baptiste D. Comte de. *Mémoires militaires, historiques et politques de Rochambeau.* 2 vols. Paris, 1809.

Rogers, John (ed.). *The Miscellaneous Works of Rev. John Witherspoon.* 4 vols. Philadelphia, 1800–1803.

Ryden, George H. (ed.). *Letters to and from Caesar Rodney, 1756–1784.* Philadelphia, 1933.

Sifton, Paul G. (ed.). "Otto's Memoire to Vergennes, 1785," *William and Mary Quarterly,* third series, XXII (1965), 626–45.

Sparks, Jared (ed.). *Correspondence of the American Revolution: Letters of Eminent Men to George Washington.* 4 vols. Boston, 1853.

Starr, Raymond (ed.). "Letters from John Lewis Gervais to Henry Laurens," *South Carolina Historical Magazine,* LXVI (1965), 15–37.

Stevens, Benjamin F. (ed.). *Benjamin F. Stevens's Facsimiles of Manuscripts in European Archives Relating to America, 1773–1783.* 26 vols. London, 1889–1898.

Syrett, Harold C. *et al.* (eds.). *The Papers of Alexander Hamilton.* New York, 1961–.

The Journal and Letters of Samuel Curwen, An American in England from 1775–1783. 4th ed. Boston, 1864.

The Works of John Witherspoon. 9 vols. Printed by J. Ogle. Edinburgh, 1815.

Van Doren, Carl (ed.). *Letters of Benjamin Franklin and Jane Mecom.* Princeton, 1950.

Warren-Adams Letters. (Massachusetts Historical Society, *Collections,* LXXII & LXXIII.) Boston, 1917 & 1925.

Wharton, Francis (ed.). *Revolutionary Diplomatic Correspondence of the United States.* 6 vols. Washington, 1889.

Willcox, William B. (ed.). *The American Rebellion, Sir Henry Clinton's Narrative of his Campaigns, 1775–1782.* New Haven, 1954.

Wrangel, Fersen U. Count de. (ed.). *Lèttres d'Axel de Fersen à Son Père pendant la Guerre de l'Indépendance d'Amérique.* Paris, 1929.

SERMONS AND PAMPHLETS

Adams, Zabdiel. *The Evil designs of Men made subservient by God to the Public Good: particularly illustrated in the rise, progress and Conclusion of the American war.* Boston, 1783.

Backus, Isaac. *The Substance of an Address to an Assembly in Bridgewater March 10, 1779.* Providence, 1779.

Bandot, Seraphin. *Discours prononce le 4 Juillet, jour de l'Anniversaire de l'indépendence.* Philadelphia, 1779.

Berkenhout, John. *Lucubrations on Ways and Means.* London, 1780.

Brackenridge, Hugh. *Six Political Discourses Founded on the Scripture.* Lancaster, 1778.

The Case and Claim of the American Loyalists Impartially Stated and Considered. London, 1783.

Chauncy, Charles. *A Sermon Preached at the Thursday Lecture in Boston.* Boston, 1778.

Clarke, Jonas. *A Sermon Preached Before His Excellency John Hancock, Esq; Governor; His Honor Thomas Cushing, Esq; Lieutenant-Governor; The Honorable Council, and the Honorable Senate and House of Representatives of the Commonwealth of Massachusetts, May 30, 1781.* Boston, 1781.

———. *Mr. Clarke's Sermon at the Interment of Rev. Dr. Cooper.* Boston, 1784.

Cooper, Samuel. *Dr. Cooper's Sermon Preached at the Dudleian-Lecture.* Boston, 1774.

———. *A Sermon preached before his Excellency John Hancock, Esq; gouvernour, the honourable Senate, and House of Representatives of the Commonwealth of Massachusetts.* Boston, 1780.

Cummings, Henry. *A Sermon Preached at Lexington on the 19th of April, 1781 Being the Anniversary of the Commencement of Hostilities Between Great-Britain and America, which took Place in that Town, on the 19th of April, 1775.* Boston, 1781.

Dana, James. *A Sermon Preached before the General Assembly of the State of Connecticut at Hartford on the Day of the Anniversary Election, May 14, 1779.* Hartford, 1779.

The Declaration and Address of His Majesty's Suffering Loyalists to the People of America. London, 1782.

Evans, Israel. *A Discourse delivered in New-York before a Brigade of Continental Troops and a Number of Citizens, assembled in St. George's Chapel on the 11th of December, 1783.* New York, 1783.

Fiske, Nathan. *An Oration Delivered at Brookfield, Nov. 14, 1781 in the Celebration of the Capture of Lord Cornwallis and his whole Army at York-Town and Gloucester, in Virginia by the combined Army under the Command of His Excellency General Washington On the 19th of October, 1781.* Boston, 1781.

Forbes, Eli. *A Sermon Preached October 9, 1760*. Boston, 1761.

Foxcroft, Thomas. *Grateful Reflexions on the Signal Appearances of Divine Providence for Great Britain and its Colonies in America, which diffuse a General Joy*. Boston, 1760.

Frisbie, Levi. *An Oration Delivered at Ipswich at the Request of a Number of Inhabitants, on the Twenty-ninth of April, 1783; on Account of the Happy Restoration of Peace Between Great Britain and the United States of America*. Boston, 1783.

[Galloway, Joseph]. *A Letter to the People of America*. London, 1778.

Gill, Jeremiah. *Thoughts on the Fast for the 10th of February, 1779*. London, 1779.

Gordon, William. "The Doctrine of Transubstantiation considered and refuted." Harvard University Archives.

Howard, Simeon. *A Sermon on Brotherly Love*. Boston, 1779.

[Inglis, Charles]. *Letters of Papinian*. New York, 1779.

A Letter on the Preliminaries of Peace. London, 1783.

Lockwood, James. *A Sermon Preached at Weatherfield, July 6, 1783*. New Haven, 1783.

Madison, James. *Sermon Preached in the County of Botetourt, on the 13th of December, 1781*. Richmond, 1781.

Mayhew, Jonathan. *Two Discourses delivered October 9th, 1760*. Boston, 1760.

Meigs, Josiah. *An Oration pronounced Before a Public Assembly in New-Haven, on the 5th of November, 1781, At the Celebration of the Glorious Victory over Lieutenant-General Earl Cornwallis at York-Town in Virginia, on the 19th Day of October, 1781*. New Haven, 1782.

Mellen, John. *A Sermon Preached at the West Parish in Lancaster, October 9, 1760*. Boston, 1760.

Minot, George. *An Oration Delivered March 5th, 1782*. Boston, 1782.

Morrill, Isaac. *A Sermon Preached at Lexington April 19, 1780*. Boston, 1780.

Murray, John. *A Discourse delivered at the Presbyterian Church in Newburyport*. Newburyport, 1779.

Payson, Phillips. *A Sermon Preached at Lexington on the Nineteenth of April, 1782*. Boston, 1782.

Powers, Peter. *Tyranny and Toryism exposed; Being the Substance of Two Sermons, Preached at Newbury, Lord's Day, September 10, 1780*. Hartford, 1781.

Ramsay, David. *An Oration on the Advantages of American Independence*. Charleston, 1778.

Rowland, David S. *A Sermon Preached at Providence, June 6, 1779*. Providence, 1779.

Smith, William. *The Candid Retrospect; or the American War examined by Whig Principles*. Charlestown, 1780.

Spring, Samuel. *The Substance of A Discourse Delivered at Westford, October 4, 1779.* Newburyport, 1780.

The State of the Clergy in Virginia before the American Revolution. London, [1783].

Stiles, Ezra. *The United States elevated to Glory and Honor.* New Haven, 1783.

Stillman, Samuel. *A Sermon Preached before the Honorable Council and the Honorable House of Representatives of the State of Massachusetts in New-England at Boston, May 26, 1779.* Boston, 1779.

Strong, Nathan. *A Sermon Preached at the Annual Thanksgiving, December 7, 1780.* Hartford, 1780.

Tappan, David. *A Discourse Delivered at the Third Parish in Newbury on the first of May, 1783, Occasioned by the Ratification of a Treaty of Peace, Between Great Britain and the United States of America.* Salem, 1783.

Wadsworth, Benjamin. *A Sermon Preached at the Ordination of the Reverend Mr. Josiah Badcock, to the Pastoral Care of the Church of Christ in Andover in the Commonwealth of New Hampshire, October 30, 1782.* Salem, 1782.

Warren, John. *An Oration, Delivered July 4th, 1783, At the Request of the Inhabitants of the Town of Boston; in Celebration of the Anniversary of American Independence.* Boston, 1783.

Whitaker, Nathaniel. *The Rewards of Toryism, A Discourse on Judges.* Newburyport, 1783.

Whittelsey, Chauncey. *The Importance of Religion in Civil Rule Considered. A Sermon Preached before the General Assembly of the State of Connecticut at Hartford on the Day of the Anniversary Election, May 14, 1778.* New Haven, 1778.

Wigglesworth, Edward. *The Authority of Tradition Considered.* Boston, 1778.

Willard, Joseph. "Persecution opposite to the Genius of the Gospel." Harvard University Archives.

Williams, Nathan. *A Sermon Preached in the Audience of the General Assembly of the State of Connecticut at Hartford on the day of their Anniversary Election, May 11, 1779.* Hartford, 1780.

Woodward, Samuel. *A Sermon Preached at Lexington, April 19, 1779.* Boston, 1779.

———. *A Sermon Preached October 9, 1760.* Boston, 1760.

NEWSPAPERS AND MAGAZINES

[Annapolis] *Maryland Gazette.* 1779–1783.

[Boston] *Continental Journal and Weekly Advertiser.* 1778–1783.

[Boston] *Evening Post and General Advertiser.* 1778–1779.

Boston Gazette. 1778–1783.

[Boston] *Independent Chronicle.* 1778–1783.

[Charleston] *Royal Gazette.* 1781–1782.

[Hartford] *Connecticut Courant.* 1778–1783.

[New Bern] *North Carolina Gazette.* 1777–1778.

Newport Gazette. 1778–1779.

[Newport] *Gazette Francaise.* 1780–1781.

Newport Mercury. 1780–1783.

New York Gazette and Weekly Mercury. 1778–1783.

[New York] *Royal Gazette.* 1778–1783.

[Philadelphia] *Freeman's Journal.* 1781–1783.

[Philadelphia] *Independent Gazetteer.* 1782–1783.

[Philadelphia] *Pennsylvania Gazette.* 1779–1783.

[Philadelphia] *Pennsylvania Journal and Weekly Advertiser.* 1779–1783.

[Philadelphia] *Pennsylvania Packet.* 1778–1783.

Providence Gazette. 1778–1783.

Salem Gazette. 1781–1783.

[Trenton] *New Jersey Gazette.* 1778–1783.

United States Magazine. 1779.

[Williamsburg] *Virginia Gazette* (Clarkson & Davis). 1778–1779.

[Williamsburg] *Virginia Gazette* (Dixon & Hunter edition and Dixon & Nicolson edition). 1778–1780.

[Williamsburg] *Virginia Gazette* (Purdie edition). 1778.

SECONDARY SOURCES

Abernethy, Thomas P. *Western Lands and the American Revolution.* 2d ed. New York, 1959.

Alden, John R. *The South in the Revolution, 1763–1789.* Baton Rouge, 1957.

Alexander, Edward P. *A Revolutionary Conservative, James Duane of New York.* New York, 1938.

Allen, Herbert S. *John Hancock, Patriot in Purple.* New York, 1948.

Austin, James T. *Life of Elbridge Gerry.* 2 vols. Boston, 1828.

Bailyn, Bernard. *The Ideological Origins of the American Revolution.* Cambridge, 1967.

——. *The Origins of American Politics.* New York, 1968.

Balch, Thomas. *The French in America.* 2 vols. Philadelphia, 1891.

Baldwin, Alice M. "Sowers of Sedition: The Political Theories of Some of the New Light Presbyterian Clergy of Virginia and North Carolina," *William & Mary Quarterly,* third series, V (1948), 53–76.

——. *The New England Clergy and the American Revolution.* Durham, 1928.

Barrow, Thomas. "The American Revolution as a Colonial War for Independence," *William & Mary Quarterly,* third series, XXV (1968), 452–64.

Barthold, Allen J. "French Journalists in the United States, 1780–1800," *Franco-American Review*, I (1936), 215–30.

Barton, H. A. "Sweden and the War of American Independence," *William & Mary Quarterly*, third series, XXIII (1966), 408–30.

Bemis, Samuel Flagg. *American Foreign Policy and the Blessings of Liberty and Other Essays*. New Haven, 1962.

———. *Pinckney's Treaty*. Baltimore, 1926.

———. (ed.). *The American Secretaries of State and their Diplomacy*. I. New York, 1927.

———. *The Diplomacy of the American Revolution*, revised edition. Bloomington, 1961.

Berger, Carl. *Broadsides and Bayonets: The Propaganda War of the American Revolution*. Philadelphia, 1961.

Bonsal, Stephen. *When the French Were Here*. New York, 1945.

Boudinot, John J. *The Life of Elias Boudinot*. 2 vols. Cambridge, 1896.

Boyd, George Adams. *Elias Boudinot*. Princeton, 1952.

Brant, Irving. *James Madison*. Vol. I: *The Virginia Revolutionist*. Vol. II: *The Nationalist*. New York, 1941 and 1948.

Bridenbaugh, Carl. *Mitre and Sceptre*. New York, 1962.

Broadman, Roger S. *Roger Sherman, Signer and Statesman*. Philadelphia, 1938.

Brown, Wallace. *The King's Friends*. Providence, 1965.

Brown, William Garrott. *The Life of Oliver Ellsworth*. New York, 1905.

Brunhouse, Robert L. *The Counter-Revolution in Pennsylvania*. Harrisburg, 1942.

Buckle, Emory Stevens (ed.). *The History of American Methodism*. 3 vols. New York, 1964.

Burnett, Edmund C. *The Continental Congress*. New York, 1941.

Calkin, Homer L. "Pamphlets and Public Opinion During the American Revolution," *Pennsylvania Magazine of History and Biography*, LXIV (1940), 22–42.

Carson, George Barr J. "The Chevalier de Chastellux, Soldier and Philosophe." Unpublished dissertation, University of Chicago, 1942.

Caughey, John W. *Bernardo de Galvez in Louisiana, 1776–1783*. Berkeley, 1934.

Christie, Ian R. *The End of North's Ministry, 1780–1782*. London, 1958.

Coe, Samuel Gwynn. *The Mission of William Carmichael to Spain*. Baltimore, 1928.

Colbourn, H. Trevor. *The Lamp of Experience*. Chapel Hill, 1965.

Coleman, Kenneth. *American Revolution in Georgia*. Athens, 1958.

Collins, Varnum L. *President Witherspoon*. 2 vols. Princeton, 1925.

———. *The Continental Congress at Princeton*. Princeton, 1908.

Corwin, Edward S. *French Policy and the American Alliance of 1778*. Princeton, 1916.

Cresson, W. P. *Francis Dana*. New York, 1930.

Crittenden, Charles C. *North Carolina Newspapers Before 1790*. (The James Sprunt Historical Studies, XX.) Chapel Hill, 1928.

Cunliffe, Marcus. *George Washington, Man and Monument*. Boston, 1960.

Dabney, William M. and Dargan, Marion. *William Henry Drayton and the American Revolution*. Albuquerque, 1962.

Dangerfield, George. *Chancellor Robert R. Livingston of New York*. New York, 1960.

Davidson, Philip. *Propaganda and the American Revolution, 1763–1783*. Chapel Hill, 1941.

DeConde, Alexander. *Entangling Alliance: Politics and Diplomacy under George Washington*. Durham, 1958.

DeMond, Robert. *The Loyalists in North Carolina during the Revolution*. Durham, 1940.

East, Robert A. *Business Enterprise in the American Revolutionary Era*. New York, 1938.

Echeverria, Durand. *Mirage in the West*. Princeton, 1957.

Eckenrode, H. J. *The Revolution in Virginia*. 2d ed. Hamden, 1964.

Edler, Friedrich. *The Dutch Republic and the American Revolution*. Baltimore, 1911.

Einstein, Lewis. *Divided Loyalties*. London, 1933.

Fäy, Bernard. "Portrait du Comte de Vergennes," *Franco-American Review*, I (1936), 143–48.

––––––. *The Revolutionary Spirit in France and America*. New York, 1927.

Ferguson, James. *The Power of the Purse*. Chapel Hill, 1961.

Fingerhut, Eugene R. "Uses and Abuses of the American Loyalists' Claims: A Critique of Quantitative Analyses," *William & Mary Quarterly*, third series, XXV (1968), 245–58.

Fleming, Thomas J. *Beat the Last Drum*. New York, 1963.

Forbes, Allen and Cadman, Paul. *France and New England*. Boston, 1925.

Freeman, Douglas S. *George Washington*. Vol. IV: *Leader of the Revolution*. Vol. V: *Victory with the Help of France*. New York, 1951 and 1952.

Gilbert, Felix. *The Beginnings of American Foreign Policy: To the Farewell Address*. 2d ed. New York, 1965.

Godechot, Jacques. *France and the Atlantic Revolution of the Eighteenth Century, 1770–1799*. Translated by Herbert Rowen. New York, 1965.

––––––. "Les Relations Économiques entre la France et les États-Unis de 1778 à 1789," *French Historical Studies*, I (1958), 26–39.

Goodman, Paul. *The Democratic-Republicans of Massachusetts*. Cambridge, 1964.

Gordon, William. *The History of the Rise, Progress and Establishment of the United States of America*. 4 vols. London, 1788.

Gottschalk, Louis. *Lafayette Joins the American Army*. Chicago, 1935.

––––––. *Lafayette and the Close of the American Revolution*. Chicago, 1942.

Greene, George W. *The Life of Nathanael Greene*. 3 vols. New York, 1871.

Greene, Jack P. *Quest for Power.* Chapel Hill, 1963.

Gummere, Richard M. *The American Colonial Mind and the Classical Tradition.* Cambridge, 1963.

Hale, Edward and Hale, Edward, Jr. *Franklin in France.* 2 vols. Boston, 1887–1888.

Hall, Charles S. *Life and Letters of Samuel Holden Parsons.* Binghamton, 1905.

Harley, Lewis R. *Life of Charles Thomson.* Philadelphia, 1900.

Hastings, George E. *Life and Works of Francis Hopkinson.* Chicago, 1926.

Hatch, Lewis. *The Administration of the American Revolutionary Army.* New York, 1904.

Hedges, James B. *The Browns of Providence Plantations.* Cambridge, 1952.

Heimert, Alan. *Religion and the American Mind: From the Great Awakening to the Revolution.* Cambridge, 1966.

Henderson, Herbert James, Jr. "Political Factions in the Continental Congress: 1774–1783." Unpublished dissertation, Columbia University, 1962.

Hendrick, Burton J. *The Lees of Virginia.* Boston, 1935.

Henry, William W. *Patrick Henry.* 2 vols. New York, 1891.

Hewat, Alexander. *A Historical Account of the Rise and Progress of the Colonies of South Carolina and Georgia.* 2 vols. London, 1779.

Hindle, Brooke. *David Rittenhouse.* Princeton, 1964.

Jay, William. *Life of John Jay.* 2 vols. New York, 1833.

Jensen, Merrill. *The Articles of Confederation.* Madison, 1948.

——. *The New Nation.* New York, 1950.

Jones, Thomas. *History of New York during the Revolutionary War.* Edited by Edward DeLancy. New York, 1879.

Jusserand, Jules J. *With Americans of Past and Present Days.* New York, 1916.

Kaplan, Lawrence S. *Jefferson and France.* New Haven, 1967.

Ketcham, Ralph L. "France and American Politics, 1763–1793," *Political Science Quarterly,* LXXVII (1963), 198–223.

Kite, Elizabeth S. *Brigadier-General Louis Lebegué Duportail, 1777–1783.* Baltimore, 1933.

Lanctot, Gustave. *Canada and the American Revolution, 1774–1783.* Translated by Margaret Cameron. Cambridge, 1967.

Lasseray, André. *Les Français sous les Treize Étoiles.* 2 vols. Paris, 1935.

Lawrence, Alexander A. *Storm over Savannah.* Athens, 1951.

Leary, Lewis G. *That Rascal Freneau.* 2d ed. New York, 1964.

Lee, Henry. *Memoirs of the War in the Southern Department.* 2d ed. Washington, 1827.

Lee, Richard Henry. *Life of Arthur Lee.* 2 vols. Boston, 1829.

Lemisch, Jesse. "Jack Tar in the Streets: Merchant Seamen in the Politics of Revolutionary America," *William and Mary Quarterly,* third series, XXV (1968), 452–64.

Libby, Orin G. "A Critical Examination of Gordon's History of The American Revolution," *Annual Report of the American Historical Association*, I (1899).

Loménie, Louis de. *Beaumarchais and his Times*. Translated by Henry Edwards. New York, 1857.

Loughrey, Mary E. *France and Rhode Island, 1686–1800*. New York, 1944.

Lovejoy, David S. "Samuel Hopkins: Religion, Slavery, and the Revolution," *New England Quarterly*, XL (1967), 227–43.

Lutnick, Solomon. *The American Revolution and the British Press, 1775–1783*. Columbia, 1967.

Lyman, Theodore, Jr. *The Diplomacy of the United States*. 2 vols. Boston, 1828.

Lyon, E. Wilson. *The Man Who Sold Louisiana: The Career of François Barbé-Marbois*. Norman, 1942.

Madariaga, Isabel de. *Britain, Russia, and the Armed Neutrality of 1780*. New Haven, 1962.

Main, Jackson Turner. *The Anti-Federalists: Critics of the Constitution 1781–1788*. Chicago, 1964.

Martyn, Charles. *Life of Artemas Ward*. New York, 1921.

Mays, David J. *Edmund Pendleton*. 2 vols. Cambridge, 1952.

Mead, Sidney. *The Lively Experiment*. New York, 1963.

Meng, John J. *Comte de Vergennes, European Phases of his American Diplomacy, 1774–1780*. Washington, 1932.

———. "French Diplomacy in Philadelphia: 1778–1779," *Catholic Historical Review*, XXIV (1938), 39–57.

Metzger, Charles H. *Catholics and the American Revolution*. Chicago, 1962.

———. *The Quebec Act*. New York, 1936.

Miller, John C. *Sam Adams, Pioneer in Propaganda*. Boston, 1936.

Mitchell, Broadus. *Alexander Hamilton*. 2 vols. New York, 1957 and 1962.

Monaghan, Frank (ed.). *French Travelers in the United States, 1765–1932*. New York, 1933.

———. *John Jay*. New York, 1935.

Montmort, Comte de. *Antoine Charles du Houx, Baron de Vioménil*. Translated by John R. Gough. Baltimore, 1935.

Morgan, Edmund S. *The Gentle Puritan: A Life of Ezra Stiles, 1727–1795*. New Haven, 1962.

———. "The Puritan Ethic and the American Revolution," *William & Mary Quarterly*, third series, XXIV (1967), 1–43.

Morgan, Edmund and Morgan, Helen. *The Stamp Act Crisis,* revised edition. New York, 1963.

Morris, Richard B. *The American Revolution Reconsidered*. New York, 1967.

———. (ed.). *The Era of the American Revolution*. New York, 1939.

———. *The Peacemakers*. New York, 1965.

Murphy, Orville T. "The Comte de Vergennes, the Newfoundland Fisheries, and the Peace Negotiations of 1783: A Reconsideration," *Canadian Historical Review*, XLVI (1965), 32–46.

McCormick, Richard P. *Experiment in Independence: New Jersey in the Critical Period, 1781–1789*. New Brunswick, 1950.

Mackesy, Piers. *The War for America*. Cambridge, 1964.

McLoughlin, William G. "Isaac Backus and the Separation of Church and State in America," *American Historical Review*, LXXIII (1968), 1392–1413.

MacMillian, Margaret B. *War Governors in the American Revolution*. New York, 1943.

McRee, Griffith J. *Life and Correspondence of James Iredell*. 2 vols. New York, 1857.

Nelson, William. *The American Tory*. New York, 1961.

Newlin, Claude M. *Life and Writings of Hugh Henry Brackenridge*. Princeton, 1932.

O'Donnell, William E. *The Chevalier de la Luzerne, French Minister to the United States, 1779–1784*. Louvain, 1938.

Oh, Wonyung Hyun. "American Opinion Relative to International Affairs, 1763–1775." Unpublished dissertation, University of Washington, 1963.

Ormesson, Wladimir, Comte d'. *La Première Mission Officielle de la France aux États-Unis*. Paris, 1924.

Palmer, Robert R. *The Age of the Democratic Revolution*. Vol. I: *The Challenge*. Princeton, 1959.

Parker, Peter J. "The Philadelphia Printer: A Study of an Eighteenth-Century Businessman," *Business History Review*, XL (1966), 24–46.

Phillips, Philip C. *The West in the Diplomacy of the American Revolution*. Urbana, 1913.

Pole, Jack R. *Political Representation in England and the Origins of the American Republic*. New York, 1966.

Preston, Howard W. "Rochambeau and the French Troops in Providence in 1780–81–82." (Rhode Island Historical Society, *Collections*, XVII.) Newport, 1923, 1–23.

Ramsay, David. *The History of the American Revolution*. London, 1793.

Ray, Sister Mary Augustina. *American Opinion of Roman Catholicism in the Eighteenth Century*. New York, 1936.

Reed, William B. *Life and Correspondence of Joseph Reed*. 2 vols. Philadelphia, 1847.

Rice, Howard C., Jr. "French Consular Agents in the United States, 1778–1791," *Franco-American Review*, I (1936), 368–70.

Richardson, Lyon H. *A History of Early American Magazines, 1741–1789*. New York, 1939.

Riley, Arthur J. *Catholicism in New England to 1788*. Washington, 1936.

Roche, John R. *Joseph Reed*. New York, 1957.

Rossman, Kenneth R. *Thomas Mifflin and the Politics of the American Revolution*. Chapel Hill, 1952.

Rowland, Kate Mason. *Life and Correspondence of George Mason.* 2 vols. 2d ed. New York, 1964.

Savelle, Max. "The Appearance of an American Attitude toward External Affairs, 1750–1775," *American Historical Review,* LII (1946), 655–66.

Scheer, George F. and Rankin, Hugh F. *Rebels and Redcoats.* Cleveland, 1957.

Schlesinger, Arthur M. *Prelude to Independence: The Newspaper War on Britain, 1764–1776.* 2d ed. New York, 1965.

———. *The Colonial Merchants and the American Revolution.* 2d ed. New York, 1957.

Sedgwick, Theodore. *A Memoir of the Life of William Livingston.* New York, 1833.

Shipton, Clifford K. *Isaiah Thomas.* Rochester, 1948.

Shy, John. *Toward Lexington.* Princeton, 1965.

Simms, William G. *Memoir and Correspondence of Col. Laurens in the Years, 1777–78.* New York, 1867.

Sioussat, St. George L. "The Chevalier de la Luzerne and the Ratification of the Articles of Confederation by Maryland, 1780–1781: With Accompanying Documents," *Pennsylvania Magazine of History and Biography,* LX (1936), 391–418.

Smith, Charles Page. *James Wilson.* Chapel Hill, 1956.

———. *John Adams.* 2 vols. New York, 1962.

Smith, Ellen Hart. *Charles Carroll of Carrollton.* Cambridge, 1942.

Smith, Fritz-Henry, Jr. "The French at Boston during the Revolution," *Bostonian Society Publications,* X (1913), 9–78.

Smith, Paul H. "The American Loyalists: Notes on their Organization and Numerical Strength," *William and Mary Quarterly,* third series, XXV (1968), 259–77.

———. *Loyalists and Redcoats.* Chapel Hill, 1964.

Sparks, Jared. *Life of Gouverneur Morris.* 3 vols. Boston, 1832.

Spaulding, Ernest Wilder. *His Excellency George Clinton.* New York, 1938.

Staples, William R. *Rhode Island in the Continental Congress.* Providence, 1870.

Stedman, Charles. *The History of the Origin, Progress, and Termination of the American War.* 2 vols. London, 1794.

Stille, Charles J. *The Life and Times of John Dickinson.* Philadelphia, 1891.

Stourzh, Gerald. *Benjamin Franklin and American Foreign Policy.* Chicago, 1954.

Sullivan, Kathryn. *Maryland and France, 1774–1789.* Philadelphia, 1936.

Thayer, Theodore G. *Nathanael Greene: Strategist of the American Revolution.* New York, 1960.

Thornton, John Wingate. *The Pulpit of the American Revolution.* Boston, 1860.

Trescot, William Henry. *The Diplomacy of the Revolution: An Historical Study.* New York, 1852.

Van Doren, Carl. *Benjamin Franklin.* New York, 1965.

———. *Secret History of the American Revolution.* New York, 1941.

———. *Mutiny in January.* New York, 1943.

Van Tyne, Claude. "French Aid before the Alliance of 1778," *American Historical Review,* XXXI (1925), 20–40.

———. *The Loyalists of the American Revolution.* New York, 1929.

Ver Steeg, Clarence L. *Robert Morris, Revolutionary Financier.* Philadelphia, 1954.

Wallace, David D. *The Life of Henry Laurens.* New York, 1914.

Walsh, Richard. *Charleston's Sons of Liberty.* Columbia, 1959.

Ward, Christopher. *The War of the Revolution.* 2 vols. Edited by John R. Alden. New York, 1952.

Weelen, Jean Edmond. *Rochambeau, Father and Son.* Translated by Lawrence Lee. New York, 1936.

Wells, William V. *The Life and Public Services of Samuel Adams.* 3 vols. Boston, 1865.

Wheeler, Joseph T. *The Maryland Press, 1777–1790.* Baltimore, 1938.

Whitridge, Arnold. *Rochambeau.* New York, 1965.

Whittemore, Charles P. *A General of the Revolution, John Sullivan of New Hampshire.* New York, 1961.

Willcox, William B. *Portrait of a General.* New York, 1964.

Wood, Gordon S. "Rhetoric and Reality in the American Revolution," *William and Mary Quarterly,* third series, XXIII (1966), 3–22.

Woods, David W. *John Witherspoon.* New York, 1936.

Index

Adams, Abigail: on French officers, 58; on 1781 peace instructions, 177–78

Adams, Andrew: on Newport campaign, 55–56

Adams, John: drafting model treaty, 8; on proposed boundaries, 25; replaces Silas Deane, 39; elected peace negotiator, 73–76, 168, 176; returns to U.S., 78–79; feuds with Vergennes, 154–60, 167; on 1781 peace instructions, 176–78, 181, 195–96; mentioned, 29, 46, 57, 80, 81, 120, 123, 124, 130, 153, 190, 206, 207

Adams, Samuel: on need for fishery, 18; on boundaries of U.S., 24–25; association with John Temple, 34–35; opinion of Gérard, 45; on D'Estaing, 57; relations with Samuel Cooper, 120–22, 124; on post-war foreign policy, 205; assessment of alliance, 213; mentioned, 41, 46, 59, 66, 67, 79, 80, 81, 119, 161–62, 169, 211

Allen, James: 17

American attitudes toward Frenchmen: before the Revolution, 2; after the alliance, 15; after Newport campaign, 53, 60–61; in the press, 112–14; toward Rochambeau's army, 136; after Yorktown, 149; after peace, 209

Americanus: relationship with Gérard, 69n

Anglicans: 5

Arnold, Benedict: in Virginia, 142–43; mentioned, 116, 123

Arrival of preliminary treaty of peace: 195–97

Austrian-Russian mediation: 155–56

Bailey, Francis: 82

Barbé-Marbois, François: analysis of Congress 85; on American colleges, 99; on Congressmen, 162; his intercepted letter, 181, 192–93, 195; men-

tioned, 77–79, 87, 127, 157, 165, 174, 192

Barney, Joshua: 195

Bartlett, Josiah: member of radical bloc, 17; on Gérard, 32; on Newport campaign, 55

Beaumarchais, Pierre Augustin Caron de: 9

Berkenhout, John: on peace negotiations, 34–35; mentioned, 40

Birth of Dauphin: 188–89

Blanchard, Claude: 123–24

Bland, Theodorick: 166, 173, 181, 199, 211

Boucher, Jonathan: 93

Boudinot, Elias: 173, 185, 192, 195

Bowdoin, James: 34

Brackenridge, Hugh Henry: works for French, 68, 118, 119, 124–25, 128, 132; articles for French, 125–26; mentioned, 206

Burgoyne, General John: 11

Burke, Thomas: Luzerne's opinion of, 81; mentioned, 18, 71

Canada: French position in 1778, 27; American demands for, 28; in 1779 peace ultimata discussions, 65

Canning, William: 136

Carleton, Sir Guy: 106, 107, 187

Carlisle Commission: 21–24

Carlisle, Frederick Howard, Earl of: head of Carlisle Commission, 21

Carmichael, William: 11, 121, 176

Carroll, John: 11–12

Catholicism: American attitude before alliance, 5; and alliance, 91, 96–97, 98; discussion of in press, 116

Chastellux, François Jean, Chevalier de: 82, 114–15, 123

Choiseul, Étienne François, Duc de: 33

Clajon, William: 172

Clark, George Rogers: 26, 36